Pillaging Cambodia

Pillaging Cambodia

The Illicit Traffic in Khmer Art

MASHA LAFONT

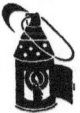

McFarland & Company, Inc., Publishers
Jefferson, North Carolina, and London

The photographs on pages 13, 14, 15, 16, 33, 74, 86, 87, 100, 106, 121, 122, 123, 124, 125, 126, 140 are repro- duced with permission of UNESCO/Anne Lemaistre.

LIBRARY OF CONGRESS CATALOGUING-IN-PUBLICATION DATA

Lafont, Masha, 1971–
    Pillaging Cambodia : the illicit traffic in Khmer art / Masha Lafont.
        p.   cm.
    Includes bibliographical references and index.

    ISBN-13: 978-0-7864-1933-3
    (softcover : 50# alkaline paper) ∞

    1. Art thefts—Cambodia.   2. Art, Khmer.   I. Title.
N7315.L34   2004
364.16'2—dc22   2004018235

British Library cataloguing data are available

On the cover: *background* ©2004 EclectiCollections; *art* from Museum of Phnom Penh; *bottom* ©2004 Clipart

Manufactured in the United States of America

McFarland & Company, Inc., Publishers
  Box 611, Jefferson, North Carolina 28640
  www.mcfarlandpub.com

Contents

Acknowledgments

In writing this book I owe a great deal to my husband, Jean-Loup, for his love, continuous support and encouragement. I also would like to thank Tamara Teneishvili for her immense help during my trip to Cambodia. Without her support it would have been impossible to complete this book. Also, I thank Dr. Jesus del Rio Luelmo for doing seven useful maps for this book. Finally, I thank Anne Lemaistre for her suggestions and her help in providing materials and photos.

Abbreviations and Special Terms

Angkor   from Sanscrit nagara, royal city or capital, the
                           Khmer capital from 10th to 15th century. The
                           territory extends over 248 miles (400 square
                           kilometers) in the region of Siem Reap with over
                           hundred temples and monuments, the most
                           famous of which are Angkor Wat and Angkor
                           Thom.

Apsara   heavenly nymph

APSARA   Authority for the Protection and Management
                           of Angkor and the Region of Siem Reap

Banteay   citadel

Cham   the people of Champa, the rival state adjoining
                           Cambodia that is modern Southern Vietnam

Conservation d'Angkor   storage rooms opened in 1908 by the French
                           scholars working in Angkor for the preservation
                           and study of the objects of art. Currently it con-
                           tains over five thousand statues, lingha and steles
                           that are stored there because of the danger of theft.

DCA	Depôt de la Conservation d'Angkor
EFEO	Ecole Française d'Extrême-Orient
Garuda	mythical half-man, half-bird on which Vishnu rode
GDP	gross domestic product
GNP	gross national product
IADAA	International Association of Dealers in Ancient Art
IARC	Illegal Antiquities Research Center
ICC	International Coordinating Committee
ICOM	International Council of Museums
IGO	international governmental organization
Jayavarman VII	the King of Cambodia (1181–1201), one of the greatest kings of Angkor, who drove the Chams out of Cambodia and erected the most famous temples of Angkor
Khmer Rouge	a revolutionary organization that seized power in 1975 and implemented a brutal social restructuring, resulting in the suffering and death of millions of Cambodians over the following four years. At the moment of writing, most of the country, apart from a few small remaining areas, is free from the Khmer Rouge.
Lingha	form of a Shiva as a phallic symbol
Lokeshvara	a divine combination of Shiva and Aalokitesvara
Mt. Meru	the mythical mountain, sacred to Hindus and

Buddhists, which is the center of the world and a dwelling place of the Hindu God Shiva

Naga — mythical serpent, often multi-headed (often represented in Cambodian art with three, five or seven heads)

NGO — nongovernmental organization

OCBC — Office Central de Biens Culturel

Pandit — a title of Sanskrit scholars studying sacred Hindu and Buddhist scripts

Sanchok — soldier

SCTIP — Service de Coopération Technique International de Police

Theravada Buddhism — a school of Buddhism (also known as southern school of Hinayana Buddhism) found in Burma, Thailand, Laos and Cambodia

Thom — large

UNESCO — United Nations Educational, Scientific and Cultural Organization

UNIDROIT — International Institute for the Unification of Private Law

Wat — monastery

Year Zero — proclaimed by Khmer Rouge in 1975, when they took power and Cambodia was isolated from the rest of the world until 1979.

Yuga — cosmic cycles according to the ancient Hindus. The cycle of four Yuga of our creation is thus counted: Krita Yuga—1,728,000 years; Treatâ Yuga—1,296,000 years; Dvâpara Yuga—864,000 years; Kalî Yuga—432,000 years. The present

Yuga is said to have begun in 3102 B.C. The cycle of 4 Yuga (Catur Yuga) corresponds to a duration of 4,320,000 terrestrial years (Mahâ Yuga).

Introduction

This book addresses the problem of illicit trafficking of objects of art from Cambodia and the impact it has on the cultural heritage of the country. It is a very complex, multi-level and present-day issue that has existed for several decades. Hundreds of objects of Khmer art, often practically whole temples, are being looted from Cambodia on a daily basis, transported via Thailand, Hong Kong and Malaysia, and sold illegally all over the world. This book is focused on the art created between the sixth and the fifteenth century in the Khmer Empire, which occupied the territory of the modern Cambodia, part of Thailand, Laos and Vietnam.

The national heritage and cultural history of Cambodia, represented and retold in the magnificent ancient temples scattered all over the country and revealing one of the highest achievements of ancient Asian civilizations, is systematically being destroyed and vandalized, depriving the long-suffering and suffocated country of its treasures.

The problem has attracted the attention of the international community, various governmental bodies, legal authorities and many other institutions and individuals on numerous occasions over the last few years. Conferences and symposia have been held to research and analyze this dilemma, attract public attention and look for possible solutions. However, the problem continues to exist.

The issue involves many conflicting interests. Being in high demand on all the continents, the pieces of looted art appear in galleries, auction houses, private collections and museums that often openly display their provenance. The collectors claim that the appreciation of art must focus solely on its aesthetic qualities, quite apart from its historical significance. They also use the argument that art is better protected in collections and museums outside of Cambodia.

Similar cases of art trafficking exist in all countries; however, hardly anywhere has it reached such a horrifying and uncontrollable scale, with similar deteriorating effects for the country at present and in the future. At the moment it still remains a serious problem that has not been properly addressed. Organizations such as UNESCO actively participate in the safeguard and protection of Cambodian heritage and attract the help of the Ministries of Interior and Foreign Affairs, Tourism, Culture and Commerce as well as the leading experts in art, law and other relevant areas. Most of the material, however, is unpublished and scattered.

Khmer art, which is in high demand, was created in the Khmer Empire and dates back to the period of the sixth—fifteenth centuries. In the fifteenth century the kingdom was invaded by the Thai army. The capital, Angkor—a large territory of 248 miles (400 square kilometers) now protected by UNESCO—ceased to exist and was forgotten. It was rediscovered by scholars from the *Ecole Française d'Extrême-Orient* (EFEO) in the 1860s. The EFEO has been working ever since on the restoration and revival of Cambodian art.

The first well-known looting incident happened in 1924, when the young French writer André Malraux and his wife decided to take out and sell some of the objects that they found during their trip to Angkor. They were caught and sentenced. The little-known writer later became a Minister of Culture in France and an active fighter against colonialism and its causes, and he did a lot for the protection of colonial art.

The present problem started to develop in the 1950s and 1960s when more Western tourists, businessmen and diplomats traveled to the Far East. It reached a global scale during the Vietnamese invasion of Cambodia and the war in Vietnam in the 1970s, with the large foreign community stationed in Thailand. Cambodian refugees who lived in the camps near the Thai border were trained to go into the temples scattered all over the jungles to look for whole statues and torsos and heads of statues. At this point a network of illegal trafficking was formed.

Now, with the war at an end, the situation remains the same. Parts of the temples were broken into pieces and transported over the Thai border to find their way to the galleries in Bangkok. There they were bought or specifically ordered by foreigners from Europe, America and Japan and exported from the country with false certificates, thereby ending up in prestigious galleries, auction houses, private collections and museums.

The scale of the operation is enormous as hundreds of objects cross the Thai border all the time without being noticed or stopped by the authorities of either country. Many temples are looted even before the art specialists find out about their existence. It is a well-established network that locally involves multiple organized and well-trained gangs, the military and high ranking officials from the administrative system, and it is well organized outside Cambodia. One of the first obstacles is the situation in the country, which is very poor. It was destroyed by the Pol Pot regime and the Vietnamese invaders, and ruled by the military with a high level of corruption, which aggravates the problem and makes it harder to resolve.

Elimination of illegal trafficking itself as one way to enhance a national cultural heritage depends on factors outside the control of the Cambodian government—chiefly on the international demand for art from the major consumer countries. Because such outside factors are unlikely to change soon, the ability of the Cambodian government to undertake a cultural heritage preservation project (considering the current economic circumstances) is not sufficient.

Since the early 1970s, the national and international traffic in and demand for art has exploded, reaching North America, Europe, Australia, and the Far East. During the last forty years, Cambodia has experienced exceptionally turbulent social, economic and political changes. These have been characterized by slow or even no economic growth, a high level of violence, and genocide, all of which nourished the pervasive growth of an illegal art trafficking industry. Many Cambodians and outside experts have observed these changes from differing perspectives and ideologies. In this research I shall attempt to develop an interpretation of this phenomenon in Cambodia.

The problem discussed in this book contains many factors that contribute to this dilemma. The main driving force is a market demand that comes from Japan, the United States, Switzerland and other countries. Many private collectors are ready to pay any price for a good piece of art, even if they have prior knowledge of its doubtful provenance. This activates the dealers and the auction houses, whose obvious interests evolve around the high profit margins that are common in this trade. There are also museums that have their own set of rules and politics and at the same time are interested in acquiring the best pieces of art and enriching their collections. There are many arguments that question the degree to which the cultural heritage of a particular country can be deteriorated by the migration of art.

Cambodia is going through a difficult time after the wars and the Pol

Pot regime. Its economic, social and political situation is chaotic. At the same time it possesses a unique cultural heritage, a large part of which is still unknown to researchers. The combination provides a good environment for the military and the middlemen to traffic art from the country, thus destroying the cultural heritage of the nation. There is a complicated network of organized gangs (rarely individuals) who are trained and equipped to get the required pieces of art. The industry is no doubt very competitive; its participants are very numerous and include not only military but also police and customs officers, peasants, the local population, diplomats and others.

Many legal and ethical measures are taken to stop the illegal trafficking and thus put an end to the illegal trade in cultural property. In order to cut it off at its roots, the Cambodian government should take stern measures supported by national police forces and by the international community. The measures taken by the government to reduce corruption, introduce law and order, and work with the international organizations, institutions and various authorities will help. Particular effort is made by UNESCO and other organizations such as INTERPOL. The temples of Cambodia need more protection and investment and a computerized database and inventory of the historical and cultural heritage should be established, listing the most precious and endangered pieces.

The illegal trade in antiquities in Cambodia causes enormous damage to the country's cultural heritage. It is obvious that the problem won't disappear completely and will continue to exist, but it is possible to reduce its scale of destruction for the country.

Note on the Information and Materials Used in the Book

I think I should say a word about the availability and quality of the data and other information and sources that I gathered and used in this book. As one can imagine, data related to the illicit trafficking of art from Cambodia are not abundant. Little research has been done on this subject. Much of the information that exists cannot be considered absolutely reliable, complete, or unified in nature. The books that have been published on this issue are somewhat scarce. A lot of accessible information comes mainly from private sources or unpublished research rather than from academic literature. The majority of the information was collected from interviews that took place in Paris and Phnom Penh; again, some of it may not be completely reliable.

Therefore, all the information I collected, summarized and interpreted for this book could have been interpreted differently by other researchers. Nevertheless, I have tried to verify and check as much data as possible and to remain objective throughout the book. However, much of the information remains inconsistent, even contradictory.

I would also like to point out that some of the main sources of information, apart from my trip to Cambodia, were articles from Cambodian (mainly) and some other newspapers. I think the use of articles and the information provided in these articles is legitimate because the Asian press in general and Cambodian press in particular provide exact data and information on many current-day issues, including this one. Therefore, I consider this source of information acceptable for my book. The bibliography not only includes references to the books used in the text but also presents a rather complete list of all the books, articles, conferences, reports, legislative texts and Internet sites written or published on this issue before 2001.

1

The Illicit Traffic of Art from Cambodia

Overview of Cambodian Art

Cambodia: A Historical Background

The study of the history of Cambodia shows many gaps. The written materials used by the Khmers in the past made on animal skin and papyrus did not survive and the only research that can be done by scholars is based on written sources that come from the stone inscriptions. Many of the stone inscriptions are broken or lost or in many cases were looted before the scholars got a chance to read them. Another part of the historical research is based on archaeological excavations, which in the case of Cambodia also present certain difficulties because of multiple illicit excavations that ruin the original source of the study. The last source is the temples themselves.

The earliest traces of the people who could make pottery in Cambodia date back to 4200 B.C. At the beginning of the Christian Era the Cambodians went through a process known as Indianization. They have remained under the Indian influence for over a thousand years. The earliest Kingdom was Funan, also now known as the pre–Angkorean period, which lasted until the sixth century A.D.[1] In terms of objects of art from this period, the archaeologists find many examples of pottery and bronze vases. Strangely enough these objects may often be found for sale in the markets of Phnom Penh and Siem Reap, in people's homes used as vases and in the galleries, but hardly at all in the museums.

The Angkorean period, during which the temples were built and the Khmer Empire gained its position as one of the great empires of the region, is usually placed by scholars in the period between 802 and 1431. This historical period is named after the capital of the Kingdom, Angkor, situated in the province Siem Reap. All the most well-known temples were built in this area. It started with the reign of Jayavarman II, who introduced a cult of devaraja—god king—which meant that the king had temporal authority on earth but also had a quasi-divine status.[2] His rule was followed by Jayavarman III and Indravarman I, who built one of the first temples—Preah Ko—and established the first baray that gave a start to a famous irrigation system in the Angkor area.

The time that is often called a classical period dates to the construction of Angkor Thom and Angkor Wat in the eleventh century. The first important monarch was Suryavarman II, who unified Cambodia and led campaigns against Vietnam. He also initiated the construction of the temple of Angkor Wat, which was devoted to the Hindu deity Vishnu. It was one of the most important periods in the history of Angkor; however, it greatly strained the resources of the kingdom because most of the war campaigns held by Suryavarman II were unsuccessful.

Other radical changes were also made by Jayavarman VII (1181—1201), who adopted Mahayana Buddhism and built a number of significant monuments in Angkor, among them the centerpiece of Angkor Thom—Bayon. After his reign the kingdom went into decline. It was attacked by a Thai army first in 1351 and again in 1431, and after that the capital moved to Phnom Penh. Angkor was rediscovered in the 1860s by French scholars, who started research in 1901. (The 100th anniversary of that research was celebrated in February 2001.)

After the location of the capital was changed, Cambodia went into decline. The country was always threatened by either Vietnam or Thailand. For a long time Thailand occupied the northern part of Cambodia, including Angkor, which was restituted only during the French protectorate. Many scholars say that the establishment of the French protectorate in 1863 saved Cambodia from being occupied by one of the two countries.

The protectorate lasted until 1963, when the country gained its independence. The recent history of the country is well known. The King of Cambodia, Norodom Sihanouk, could not remain in power, and Cambo-

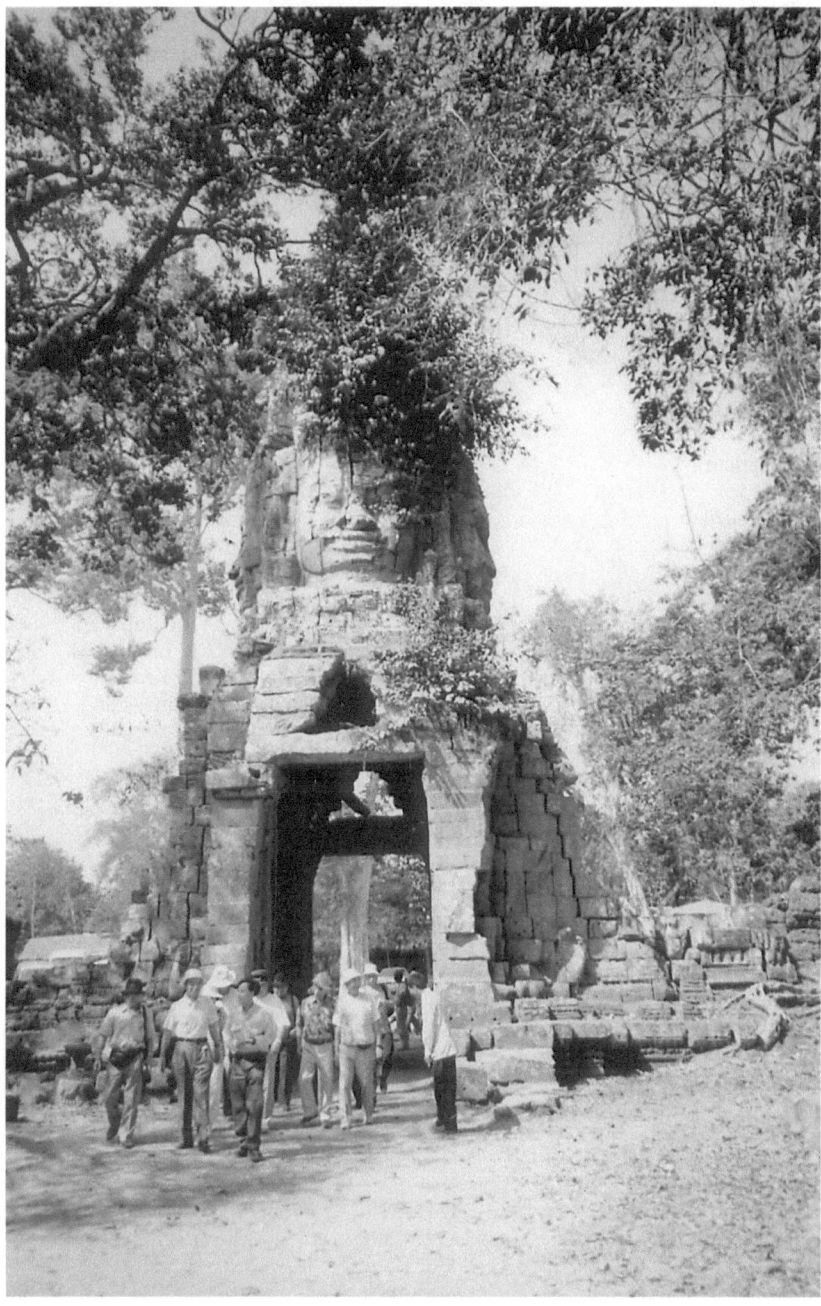

Entrance gate; Temple of Ta Prohm; end of the twelfth century; built during the reign of Jayavarman VII.

dia was finally taken over by the Khmer Rouge (1975—1979). Between 1979 and 1990 Cambodia was a communist country and was largely supported by the former Soviet Union. Since the fall of the U.S.S.R., the country has tried to establish a democracy.

ANGKOREAN MONARCHS

King	Dates of Reign	Temples Built in the Territory of Angkor
Jayavarman II	802–50	
Jayavarman III	850–77	
Indravarman I	877–89	Preah Ko
		Bakong (Roluos)
Yasovarman I	889–910	Lolei (Roluos)
		Bakheng
Harshavarman I	910–28	
Jayavarman IV	928–42	
Harshavarman II	942–44	
Rajendravarman II	944–68	Eastern Mebon
		Pre Rup
		Phimeanakas
Jayavarman V	968–1001	Ta Keo
		Banteay Srei
Udayadityavarman I	1001–02	
Suryavarman I	1002–49	
Udayadityavarman II	1049–65	Baphuon
		Western Mebon
Harshavarman III	1065–90	
Jayavarman VI	1090–1108	
Dharanindravarman I	1108–12	
Suryavarman II	1112–52	Angkor Wat
		Banteay Samré
Harshavarman IV	1152	
Dharanindravarman II	1152–81	
Jayavarman VII	1181–1201	Angkor Thom
		Ta Nei
		Peah Khan
		Preah Palilay
		Ta Prohm
		Banteay Kdei
Indravarman II	1201–43	
Jayavarman VII	1243–95	
Sri-Indravarman	1295–1307	
Sri-Indrajayavarman	1307	
Jayavarman Paramesvara	Mid–1300s	

Cambodian Cultural Heritage

Cambodian cultural heritage is unique. The art that was created by the ancient Khmer civilization cannot be found anywhere else in the world. The French archaeologist Bernard-Philippe Groslier, who was responsible for Angkor between 1908 and 1975 (at which point he was forced by the Khmer Rouge to leave), expresses his emotions about Angkor (the territory of 248 miles [400 square kilometers] near Siem Reap province with over seventy temples, the best known of which are Angkor Wat and Angkor Thom) by making the following comparison: "Imagine," he wrote, "that within the city limits of Paris, between La Défense and the Place de la Nation, you found thrown together Versailles, the Place des Vosges and the palace of Fontainebleau and, surrounding these, the cathedrals of Notre-Dame, Chartres, Reims, Amiens, Bourges and Strasbourg flanked by all the churches built in Paris before the nineteenth century."[3]

Not much is known about the Khmer civilization, and every source that disappears places scholars further away from discovering facts about the lives of the Cambodian people in ancient times. Apart from that, the temples of Angkor are not only simple constructions that served religious purposes; they also hide multiple levels of the Khmers' knowledge and contain cosmological meaning and significance. Here the parallel may be made with the temples of Egypt and the Maya civilization. Each statue, each bas-relief carving has a meaning and is placed according to this meaning; when it disappears, the meaning is lost. The statue that is displaced loses its power as well as its religious and theological significance, and the temple loses the composit parts that gave its existence the cosmological and religious importance for which it was constructed.

Analyzing the construction of the temples itself, one can see that the materials used were laterite, bricks, sandstone, stucco, timber and metal. Of course, apart from being destroyed by the looters, there is natural destruction caused by the effects of age, of vegetation and weather. Fortunately there was not much destruction done by war. Although the materials used for construction were resistant, the temples have suffered from the effects of moisture, micro-vegetal growth and bacillus.[4] Only one temple, Preah Ko, in Ruluos was used as a storehouse for salt, which had its negative effect on the brickwork.

To explain why the Cambodian cultural heritage is so unique and why its destruction may lead to a total disappearance of the cultural heritage of the country, we take as an example the temple of Angkor Wat. The following description is a study of the temple that was made for years by the leading scholars in this field. The temple of Angkor Wat is one of the

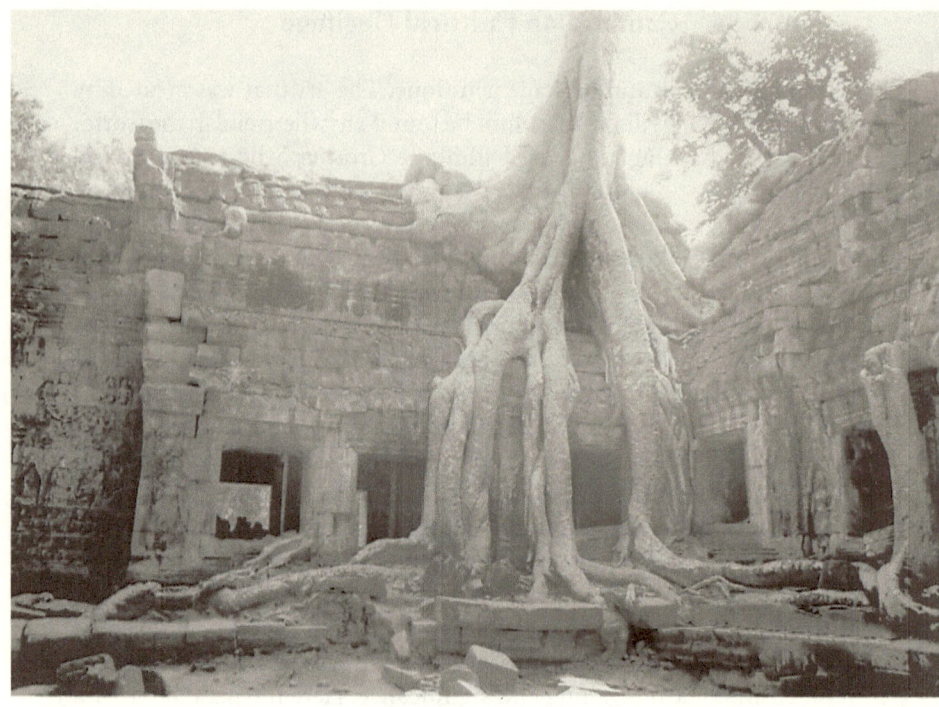

Temple of Ta Prohm; end of the twelfth century; built during the reign of Jayavarman VII.

most mysterious temples in Angkor. It opens to the west, while all the other temples open to the east. In addition, all of its bas-reliefs stretch by more than a mile in the outer galleries in a counterclockwise direction, while the galleries in the other temples usually follow a clockwise direction. The reversed direction and west-facing door are usually associated with the dead for meteorological reasons; the temple was probably constructed as a tomb.

David Chandler describes in his book the study of the dimensions of the temple, started in the 1970s by Eleanor Moron, who showed that the distance along an east-west axis suggests that the construction of the temple reflects the four ages or *yuga* that come from Indian philosophy.[5] The first of these, the Krita Yuga, the golden age, lasted 1,728,000 years—the distance between the western entrance and the central tower measured in *hat* (0.4 meter), the next three stages lasted 1,296,000; 864,000; and 432,000 years, which were exactly the other components measured along the axis.

At the moment we are living in the last stage, Kali Yuga, after which the world will be destroyed and will be rebuilt by Brahma again accord-

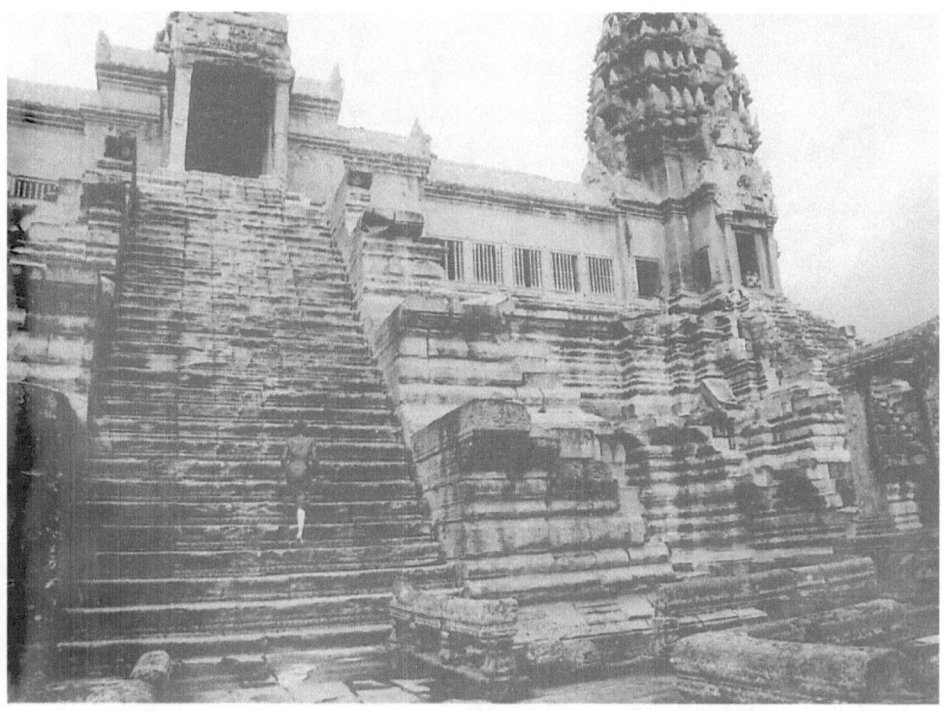

Temple of Angkor Wat; twelfth century; built by Suryavarman II.

ing to the four yugas. When the visitor enters the temple from the west, he moves backward in time, approaching the first of the ages, the golden age. The research done in the temple by astronomers showed an astronomical correlation within the temple. The observer standing in front of the western gates can see the sunrise over the central tower of Angkor Wat.

Like some other temples, Angkor Wat replicates the universe. The four levels of the architectural plan show what the Khmer people thought the universe looked like. The central tower is Mt. Meru (the dwelling place of the Hindu god Shiva), which is surrounded by the continents (the lower courtyards) and the oceans (the moat). The discovery of the cosmological meaning of the temple showed that the temple was coded as a religious text, which could be read by visitors while they walk from the western entrance to the east. The religious and astronomical texts used by the Khmers have disappeared, but the architecture on which the temples were based have remained. Obviously, the simple people or the slaves were not aware of these meanings that were known only to the learned pandits,[6] but the written sources say that even the poorest slaves were astounded by the temple.

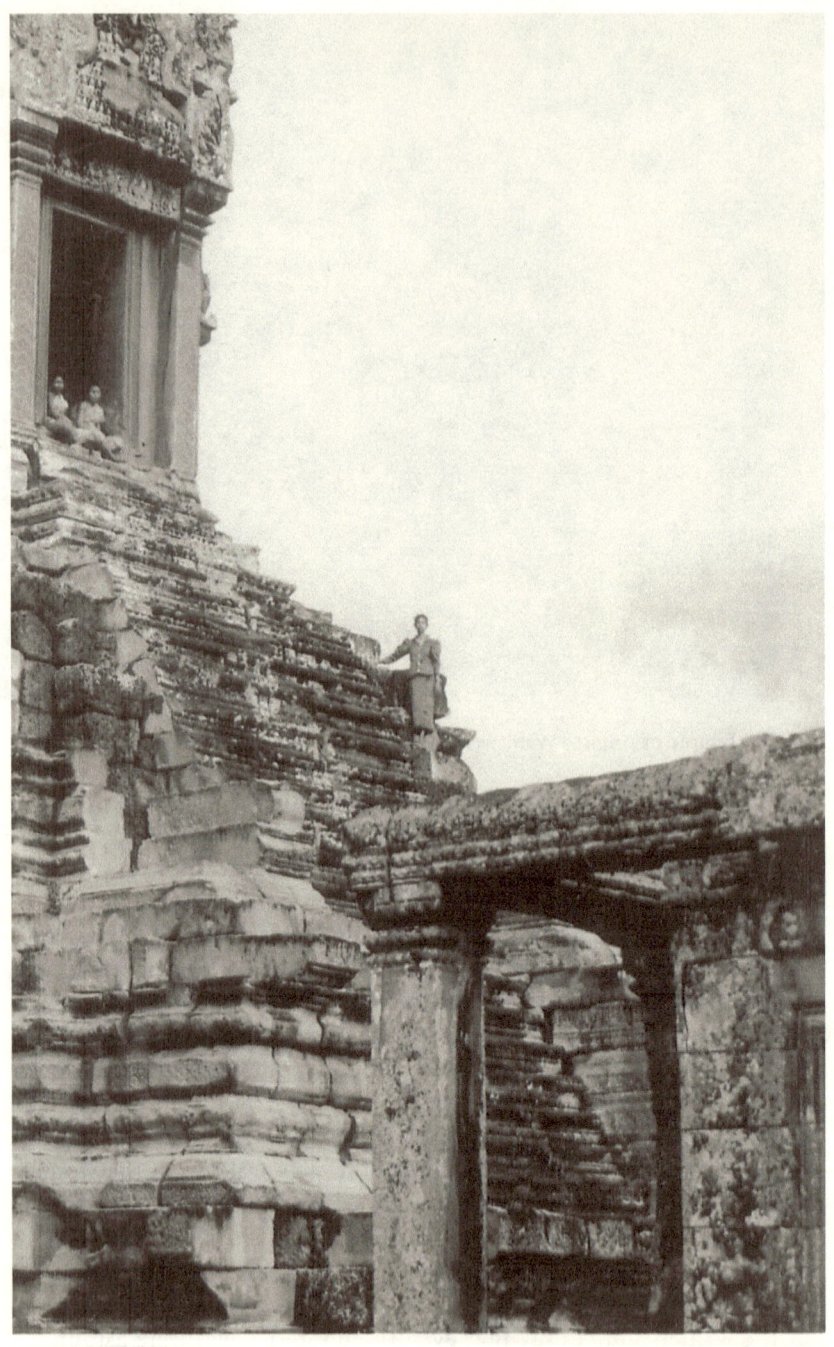

Temple of Angkor Wat; twelfth century; built by Suryavarman II.

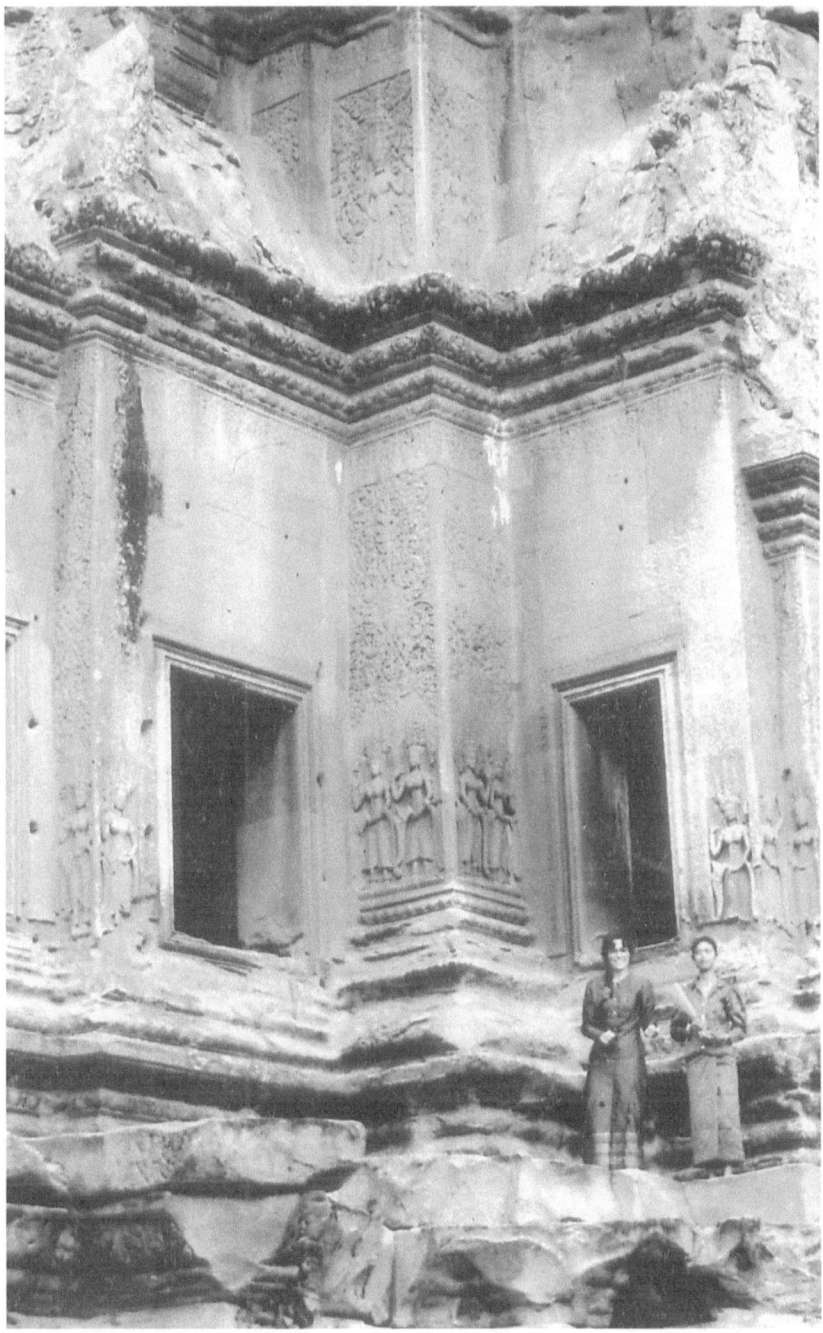

Temple of Angkor Wat; twelfth century; built by Suryavarman II.

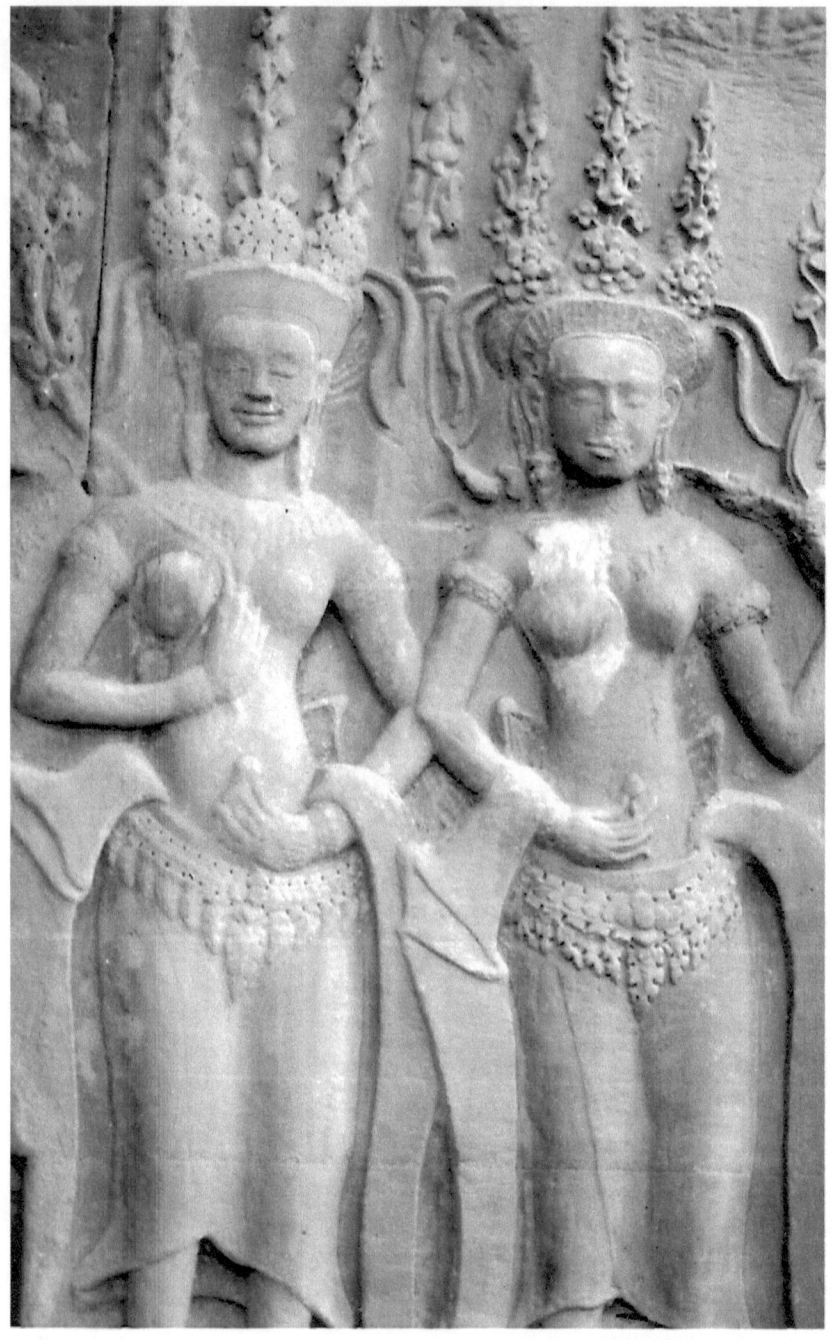

Apsaras; Temple of Angkor Wat; twelfth century; built by Suryavarman II.

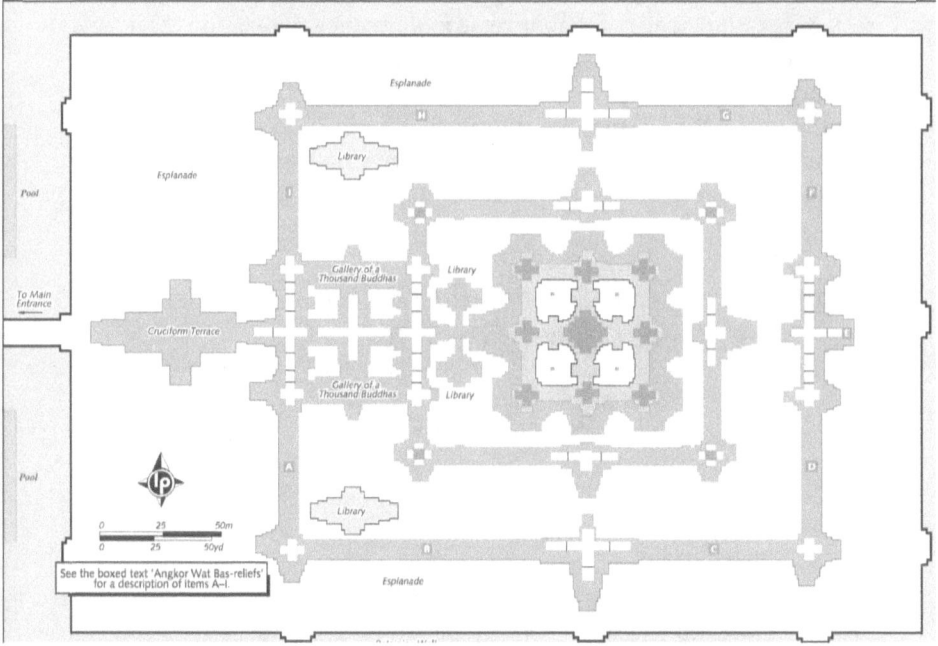

Figure 1. Central Structure of Angkor Wat. Reproduced with permission from *Cambodia*, 4th ed. ©2002 Lonely Planet Publications.

For the Cambodian people the temple has always remained a symbol of the country. Even after Angkor was abandoned as a capital the people continued to live there, as they do now, and continued to come and to pray in the temples. The temples were never forgotten or abandoned by the people. However, the temples are not seen by the people as a wonder of the world but as a part of the national history. Even during the Pol Pot regime, the towers of Angkor remained on the flag as a main symbol of national pride. In one of his speeches Pol Pot said, "If our people can make Angkor, they can make anything."[7]

Khmer culture became popular in the West only in the last few decades. When objects of art arrived in France in 1873—1874, they were not well accepted or understood by the European public. They were refused by the Louvre and some other museums in Paris and were finally displayed in one of the museums in the country until 1925, when the Guimet Museum (which posesses the richest collection of Khmer art) was opened in Paris. The real destruction of the Cambodian cultural heritage started in the 1970s, when all the freestanding statues, carvings, bas-reliefs and parts of the temples started to disappear, first from Angkor and then from other temples.

It is evident from the above that there is no analogous cultural expression of the knowledge of the universe in any other civilization. Each of its elements is very valuable and, if lost, disappears completely without leaving any clues or connections with the rest of the chain. The profound knowledge of the Khmer civilization that we still do not have in full is important not only for Cambodia but for the whole world because it helps the understanding of the universal development of mankind.

Migration of Art in Cambodia During Pre-colonial and Colonial Periods

Pre-colonial Period

We can say that illicit trafficking of Khmer art did not exist during the pre-colonial period or, in other words, throughout the history of Cambodia until the middle of the nineteenth century when Cambodia became a part of French Indochina. However, certain movements of Khmer art did take place, during which the Khmer statues left the country and can now be found in Thailand, Burma or Laos.

Most of the Southeast Asian region shared the same religious beliefs. Buddhist statues were considered sacred just as they continue to be sacred now. For this reason, many wars in the region were fought to seize Buddhist statues. The winners tried to acquire and take out of the country as many statues as they could. The number of sculptures seized would determine the significance of the victory and the blessing of the gods. Therefore, it can be assumed that already in the early ages there was a certain migration of Khmer art within the region. The loss of the Buddhist statues was very painful for the country and its people. In fact, even now it is prohibited to sell for export and take out of the country the statues of Buddha. This law is true for most of the countries in this region with the exception of Cambodia, where tourists can buy statues of Buddha and take them out of the country.

In his book *Angkor la Forêt de Pierre*, Bruno Dagens describes the most well known of such episodes in the history of Cambodia. In 1431 the Thai army won the war over Cambodia and was thus entitled to take many of the Khmer Buddhist statues to Ayuthaya, then capital of Thailand. In 1569 the statues were transferred to Pegu; in 1600 they were moved to Mrohaung, capital of Arakan; and in 1734 they finished their journey in Mandalay.[8]

Colonial Period

How Angkor was rediscovered in the 1860s has already been mentioned in the previous section. The drawings of Angkor, which were made during the first trip of Henri Mouhot, opened Angkor to France and the entire world and had an enormous effect on the public. Since then many French scholars have worked in Angkor. The main projects were started at the end of the nineteenth and beginning of the twentieth century. It was actually in February 2001 that the EFEO celebrated its 100th anniversary of work in Angkor. Much has been written and said about the role of the French Protectorate in Cambodia. There is much criticism as well as much praise. Everybody, however, agrees that the main achievement of the French Protectorate was the return to Cambodia of its magnificent past—a belief in it and an advanced knowledge about it.

It is important to point out that when Henri Mouhot (first of the French scholars to see the temples) was shown the City of Temples, then lost in the middle of the jungles, Angkor was not forgotten or unknown by the locals. Many of the temples were used for prayers. The large community who lived in the territory of Angkor continues to live there now. However, it seemed that the Cambodians did not really care about it or did not have much interest in it. Therefore, it was really the French scholars who rediscovered it and returned it in its full glory to Cambodia. Needless to say, the images of temples lost in the jungles captured the minds of the Europeans. As for the Cambodians, who were at the time colonized by France, one can assume that the idea of the fallen kingdom that remained the national identity of the country was probably somewhat symbolic.

Cambodia was one of the last colonized countries whose art captured the attention and interest of the Europeans. The idea of collecting and acquiring foreign art has existed since the seventeenth century. Auction houses were established in Europe at the end of the eighteenth century. Sotheby's was established in 1744 and had originally auctioned books, coins and antiquities; at the same time their competitor, Christie's, dealt mainly in Old Master paintings and drawings. By the end of the eighteenth century, the market was auctioning antiquities from colonized countries brought in by travelers. Many objects of art were arriving in England from India. Under Napoleon a great influx of Egyptian, Greek and Roman antiquities came into Europe, especially after the Nile Campaign of 1795. Major archaeological discoveries were made in Herculaneum, Pompeii and the tomb of Tutankhamen in Egypt.

Then unknown antiquities seemed to attract everybody's attention. Now there are many quarrels and demands for restitution, but at the begin-

ning of the twentieth century tourists were glad to bring souvenirs back
to their countries. It is hard to assume that they intended to destroy somebody's cultural heritage. The attitude to this issue was really different at
the time. It could also be true that many Europeans did not understand
and underestimated the Khmer culture. The element of the unknown and
the mysterious also pervaded in antiquities, especially with the secrecy
surrounding the Angkor temples discovered in the jungles.

The question of the migration of art during the epoch of colonialism is a cause of many discussions at the moment. Europeans are often
accused of not understanding the art of the nations they have colonized,
of destroying the real values of the nations, and of paying little attention
to their cultural heritage at the moment when they either did not have the
choice or the potential or were trying to become more modernized and
catch up with Europe.[9]

Within the first decade of the twentieth century tourism was already
fully developed in Cambodia. At the time Cambodia was visited by many
well-known French writers, poets, and activists. A magnificent travel journal—*Un Pèlerin d'Angkor*—was left by Pierre Loti who was one of the first
to visit it.[10] Among other visitors were Paul Claudel and many renowned
photographers, artists, painters, and scientists.

Already at this time the first objects of art were stolen from Angkor.
It is impossible to say how many sculptures and of what value left the
country at this moment. Of course the scale of these operations did not
have anything in common with the pillage that goes on now. However,
undoubtedly, there were many instances whereby many objects left the
country.

The most "famous" of these incidents happened with André Malraux.
The story has been repeated and published on many occasions. In 1923 it
seemed that his case was made a publicized example for others. Undoubtedly, it could not be the only such occasion of theft, but the authorities
decided to make Malraux a publicized example of the multiple thefts.

Malraux, a young French writer, while traveling in Cambodia with
his wife and a friend, tried to take statues from the temple of Banteay Srei
for the purpose of sale. He was caught and kept in custody in Cambodia,
while his wife went to France to attract the attention of the French public and their influential friends to the incident. Malraux was finally allowed
to leave Cambodia. In the 1960s he became French Minister of Cultural
Affairs and a fighter for the independence of colonial states and protection of their cultural identity.[11]

This, for example, is how the story was interpreted by the French
writer Paul Morand in his diary: "*L'enlèvement des bas-reliefs de Banteay*

Srey en décembre 1923 ne constituait pas un vol, s'agissant d'un bien à l'a-bandon sans propriétaire. Mais l'administration coloniale, les ayant saisis dès l'arrivée à Phnom Penh, devait nécessairement faire valider cette saisie par la condamnation de Malraux: trois ans de prison ferme, ramenés à un an de prison avec sursis par la cour d'appel de Saigon le 8 octobre 1924. C'est seule-ment par un décret de 1925, sous le gouvernement d'Edouard Herriot, que fut instituée une protection des monument anciens d'Indochine."[12]

What it says, in fact, is that until 1925 there was no law protecting the cultural heritage of Cambodia, until the adoption in 1925 of *Législation relative au classement, a la protection et a la conservation des monuments historiques et des objets d'art de l'Indochine Française.*[13] At the same time, by the 1920s the number of tourists visiting Angkor was already rather significant. It continued to increase until the end of the 1960s, when Cambodia was no longer a French colony and civil disturbances started at the beginning of the 1970s. One can imagine tourists and, of course, many administrative officials who worked or passed by Cambodia bringing back to France hundreds of souvenirs of their trip. Many of these souvenirs went to museums; however, many stayed in private collections or were sold to antique shops.

It was becoming more and more fashionable to travel to Indochina. In 1907 about two hundred people visited Angkor in a period of three months.[14] To protect the temples from visitors, the first bungalows for accommodation of tourists were already founded at the beginning of the century outside the territory of Angkor Wat. By the beginning of the 1920s tourism was already well established. Most of the tourists were French; however, the number of visitors from all over the world was becoming rather significant.[15]

The attitude toward the temples of Angkor was changing. They were gradually becoming less mysterious and attractive; they lost their enchanted beauty that had attracted so much attention. Another famous French writer, Jules Roy, mentioned in his diaries a trip to Cambodia in the 1960s. He described that he took a small stone from one of the temples to give as a present to his girlfriend. He described how he took it out of the temple hidden in his clothes and when he looked at the piece in a hotel room, he discovered that the stone had lost all its beauty and mystery.[16]

Such small notes of the various trips found in the diaries of the French writers of the epoch allow for the assumption that it was popular and maybe even fashionable to visit the Angkor temples. We will not assume here that all travelers tried to acquire pieces of art to take back to France. However, it is clear that numerous incidents of this kind did take place. The majority of such objects were of little value and were not of any major historical significance. They were not the fabulous statues and statuettes that are disappearing from the temples now, totally destroying the cultural heritage of the country. Certain objects of art, however, that left Cambodia at the time were of very significant value. Most of them, though, were destined to go to museums, like the Guimet Museum, where they can still be found now. A certain portion of them went to private collections.

Post-colonial Period/Modern Times (1970—Present)

The Reasons for the Growth of
Illegal Trafficking of Art in Cambodia

Art is exported illicitly from just about any country in the world. Such unprecedented pillage as took place in Cambodia over the last few decades raises several questions on the background of this trade. There are many factors that could explain the development of the trade inside Cambodia and explain why Cambodia developed such an international advantage in the illicit trafficking of art.

First and foremost, Cambodia possesses a unique cultural heritage, most of which has been researched and studied by French scholars working in Cambodia. Another reason is that most of this heritage, over a thousand of the unknown temples and unexcavated sites that are often known only to the local people, are situated in the middle of the vast forests and jungles with no roads and no means of access. Often even the local administration does not have good means of transportation. The regions are very isolated and many of them have remained heavily mined after the wars, which also makes it difficult for archaeologists and the police to have access to or guard the temples. The geopolitical location is also quite important. Cambodia is located next to Thailand, which over the last decades has been a route for contraband and trafficking of drugs, arts, and gem stones and still remains among the first-ranked cities for organized crime and the underground art trade.

On the other hand, the trade has also grown due to a number of historical factors that have created a favorable environment for illegal trade in the country, such as the administrative system whose infrastructure is dictated by the traditional Cambodian system. Another element consists of recent political events, which cannot be overestimated. Cambodia has suffered probably more than any other country in the last decades from the Pol Pot regime and constant wars that have brought great destruction,

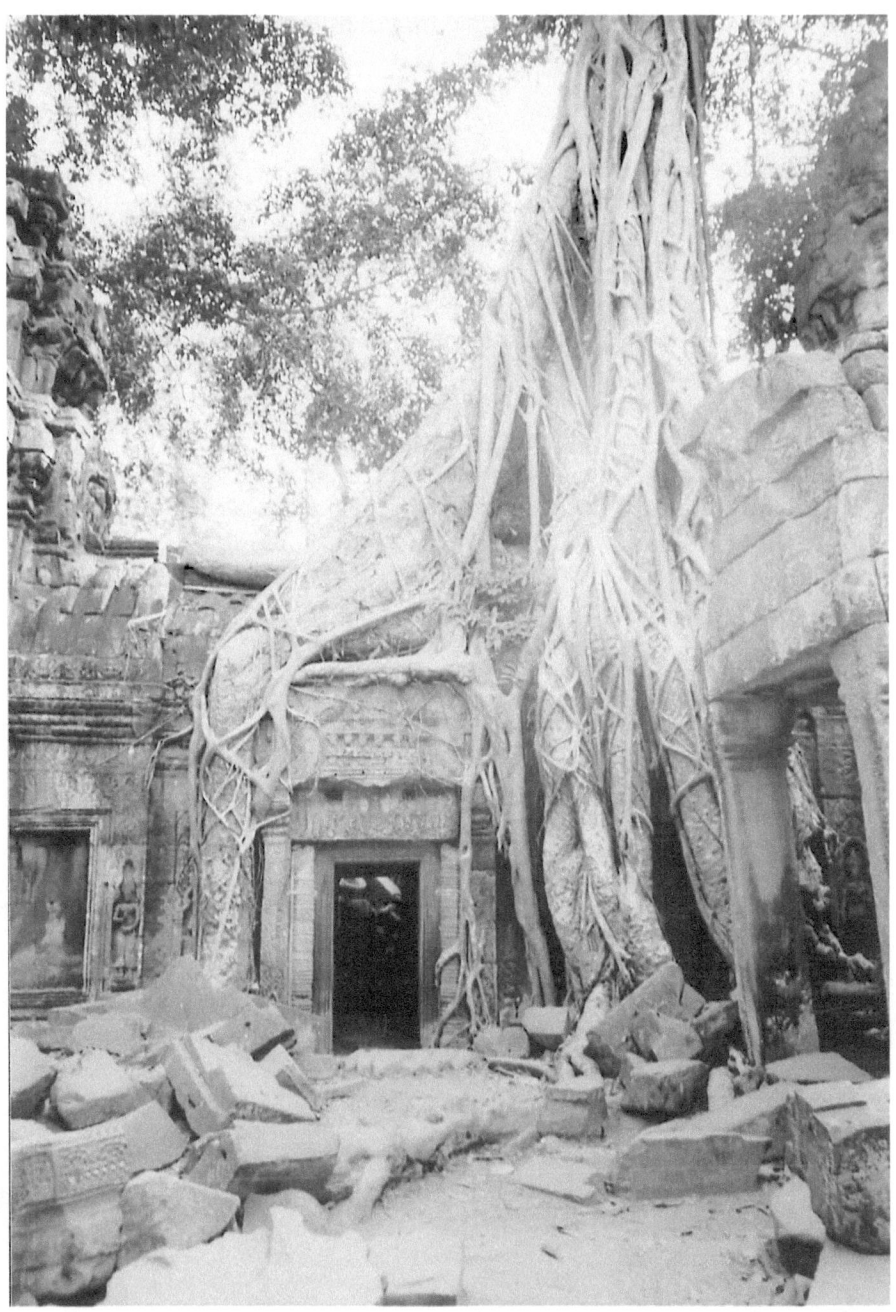

Temple of Ta Prohm: end of the twelfth century; built during the reign of Jayavarman VII.

worsened poverty, and a poor economy and have destroyed people's lives and social systems and have brought about new misfortunes.

Cultural Heritage

Analyzing the first group of reasons, one finds that the Cambodian cultural heritage possesses many magnificent temples that contain rare objects of art. Scattered all over the country they remain for years far out of sight, neither safeguarded nor protected. There are as well many temples of lesser quality that still hide many significant works of art. Another important aspect in Cambodia is that its nineteen regions are very isolated. There is often no effective connection between the provinces. The population density in some of them remains low. As the territories are not visited regularly by the authorities, foreign visitors or tourists, the risk of theft is high. At the same time there are many unexcavated sites and unknown temples. Dozens of temples in the provinces are often known

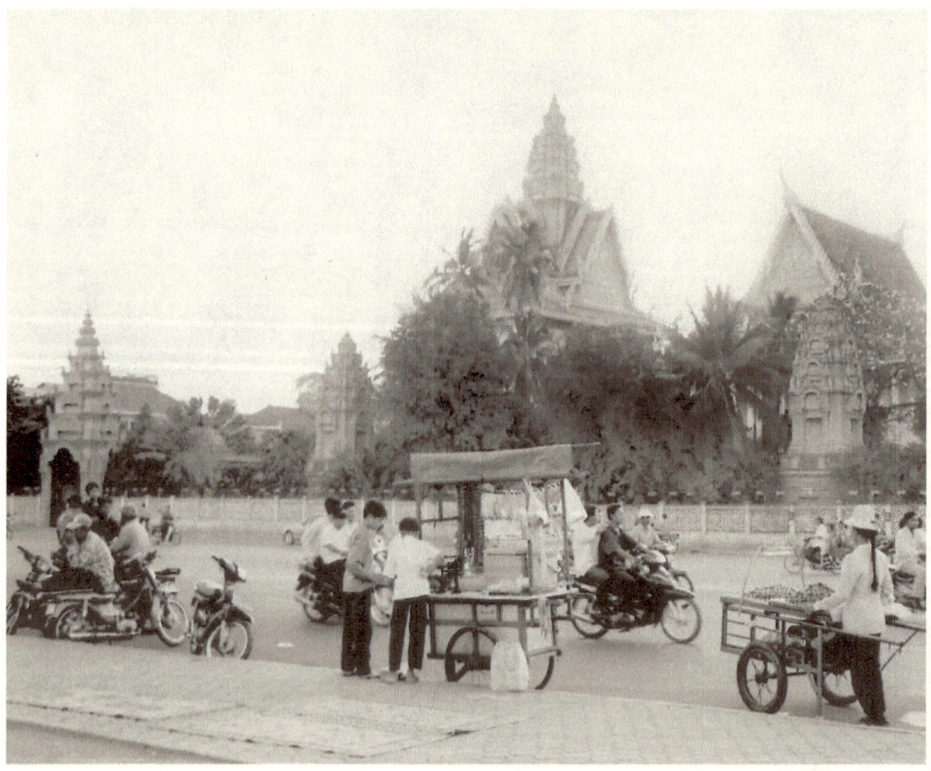

Vendors and motorikshas in front of the Wat Ounalom; center of Phnom Penh.

only to the locals. Even in cases where the temple is known to the Cambodian authority or to foreign scholars working in the country, its isolated location makes it hard to protect.

Another very important element that contributes to the growth of trafficking and is unique to Cambodia in comparison with the rest of the region is that the prices at which art can be obtained in Cambodia are very low, even compared with the neighboring countries, Laos and Vietnam. High prices make the profit margins of the middlemen larger than in any other country in this trade. At the same time, the majority of the participants involved in the trafficking web agree to do any work for a few hundred dollars, and often less than that. A similar situation exists only in Nigeria, where large numbers of artifacts are obtained by dealers at relatively small prices.

Another reason that this trade is convenient is that the border between Thailand and Cambodia has served for centuries as a way of communication between the two countries for transporting various goods. The contraband (which has a long tradition in Cambodia) of many consumer goods was institutionalized at the end of the 1970s and promoted the development of a flourishing business that gained legitimacy and destroyed the social stigma attached to this activity. This trade contributed to the establishment of links between Cambodian and foreign smugglers and allowed Cambodians to gain experience and develop further know-how in these transactions. It is practically impossible to stop the trafficking between the two countries or to do anything about it.

Cambodian Traditional Administrative System

Widespread corruption, political problems, the absence of any clear administrative system, and a lack of expertise are just some of the factors that help to explain the growth of illicit trafficking in Cambodia.

The Cambodian administrative system differs significantly from its French equivalent. The common belief is that when the French arrived in Cambodia in the nineteenth century, they found an administrative vacuum and that since ancient times Cambodia had never had a proper administrative or governmental system. Research conducted recently by scholars shows that the administrative system has in fact existed in this society for centuries.

It is true, however, that when the French came and established the protectorate in 1863 they found a system that was not compatible with the norms of European society and established the French administrative system, which continued to co-exist with the traditional one but was never really adapted into the local system. When analyzing the modern Cambodian system one can see many parallels with the past that help us to understand the main tendencies in the society.

As the regions in Cambodia have always been isolated, the governors in the provinces have had a lot of power and were treated by the local people almost as kings. The governors, while showing themselves as the most obedient servants of the king, have tried to take as much as they can from their positions. "Even the idealized theory provided that some of these provinces should fall outside the king's control for general administrative matters.... Probably an even greater qualification to the king's temporal power was that exercised by the great officials in the outer provinces...they frequently exercised the powers and enjoyed the privileges which might normally be expected to belong only to a king."[17]

Just about everybody in the country including the police, the army and politicians are trying to make extra money to have a better life and a better position in society. Bribes have always been considered the norm. Bribes are so common and cover every part of daily life that one does not even notice where the bribery starts and ends. Since early times the country had countless numbers of officials who had titles but no specific functions and who took personal levies from the people. In modern times the Khmer society continues to resemble a relationship of patron-client.

Corruption is a part of the traditional culture of the country. It exists in traditions and defines relations between people and classes in the society. For example, for centuries a level of civil servants was composed of the Mandarins, who did not have any official responsibilities but simply collected money from those who were on the lower levels of the hierarchy.

Power and wealth are other important components of Cambodian society. On the one hand, the country has always experienced economic difficulties, while on the other, the people in this region enjoy showing off their power and wealth. The drive to acquire these two attributes is very strong; they are almost always obtained by means that would be considered doubtful to Western understanding.

Such an extreme level of corruption explains in some ways the facility of trafficking in the country and reflects the destruction that exists in the country on a governmental level. When any civil servant working in the ministry, in the customs or in any other governmental structure earns between ten and twenty dollars a month, this employee is ready to cooperate with art buyers and traffickers for any amount of money. Because the number of educated and professional people is still rather low due to such poor salaries, the people who manage to receive a good education and speak foreign languages try to find work in private and international sectors, where the salary easily exceeds one hundred dollars a month and can be as much as one thousand dollars a month. Therefore, another important element is that the people who end up working in the ministries are those who are often underqualified to get any better work.[18] "Civil servants regard the state as a foster father. Considering public property as their own, they developed a habit of helping themselves to the office supplies."[19]

In modern days the character of the system has remained practically the same. The rich and powerful are highly respected and the poor and weak are rejected and not supported by society. The Khmers continue to live with their own idea about the functioning of the administrative system that together with the traditional hierarchical system of relations established by the canons of Theravada Buddhism, has many effects on what happens in the country and in society. The worsened attitude is explained by the way society has been affected by the regime of Pol Pot and the Vietnamese invasion.

Consequences of the Pol Pot Regime

When analyzing the Cambodian society and the life of the people today, one should not underestimate the way the Pol Pot regime changed the society. The Khmer people often talk about losing their culture after going through four years of genocide, when all the professional and intellectual people were either killed or left the country. The Cambodians who now live abroad in Europe and America as well as the Khmers who live in Cambodia express their fears that the Khmer as a people will cease to exist.[20]

One sees destruction in all parts of society. The dissolution of the system of social relations has changed the lives of people in the villages and in the cities. The society has been broken into parts. Many of the relationships and traditions that existed have been changed or have completely disappeared. Although the changes have not been studied yet in depth, they are evident in relationships that were modified after people had spent years in the refugee camps on the Thai border or in the labor camps where they were forced to work during the years of the Pol Pot regime.

If the fear that the Khmer people have ceased to exist can be overexaggerated, it is true that the Khmer culture was substantially damaged during the four years of the Democratic Kampuchea. The losses are evident in all the spheres of life: economical, technical, administrative, judicial, artistic and scientific. One can give thousands of examples from the lives of Cambodians of today that show the lack of the most simple and basic infrastructure in the country. For example, all the people who work today in administrative positions constitute the first, or in some cases the second, generation of civil servants, who started to work a mere twenty years ago in the 1980s. Many of them received education in the former Soviet Union. Practically all records, documentation, and papers were destroyed by the Khmer Rouge together with the knowledge and the techniques of work. The new generation of civil servants has nothing to rely on.

Another important factor behind the country's advantage in the industry has been the process of delegitimation of the regime. Delegitimation is another element that makes Cambodia such a convenient location for illicit trade. It is one of the factors that lowers the trade's risk. The legal system is just one of the areas being established in Cambodia practically from the start. All the events of the last thirty years have contributed to that factor in Indochina. The events in Cambodia were without doubt much more violent. The high level of violence implicitly lowered the value of human life and made Cambodians more prone to use violence to solve their conflicts, a useful trait in a high-profit, high-risk business in which conflict cannot be resolved through legal channels.

The field relevant to this paper—the protection of cultural heritage— has only recently been developed. There was no law for the protection of cultural heritage. The first attempt to write such a law was made in 1994 with the help of Swiss lawyer R. Fraoua, who was invited to Cambodia. Significant professional help was also provided by UNESCO and international lawyers working in UNESCO. The Cambodians themselves could not write such a law due to the lack of professional knowledge and the absence of qualified lawyers.

The law that now exists is, however, ineffective because there are no sub-decrees that may put it into force partly because there is nobody who can write it and partly because Cambodians themselves are not willing to make the necessary efforts and accelerate the process. For example, there are no sub-decrees outlining the procedures for importing and exporting objects of art from the country. That makes the efforts to combat illicit trafficking of art practically useless because nobody can legally explain how to import or export art from the country. Even if the law existed in Cambodia, it would be difficult to make people follow it, considering the level of corruption and delegitimation in the country. Without the law the attempts to stop trafficking are practically impossible.

Much destruction has been done in the cultural sphere; for example, many skills known only to certain individuals have disappeared. That includes many artisan skills known only to certain people, and prayers and Buddhist chants known only by certain monks. Traditional dancing,

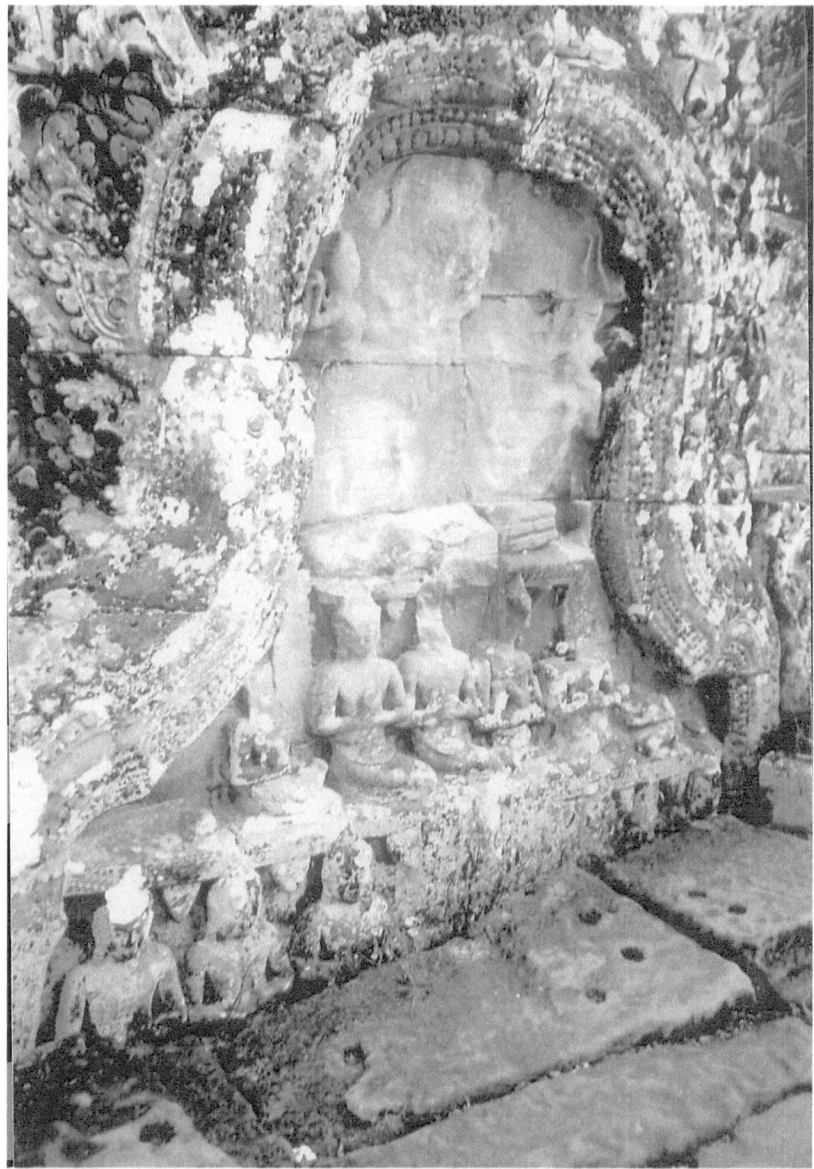

Bas-relief at the temple of Bayon; twelfth century; built during the reign of Jayavarman VII.

weaving, and work done by particular craftsmen were completely lost after these people were killed during the years of Pol Pot. Many documents, texts and books were destroyed by the Khmer Rouge. For example, the National

Library has only three hundred unduplicated titles left. Before 1975 Cambodia had thirty-six archaeologists; after 1975 more than half had left the country, and of those who stayed only three had survived in 1979.[21]

P. Dyphon writes: "Between 1975 and 1979 the holocaust of Pol Pot and the Khmer Rouge destroyed not only between 2 and 3 million lives, but uncountable artifacts bearing witness to Cambodian culture and civilization. I can give examples of such destruction that I myself witnessed: the decapitation of the large statues of Buddha and the crushing into dust of the smaller ones; the burning of the handsome ceremonial costumes used in dance and weddings; and the confiscation of our personal jewelry."[22]

Analyzing all the factors mentioned above, one can see that there is a basis for the establishment of illegal trafficking of arts. For a long time Cambodia has had a set of conditions that have minimized the risk for the traffickers, attracted the continuation of the trade, allowed the trade to develop a network and promoted the trade on the international market. One of the most important elements is the process of delegitimation, followed by the bureaucratic administrative system and corruption both in public and private sectors. Similar features exist in other countries in this region because many states are weak and incapable of controlling their territories.

However, by comparing Cambodia to other countries, one finds that much difference has been made by the years of Pol Pot regime, which destroyed the social system and eliminated or lowered many of the values, including the value of human life. All these factors as well as the low prices for objects of art and low value of labor in the country give Cambodia an "advantage" on the international level.

The Art Trafficking System

The discussion of illicit trafficking of art raises many questions. Who are the participants? How and when did the trafficking originate? How do the objects of Khmer art manage to leave Cambodia unnoticed in such vast quantities? How do they reach other continents? Who are the intermediaries and who exactly is making a profit from this trade? Is it possible to analyze and address the real scope of the problem? It is virtually impossible to provide accurate answers to these questions. The vast network that has worked so actively to plunder the Cambodian heritage over the last thirty years and even before that operates in such a secret way that no definitive statement can be made concerning the real extent of this

MAP 1: SOUTH EAST ASIAN REGION (Jesus del Rio Luelmo)

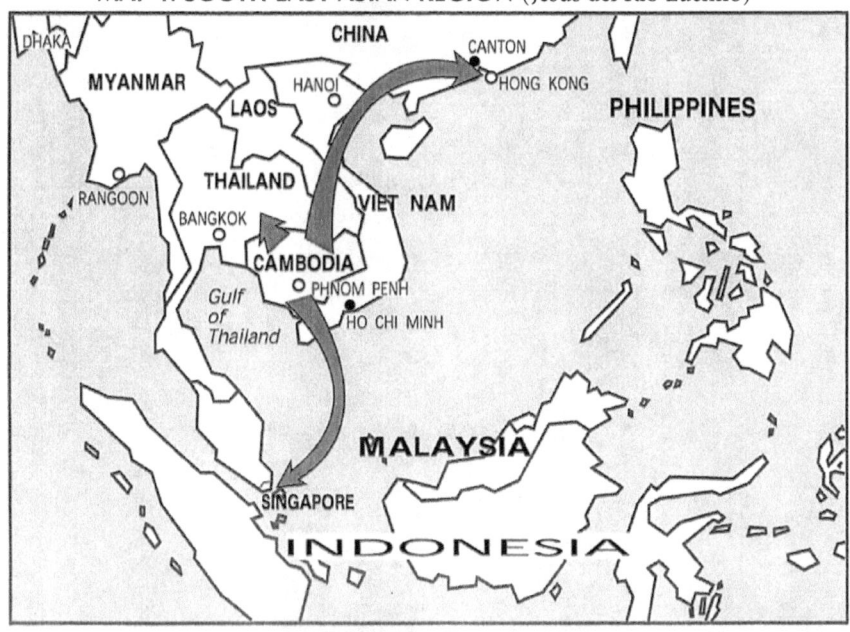

MAP 2: CAMBODIA (Jesus del Rio Luelmo)

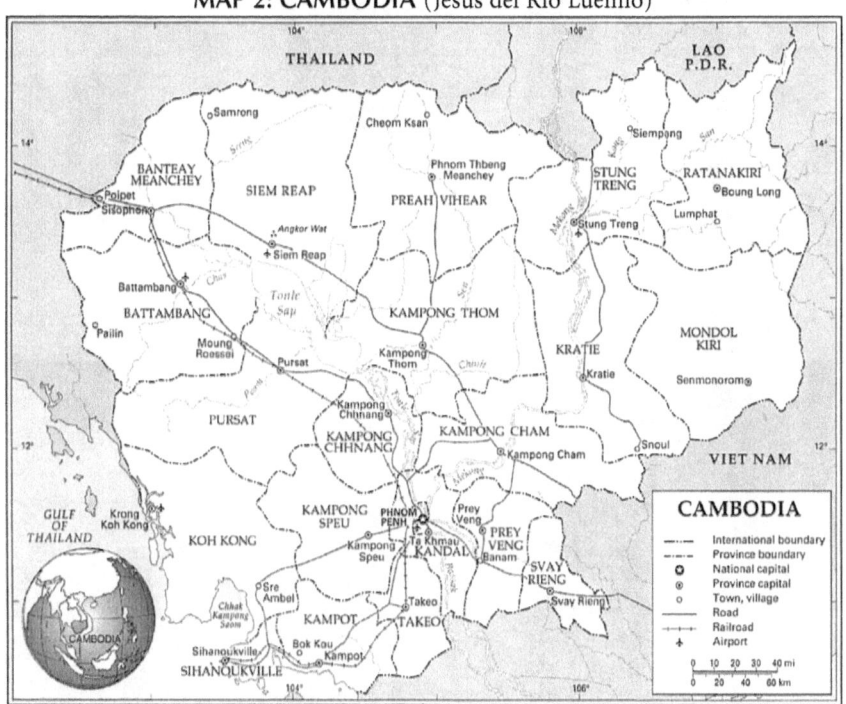

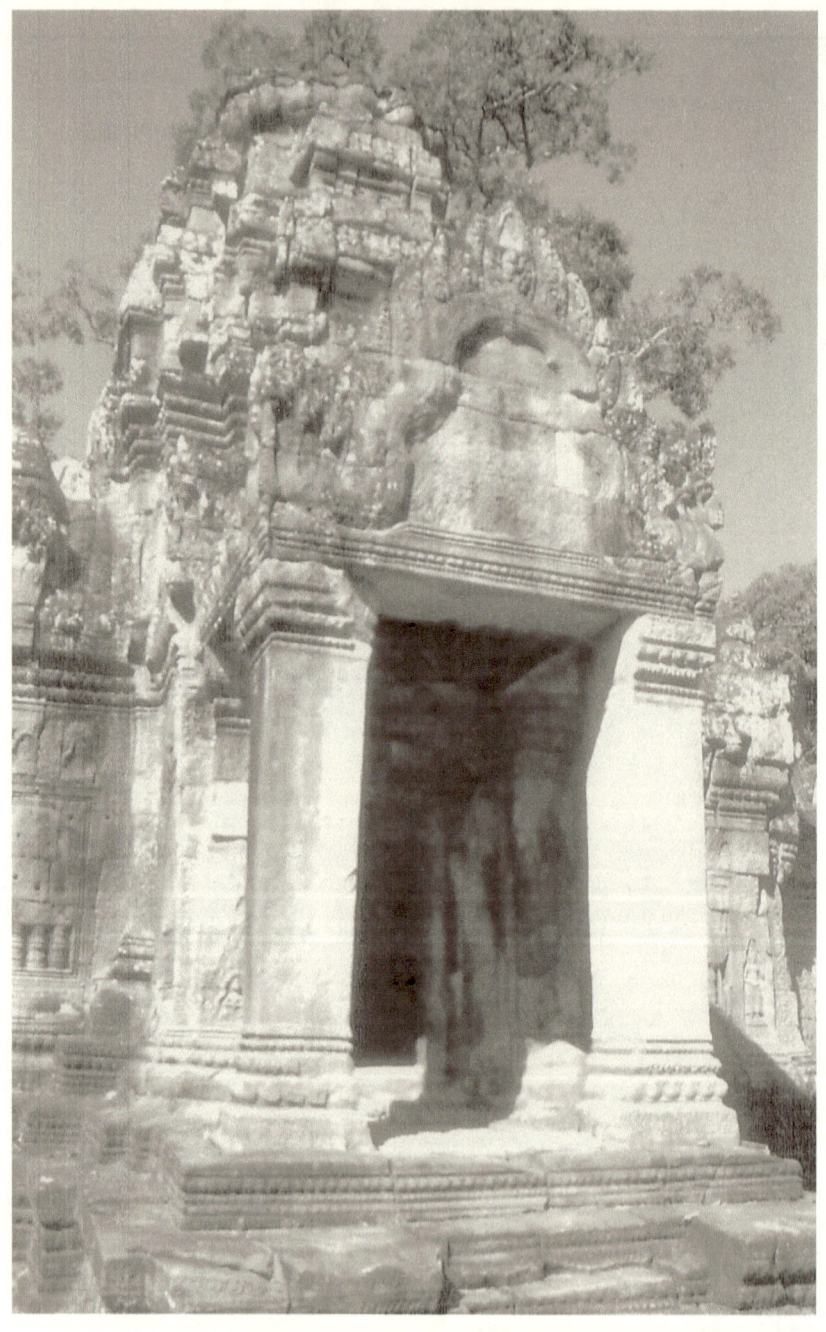

Temple of Preah Khan; twelfth century; built by Jayavarman VII.

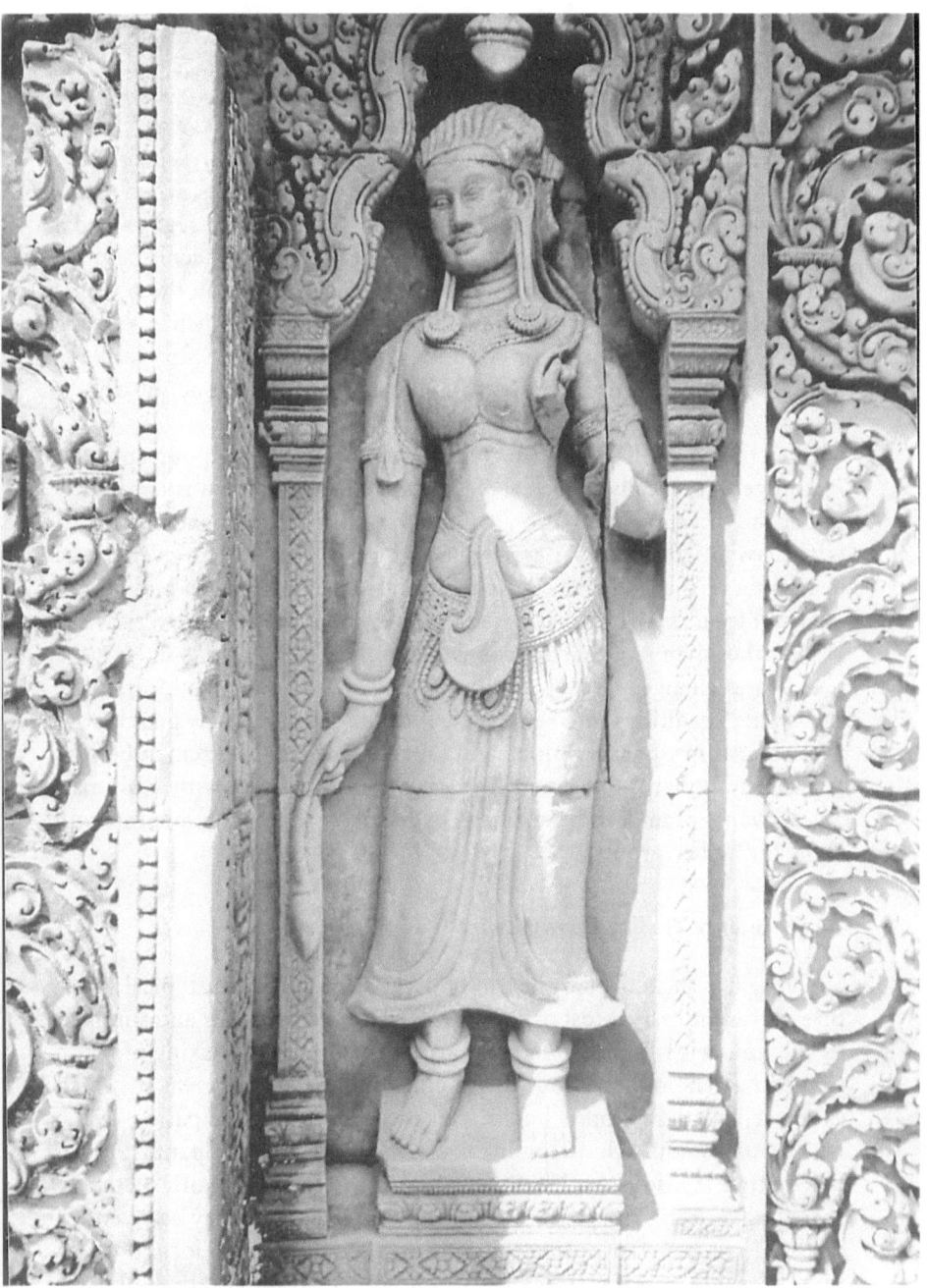

Temple of Banteay Srei; end of the tenth to beginning of the eleventh century; built by Jayavarman V.

trade. Nor can responsibility be apportioned fairly among the parties. It is quite clear, however, that these problems exist.

In this section I will explain the development of illegal trafficking in Cambodia. To analyze it one must understand the country's processes of change; the main structural changes experienced by society, such as the effect of the Khmer Rouge; the impact of external changes, when Cambodia—after being through years of civil wars, the Pol Pot regime and a decade under the influence of the former Soviet Union—suddenly became, if not a part of the international system, at least open to all the possible financial, political and economical influences from the outside; and the political situation in the country and response to it, which still gives the military a lot of freedom, power and the ability to do just about what it wants.

At the turn of the century Cambodia was a rather poor country. Placed geographically between Vietnam and Thailand, it was constantly under the threat of occupation. Although trafficking happened throughout the twentieth century, it was not a major public issue. However, by the beginning of the 1970s, the scale of operations had changed and generated an illegal export boom. It was a problem that developed over several years rather than one that appeared overnight.

Times change. Twenty or thirty years ago, dealers would organize full-sized expeditions into remote parts of the country. Many people who participated in the expeditions and witnessed the pillage remember the trucks arriving at the site and leaving later fully loaded with sculpture. Today, works of art can be acquired by means that are less elaborate and allow for higher profits.

The Structure of Illegal Trafficking

Illegal trafficking of art in Cambodia appears to have the typical structure of this industry. Most of the objects of art are provided and supplied by the military, who are the main participants in the trafficking of art in Cambodia. The military loot the temples situated in the areas in which each particular division is based. The predominant participation of the military does not exclude the involvement of other participants. Part of the looting is also done by organized groups of people, often created specifically for this purpose. The list of potential looters may be extended further to include various categories of people such as the local population, peasants, monks, trained gangs, tourists, administrative officials, diplomats, and foreigners working in Cambodia. The categories of traffickers mentioned above include people from all sectors of the soci-

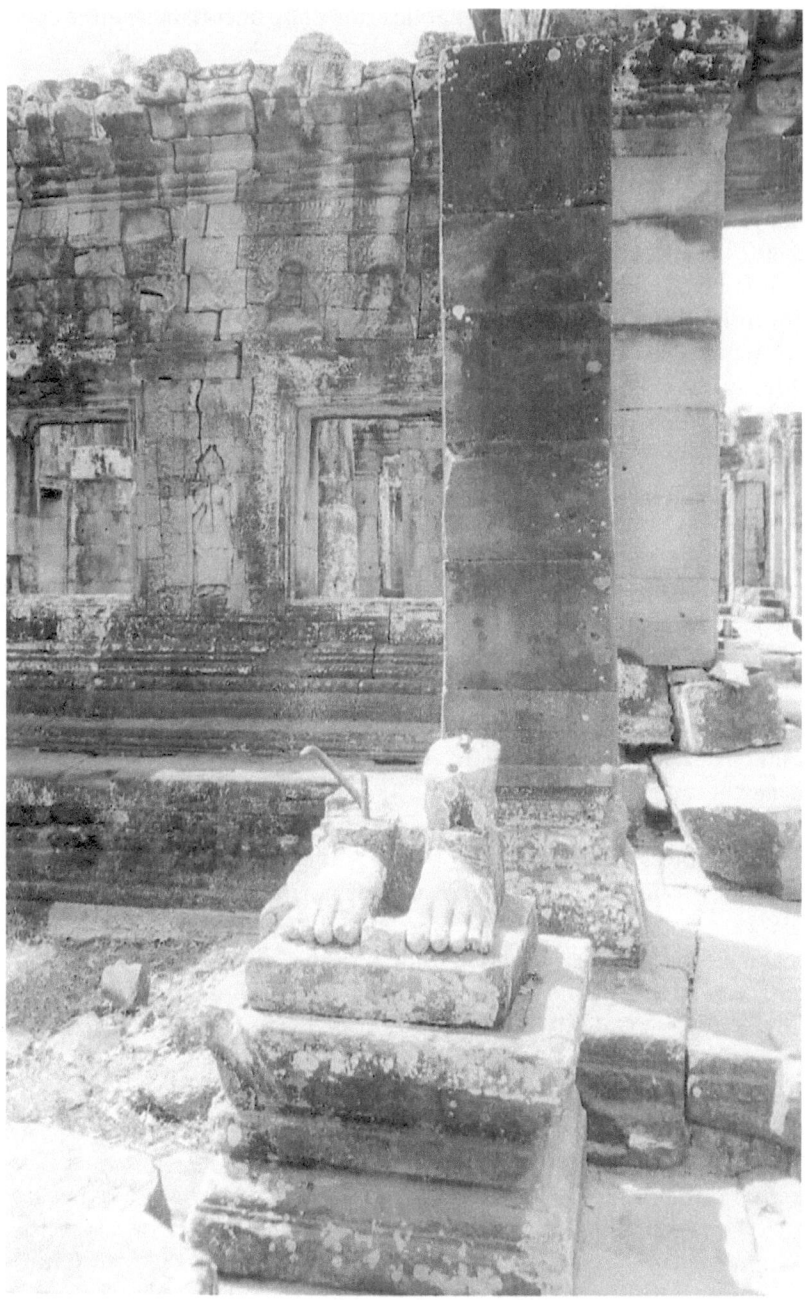

Temple of Banteay Kdei; end of the twelfth century; built during the reign of Jayavarman VII.

ety. One can therefore assume that this side of business can be quite competitive.

Nevertheless, the dominant role played by the military in the trafficking of art cannot be overestimated. In Cambodia, as in many other countries of this region, the military is a strong and well-organized body that has a certain degree of power within the country, a necessary grip over the political situation, and a high degree of authority within the government. The majority of the top and middle level military officials are active politicians; many of them occupy significant positions in Cambodian political life and participate in policy formation together with the government. The whole structure of illicit trafficking is most evidently directed from Phnom Penh by a few top military officers who are responsible for the majority of the operations that are executed by groups of soldiers all over Cambodia. The names of participants are known to the authorities, but for a number of reasons these people cannot be held responsible for their activities.

The main legal problems with illegal trafficking are connected to the absence of proof. By the time the authorities have noticed a particular piece of art is missing, it usually has already disappeared from the country along with any possible trace that may have helped to find it. For example, when a piece of Khmer art is found in Thailand, in a prestigious American gallery, or indeed in any other place, the Cambodian authority cannot provide any evidence that this object is a part of the cultural heritage of the country. Certain difficulties also arise through similarities that exist between objects of art from Cambodia and from the neighboring Thai provinces.

For a long time the northern and the northwestern parts of Cambodia were under the control of Thailand. Notwithstanding the fact that many pieces of Khmer art are unique for the region, the artistic similarity is often used by the buying side as an "excuse"—an absence of proof of the provenance. Also, most of the time the particularly exceptional pieces of art are not offered for sale right away. They may be kept in storage for a rather long period of time, often for years, before they appear on the market.

From the top military officials in Phnom Penh, the orders are dispersed throughout the nineteen provinces. The provinces are rather isolated because of the absence of roads and lack of basic infrastructure within the country and for historical reasons, such as the fact that the provinces were always more dependent on local administration than on the authorities in Phnom Penh or the king. The following quote from a journalist who recently visited Cambodia gives a recent description of road conditions in Cambodia: "Many of the bridges along the way had been blown up, and we had to drive on wobbly planks laid across the wreckage. Long stretches of road were underwater, and the rest of the highway was crated with potholes twice the length of our four-by-four."[23]

The trafficking of art is considered the least dangerous kind of illicit trafficking in Cambodia. Often the traffickers may combine several activities such as trade in arms, drugs, sex, slaves, gems and cars. The profit margins in art trafficking compared with most of the illicit activities, in fact, may not be so high. Nevertheless, the trade is evidently profitable for its participants. Depending on the type of activity, it makes all of the country's borders with Thailand, Laos and Vietnam and the Cambodian ports in the Gulf of Thailand and South China Sea possible trading points for traffickers.

The military operate in small groups of four or five people under the command of a general or a lesser military authority who may be in charge of the area and provide necessary protection. It can be estimated that there are between five hundred and seven hundred soldiers operating in Cambodia; in any case the figure does not exceed one thousand. About ten gangs operate in the area of Angkor, which remains the most important area for dealers.[24] The relationship between the members of the groups, the groups themselves and the mafia on the Thai border is well organized.

The mafia on the Thai border—the officials and police who work at the checkpoints—also have their own strict rules of coexistence within this system. The head of the Police Heritage Service, based in Angkor for monument protection, says that he knows of ten groups working in the area and in the northwest who are probably responsible for the looting in the area of Siem Reap. The leaders of the groups, however, are not known, and any group member who may get caught does not give away names.[25]

Most of the operations are done at night, particularly in the area of Angkor, which is well protected by the special police unit, Police of Cultural Heritage at Angkor. In more isolated temples, however, the looting also goes on during the day. In Angkor, the statues are often stolen during heavy rains, when the guards leave the site to stay in dry places. It is also possible to assume that guards may cooperate with the looters.[26]

The growth in illicit trafficking of art has been visible on the international arena since the 1980s when the situation in the country was quite confusing. The Vietnamese still occupied the main towns, while the countryside was largely controlled by the Khmer Rouge. To finance the anti-Vietnamese movement, Khmer Rouge soldiers sold the forests and the statues situated in the regions they controlled. At that time many pieces of Khmer art appeared in European auction houses without much resistance from the Cambodian or international authorities.[27]

A significant increase in activities has happened over the last ten years, when Cambodia was opened and Angkor was rediscovered; trucks loaded with tons of artifacts could cross the border every day. Starting in 1993, the political situation in Cambodia became relatively stable. (There was much instability in 1997 when there was a danger of a military coup and many foreigners left; most of them have come back.) At the same time, the trafficking of art has not only continued but also increased in a large proportion. In 1993 the Conservation d'Angkor was attacked twice, losing more than a dozen of objects of art in the first attack and about fifteen in the second attack. However, most of the people who participate in the trade insist that the last two years have seen a decline in this activity.

At present the main checkpoints on the border used by the traffickers are Pailin on the western side of the border, Poipet on the northwest and Preah Vihear on the north. At the moment it is estimated that the trucks cross the border as often as once or twice a month; this information, however, cannot be verified. It is possible, though, that the traffickers are changing routes and many objects are going by boat via Singapore from Koh Kood, an island in the south of Cambodia, or directly from the Cambodian port of Koh Kong to the Thai port of Samut Prakan. This route is recently under suspect; as of July 1999, police had stopped forty-three pieces of Khmer art that were heading to Singapore.[28]

At each stage of the process, there is a decline in the number of participants. Throughout the chain one can observe the sellers or suppliers, the buyers and the people who resell the goods later—all these people are involved in trafficking activities in the territories of Cambodia and Thailand. Many of the art dealers who arrive at the distribution point at Paillin or Preah Vihear to get first-hand access to the materials to be send to Bangkok or other places have their own boutiques and art galleries in Bangkok. Previously at various border points one could see many foreign art dealers who would come directly from Japan, Europe or elsewhere or Cambodian dealers living outside the country, who would search for pieces of art for private collections.

Still widespread, though diminishing since the beginning of the 1990s, is the practice of specifically ordering objects of art by certain clients. However, no statistics reflecting the reality of the situation can be obtained.

When an art dealer places an order, he usually shows up at the border with the photograph of a torso or a head and may ask to obtain precisely this piece or a similar piece of art. In some cases tourists or collectors request the artifacts from known temples that they might have visited,

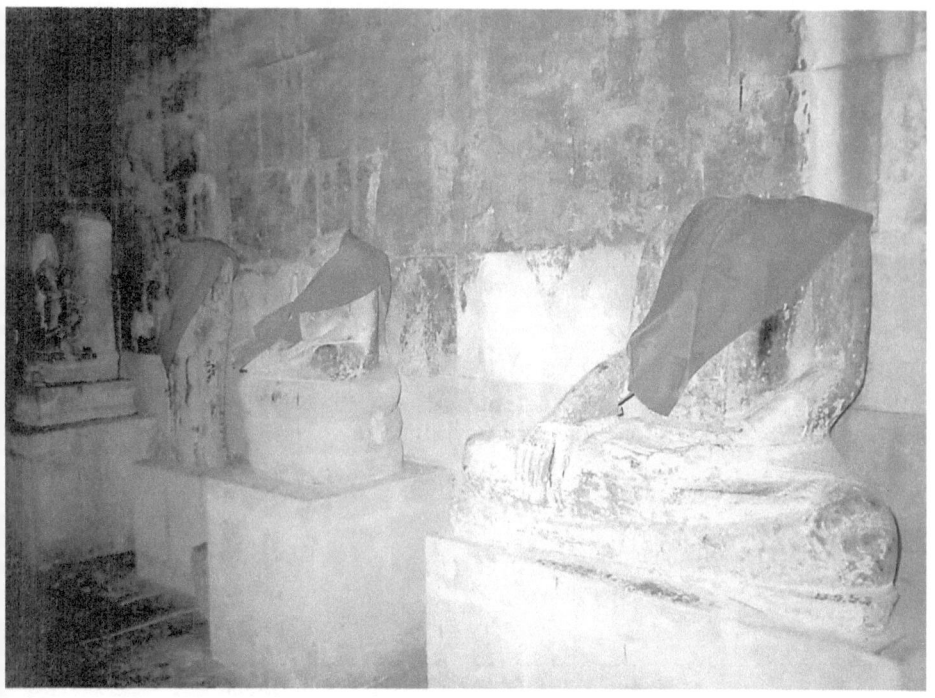

Beheaded Buddha; Angkor Wat; twelfth century; built by Suryavarman II.

such as the Temples of Angkor; these, however, have recently become harder to access.

In other cases soldiers are free to search for an identical piece in the temples they know. In both situations the gangs focus on a particular target. In special situations participants may involve somebody who knows and understands Khmer art. The whole operation might take between a couple of days and a few months, depending on the distance and the accessibility of the monument. There are many cases when the army videotapes and documents the temples and the sculptures and sends the material to the dealers in Bangkok or other neighboring countries.[29]

Two other types of looters, rare in Cambodia, include the gangs (or looters specially trained to pillage the temples) and groups of trained soldiers organized with the sole intention of obtaining certain objects of art. In the case of Cambodia, where the trafficking of art is concentrated in the hands of the military and the areas of control are defined, these types are practically nonexistent.

The areas of control are strictly divided between the soldiers. The illegality of the trade affects to some degree the structure of the trade as

MAP 3: CAMBODIAN NORTHERN BORDER WITH THAILAND

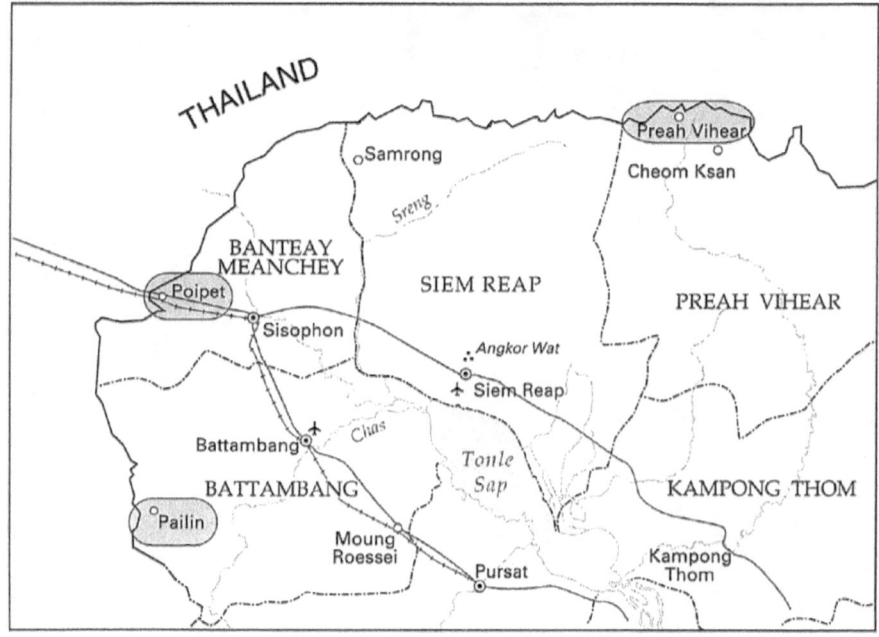

MAP 4: CAMBODIAN SOUTHERN BORDER

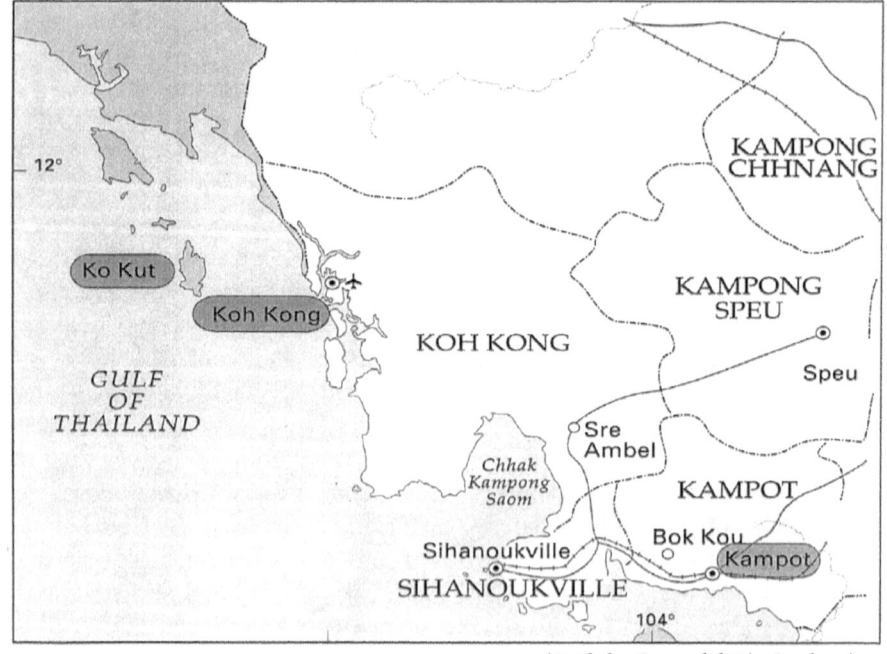

(Both by Jesus del Rio Luelmo)

well as the behavior and the strategies of its participants. It encourages risk-minimizing behavior at each stage, the location chosen, and the relationships among the participants. Some roads may be closed or blocked by Thai and Cambodian loggers or be of limited access, which somewhat reflects the level of corruption among the Cambodian security services. Even the most experienced officials say that the group leaders are neither known to the police nor to the buyers. Therefore, even if the looting may seem to be semi-open and the administration, police and the local people are aware of it, the most important members of the structure of trafficking operate very discreetly.

The relationships among the members of a gang, the gangs themselves and the dealers are, of course, based on trust because loss of the deal means loss of the piece of art and of profit. The level of competition among the groups that loot the temples is hard to determine since their exact number and coordination among them is unknown. However, knowing the character and the temper of the Cambodian people, one might assume that the relationship is very hierarchical and the rules are well outlined. There are no fights or high-level violence within or among the groups; nevertheless, there is a certain degree of violence associated with trafficking.

Most of the problems arise on the financial basis, when the groups or their members cannot divide the money. It is interesting to note that to solve the conflict, the members of the group that are being punished may be sent to jail. In fact, Cambodians are rarely known for solving problems by killing each other but rather by choosing other methods that may be very cruel and elaborate. In any case, no matter how the structure of the trade may vary, the most important features of this trade are determined by illegality.

Not all art is transported directly outside the country. Many objects can be bought in Cambodia in Phnom Penh and Siem Reap. The markets that offer souvenirs to foreigners will always have pieces of art for sale. In particular, shops selling copies of Khmer art will always have a few pieces to offer; one may look for them in one of the numerous boxes that are kept in the shop. This is true not only of bronze or wooden pieces but also of pottery or long leaves of papyrus that were used to write the history of Cambodia. Stolen from archaeological excavations, they are sold on the market as souvenirs and for the purpose of transportation they are often cut into to pieces. About five years ago the trade in Cambodia was more open; now the sellers are much more discreet, but the trade still continues. Among the sellers one can often find Thai citizens who actively participate in the art trade. Recently the art dealers in Cambodia are being very careful because they are prosecuted by the government and the police.

Cases when the sellers get arrested for trading art in Siem Reap or Phnom Penh are rather common.[30]

The looting is not done without the help of the local people who live in the area and know all the monuments that are often unknown both to researchers and to the military. In the 1960s the peasants handed over Khmer art objects to the government. In Battambang province officials and scholars accumulated so many objects of art that they opened a museum in the province under the supervision of Madeleine Gigot. This was destroyed by the Khmer Rouge in the 1970s. At the beginning of the 1970s, when war and instability started to destroy the country, many peasants hid the statues, trusting neither the Khmer Rouge nor other invaders.

After 1979, when the country was on the verge of starvation (in Phnom Penh the family of an official was allowed thirty-five pounds [sixteen kilograms] of rice per month) and the discovery and subsequent sale of objects of art could earn enough money to support the entire family or even a village for a year, the local population began to work together with the military. The soldiers would always buy these pieces from locals. Many peasants also enjoyed the protection of the military, which they received in return for helping to loot pieces of art.[31] It is possible to understand the people whose lives were so difficult that they were willing to go to any means to make money. It is also true that they were not aware of the importance of these objects of art, nor did they realize their value and certainly did not understand the notion of their national heritage.

French scholars from the EFEO estimate that there is not a single temple in the researched area that was not destroyed. It is estimated that over the country about ninety-eight percent of the temples are destroyed to a certain extent or even entirely stripped of their sculptures and images.

Another type of attack, which is practically nonexistent anymore, is a direct attack by the military on the storage rooms. The Angkor Conservation Compound was built by the French in 1910 in Siem Reap to store and protect the most valuable pieces of art. Three huge storage rooms were used for storing more than five thousand statues first in view of their restoration and then, when the French were asked to leave in 1973, in view of their protection (allowed by the Vietnamese authorities). When the rooms were reopened in 1980, five hundred objects were missing, including statues of great value. Some of them were found later in museums and galleries in North America and Europe.

The curators working in the Angkor Conservation Compound mentioned that on a number of occasions they were approached by the military, who threatened to loot the temples if they did not receive protection money. Objects continued to be stolen until recently from the Angkor

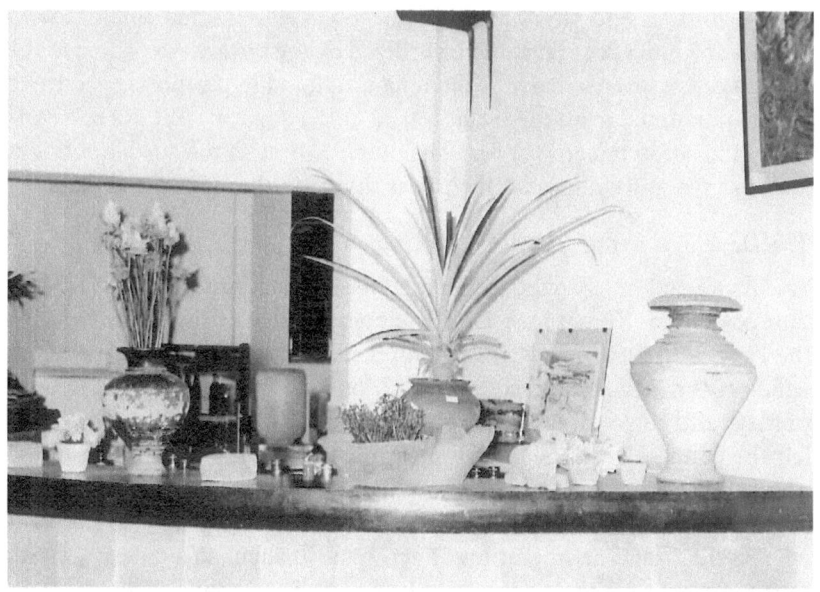

Pre-Angkorean vases.

Conservation Compound. This type of attack is rare now, after a full inventory of the Angkor Conservation Compound was completed by the employees.

On one occasion, the military even approached directly the members of UNESCO. In 1993—1994 there were several direct attacks by the local military. Richard Engelhardt, then Director of UNESCO in Cambodia, was threatened as a representative of UNESCO. The local commander came to see him to ask him not to install lights in the compound, which would make it easier for the soldiers to steal the statues. The lights were, of course, installed.

The importance of the trade has also encouraged the participants to influence the policy of bribing politicians to finance private armies. The participants may have connections in official institutions, ministries, customs or army. Often the groups have all the necessary equipment to conclude the deal. They may use all sorts of technical equipment including sport planes, which may be used in advance to photograph the objects of art or transport the pieces.

Once over the border, the objects are sold to dealers who are waiting for them at that point; most of them have shops in Bangkok. The trade is primarily done on the basis of first come, first served.

When the objects of art get to Bangkok, the price on them increases several-fold. Already by the end of the 1970s dealers had catalogs with objects of Khmer art that could be ordered by the buyers. According to the owners of the shops, many of them had diplomatic passports. The River City had boomed from the 1980s. Called an art supermarket, it has a convenient location next to the best Thai hotels. Some of the small boutiques look like real museums with the prices shown in thousands of dollars.[32]

The Development of Illegal Trafficking

As already mentioned, trafficking itself has a long history. The volume of trade in Khmer objects of art appears to have grown somewhat in the 1950s and 1960s in response to an increase in international demand, which at this stage remained indirect. More and more foreign diplomats, tourists, and elite visitors on the governmental level visited Cambodia and left the country with the official presents, which only in rare cases were not Khmer objects of art. This movement of art had not yet turned into a trade.

At the time, the migration of art was still small and did not attract much attention either domestically or internationally. The problem became evident in the 1970s in response to an increase in outside demand. It was initiated by American soldiers and officials based in neighboring Thailand during the Vietnam War on the one hand and by the Cambodian army that needed money to fight the civil war on the other.

The period between 1970 and 1975 saw some violent attacks on the storage rooms of Angkor, where the best statues were preserved. The attacks were made by Vietnamese and Khmer Rouge soldiers. After staying intact for centuries, Angkor was in danger after just a few years of war. The years of the Pol Pot regime did great damage to the cultural heritage of the country. Many witnesses and scholars, however, insist that the soldiers of the Democratic Kampuchea continued to respect the temples. Many statues were more damaged by acts of vandalism or ignorance than by intentional destruction or looting for sale. On the contrary, many soldiers recognized Angkor as the Cambodian heritage and respected the labor of the people who worked on these objects. If we look at the communist flag of Cambodia, we will see that it contains the Towers of Angkor, which remained even during the years of the Pol Pot Regime.

Nevertheless, between 1976 and 1977 there were other attacks on the Angkor Conservation Compound during which all the conservators were killed and dozens of priceless statues disappeared.[33] Some of the monuments were damaged and destroyed by the soldiers who were based in Angkor. The territory of Angkor was also damaged and turned into agricultural fields.

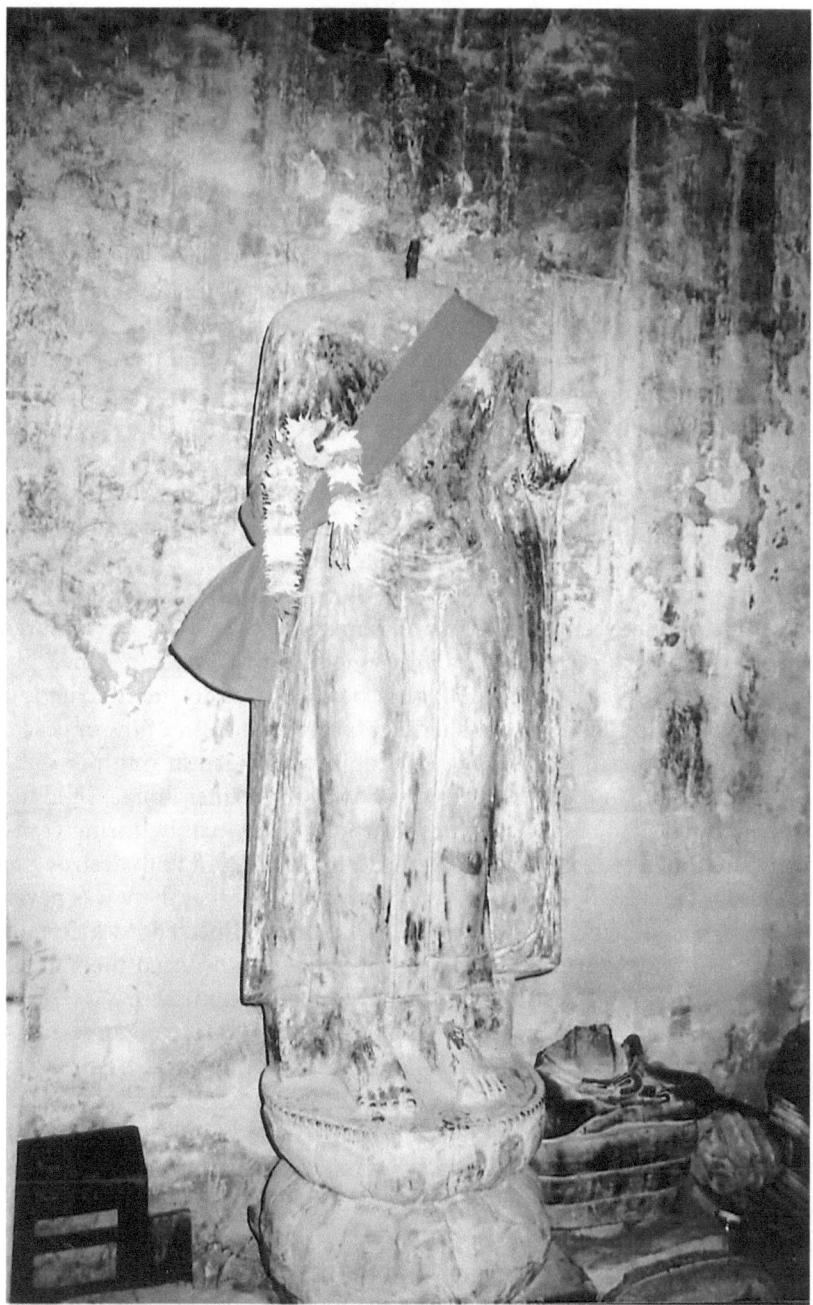

Beheaded Buddha; Temple of Angkor Wat; twelfth century; built by Suryavarman II.

The Japanese scholar Yoshiaki Ishizawa, who was the first to visit Angkor after the Pol Pot regime, wrote: *"Tout en étant consternés par ce changement brutal...au bord du bassin méridional, dans les buissons et les herbes qui poussaient à hauteur d'homme, nous avions découvert les débris d'une trentaine des statues du Bouddha et d'autres divinités, corps décapités, têtes et membres brisés et dispersés; il est probable qu'on ne les avait transportés là que pour les détruire."*[34]

Pich Keo—ex-Director of Conservation d'Angkor, ex-Director of the National Museum in Phnom Penh, and Professor of Archaeology at the Institute of Fine Arts in Phnom Penh—said that it was only in 1980, one year after the liberation of 1979, that he received a small van from the Ministry of Culture so that he could go around Siem Reap to examine the situation (all he had had for one year to move around Angkor was a bicycle) and to go to the Angkor Conservation Compound. When he opened it in 1980 for the first time after four years, he saw the destruction done to the statues. "Certain statues were broken, heads which had been broken off and restored before 1975 were beheaded again. The Museum of Battambang was practically emptied by the Khmer Rouge, they had sold it to Thai dealers. Between April 1975 and January 1979 they took sculptures from Battambang to the border in exchange for arms and medicine."[35]

However, this destruction cannot be compared to the destruction done to the Cambodian cultural heritage by the military in a time of peace. The attitude toward the Buddhist art objects changed during the Vietnamese invasion and the continuing war with the Khmer Rouge. Used for worshipping, many of the temples lost their value mainly during communism, which eroded religion, although the soldiers did not destroy the statues of the past. Some reports of the civil war say that there was never a war in the archaeological areas and all parties respected, to a certain extent, the temple area. In some cases the fighting between the Khmer Rouge and Cambodians stopped when the soldiers came across a temple or some archaeological findings. In the time of the Khmer Rouge, destruction of the cultural heritage came not only from looting but also from vandalism. The soldiers destroyed probably many more statues simply as an act of destruction than they took for sale in Thailand.

Certain damage was done to the temples at the time when soldiers stored arms and food in the temples and warehouses and mined certain areas around the temples. In some of the storage places that were used for arms, the Khmer Rouge burned all the materials, books or records that were stored there. Zones located next to war activities created favorable conditions for the gangs who were in touch with the dealers in Bangkok. The main trafficking we are talking about today started probably as early as 1977—1979. It is then that the first Polaroid snapshots and even catalogs started to appear with the orders that the art dealers were placing with Cambodians living in the camps. One witness tells the story that, in 1978, the Khmer Rouge criminals set a fire in one of the camps on the Thai border, which revealed a storage place containing Khmer works of art.[36] After the National Liberation in January 1979 the easiest way to make some money in the impoverished country was to sell and traffic everything that could be found. The goods for sale were often packed in governmental documents and papers found in the ministries that had survived the Pol Pot regime. "Another method of primitively accumulating business capital was pillage. As the population flowed back into Phnom Penh in 1979, everything still intact was fair game. Surviving libraries were looted and their contents put on sale or, in the case of dossier and newspapers, used for wrapping parcels. Many other articles for use or resale were available from both former government offices and private houses left untouched since 1975...."[37]

The period between 1979 and 1986 was relatively quiet for the art trade. The analysis of various materials shows that the actual trafficking started after 1986 and gained momentum at the beginning of the 1990s. In the mid-1980s Khmer art became highly reputable on the American market. Finally, the trafficking has increased significantly since the 1990s. At present the number of objects of stolen art exceeds hundreds of thousands and is on the increase. If between 1993 and 1998 police seized forty pieces of art, in the first half of 1999 the figure was one thousand.[38]

Until the last few years the shops in Bangkok directly exhibited pieces of Khmer art, and only the events of the last two to three years have forced them to hide the objects in back rooms. Even a few years ago, one could come across precious statues in the galleries of Bangkok with an average price of two million dollars, and many statues proved to be from the area of Angkor. The situation in Cambodia allowed groups to go to the temples situated not far from the border with Thailand to look for statues, which became in great demand. The origin of trafficking development can be traced to the subsequent search for a new source to supply the U.S. and European market.

The art dealers in Phnom Penh point out that in the last two years the numbers of objects of art that have passed over the Thai borders have significantly decreased. If a few years ago one could see new objects of art on the border every day, the present level of trade has dropped by more than half. Sometimes the trucks do not go more than twice a month. However, it is obvious that the participation of the Cambodians in the trafficking of art has not stopped and the important question that is yet unanswered is what are the new routes used by the traffickers.

The information gathered by scholars shows that there is an equal amount of looting in all regions of Cambodia. The temples are pillaged not only in the north and northwest but everywhere around the country. One can assume that the Thai border is a convenient but not vital way of transportation. Most probably there is a sharp increase in trafficking through other routes such as Laos, Vietnam, the Cambodian seaports via Hong Kong and Singapore and often back again to Thailand before leaving the region of Southeast Asia.

None of these routes has yet been "confirmed" by the police or any other sources and the new techniques used by the traffickers remain unknown. Also, Khmer art still remains hard to transport and presents certain smuggling difficulties because of its relatively heavy weight and its differing values, if it is compared with the rest of the categories of products that are traded illegally.

The Central Trafficking Route on the Thai Border

The trafficking of art over the border with Thailand has remained a significant issue in the politics between the two countries as well as on the international level for several decades. The border issue, however, has existed for much longer. Various kinds of exchanges as well as legal and illegal trade have existed for centuries at the Thai border, which is about 807 miles (1,300 kilometers) long. Since ancient times, the local population has migrated between the two countries for political and economic reasons and even at present the area remains ethnically mixed. Many of the border people may not even be sure which country they belong to.

It has become a main trading point between the two countries and one of the most important trade routes in the region since the 1970s. The actual scale at which all sorts of trade and various exchanges were going on changed dramatically during the Vietnamese invasion, particularly after the Vietnamese army occupied Cambodia, and during the war in Vietnam with the American army based in Thailand. At times of such instability, large groups of Cambodians were forced to leave their homes to live in refugee camps on the Thai border. The camps were stretched along the border, growing with time in size and capacity. In 1979 they were up to 248 miles (400 kilometers) long.

As mentioned above, the art market has been growing since the 1950s and 1960s. However, at that time it was still very small. From the 1920s when tourism first developed in Cambodia until the 1960s, it was more a case of some officials or a small number of tourists who were presented with a piece of art or who took a few pieces away as sou-

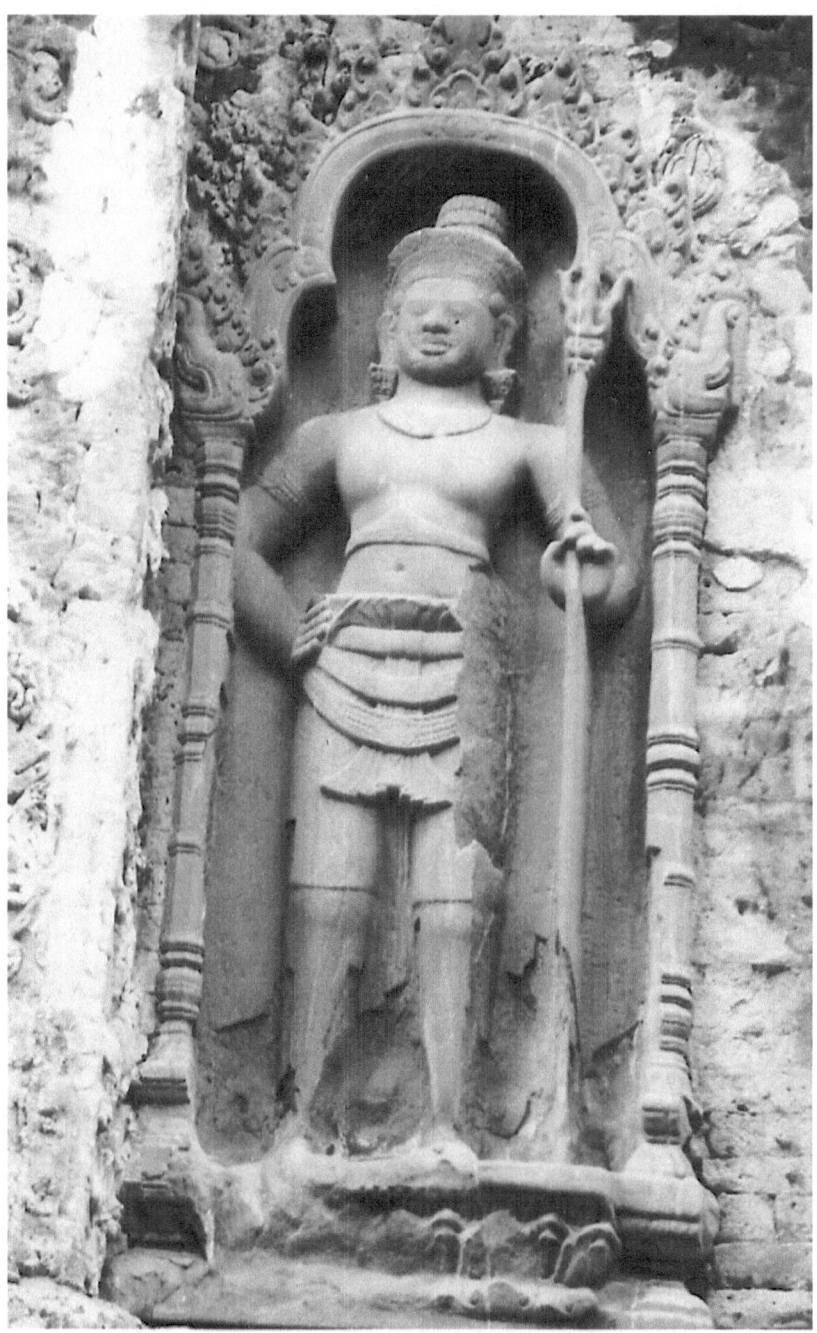

Guardian, Temple of Preah Ko.

venirs. The situation changed dramatically in the 1970s. The main reason for that was the demand of the international market and demand
from Bangkok. The demand came from dealers, tourists, and foreigners who started to arrive in Thailand. Also, the presence of the American army based in Thailand during the war in Vietnam affected in many
ways the economic infrastructure of the region and of Thailand particularly.

The scale of trade at the border started to grow and quickly reached
unprecedented dimensions. Since 1979, the economy has started to revive
in Cambodia. The introduction of the American dollars in the early 1980s
has practically excluded the use of Thai and Vietnamese currencies. The
border trade at that time was in fact very helpful for the stabilization of
the Cambodian economy. Thai goods were always available in the country, which could not produce much at the time. The trade was good not
only for the entrepreneurs but also as usual for the military of both sides.[39]

Practically all the famous temples are situated next to or not far from
the Thai border. As one can see on the map, the region of Siem Reap with
the Temples of Angkor is not very far from the Thai border and is no
doubt the most famous temple region. These temples contain the best
pieces of Khmer art and are more in danger of attack or even complete
destruction than any other temples. In fact, since the times when they
were supervised by the EFEO, the looting of objects of art meant mainly
the pillage of the famous Temples of Angkor and did not include any other
temples in the country.

All of them (about forty temples including Banteay Srei, which is
about 13 miles [21 kilometers] to the northwest of Bayon, one of the central temples on the territory of Angkor Wat) were very well known, studied, and described before 1975. The French scholars who used to work in
Angkor before 1975 and who knew all the pieces of art are still able to
define unmistakably which temple and which part of the temple the object
in question came from. On a number of occasions Bruno Dagens, who
organized the first inventory in Angkor, was able to attribute pieces of art
in the auction houses and museums.

Trafficking did not stop there. In the Siem Reap region there are about
two hundred eighty temples altogether and there are over a thousand temples scattered all over the country, which is half the size of Germany. Some
of the temples next to the Thai border are just as well known (Banteay
Chmar, Koh Ker, etc.); the rest of them, however, are often known only to
locals. With an increase in demand for objects of Khmer art, the temples
are being stripped of the statues and all freestanding objects or those parts
of the temple that can be moved away or broken apart. The quality of the

Map 5: REGION OF SIEM REAP

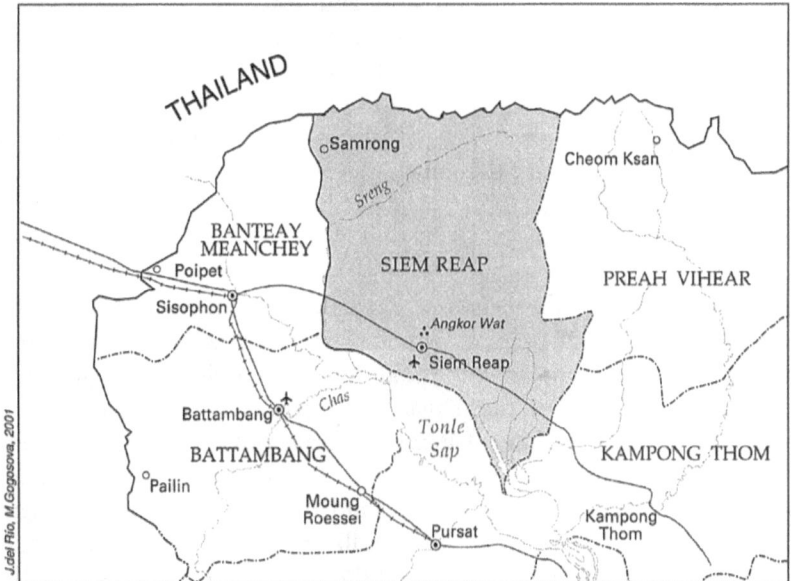

objects, of course, varies as do the artistic importance and state of preservation of the temples and of the pieces they may contain.

The quality or the condition of the pieces of art may significantly vary. Most of the temples scattered throughout the country are not as significant as the main Temples of Angkor. Different epochs, different styles and different materials that have reacted differently to time and climatic conditions are still, however, in demand. When the Vietnamese troops invaded the country, many people fled to the border and thousands of Cambodians gathered in the camps that served for the anti-Vietnamese movement. People spent months and often years there. It is obvious that trade developed at these sites. People needed food and shelter. Groups of people were also trained for the resistance movement. The camps were supported by China and Thailand. A part of the trade that developed on the sites included trafficking of the objects of art. The demand dictated by the international market came from the local dealers. The Thai military also had their share in the process.

Teams of Cambodians were trained to go into the country and into the temples and bring back the objects. The temples that were mainly attacked, and therefore suffered the most, were the ones in the northern and the northwestern parts of the country, the Siem Reap region and the temples closer to the border with Thailand. The trade went well for years.

In the late 1980s when the Vietnamese withdrew from Cambodia, the trade continued. As the camps stood empty and peace was established in the country, the trade went on.[40] Thus the whole network established in 1979 continued to function. The Cambodians needed the money; the Thai traders needed antiquities. During the 1990s the size of the operations increased again. Multiple events and witnesses mentioned below confirm that the situation remains the same.

The Temple of Banteay Chmar

One of the most well known examples of theft from the temples, which sadly shows the present state of affairs and reflects the administrative and social relations between the authorities as well as the illegal activities of the military and the mafia on the border with Thailand, is the famous case of the Temple of Banteay Chmar (Castle of Cats). Banteay Chmar is a beautiful and elaborate temple situated about 9.3 miles (13 kilometers) from the border with Thailand and, therefore, has one of the highest probabilities of being looted by the military, Thai traffickers, or anyone.

The temple, although it attracted the attention of scholars since the beginning of the last century, has never been well studied, largely because of its isolated location. According to the inscriptions, it was built in the second half of the twelfth century and the beginning of the thirteenth century by the King of Angkor, Jayavarman VII. It was devoted to his son Srindrakumara and four Sanchoks who died in the battle against Champs.[41] Even at the time of construction, the location was already somewhat inhospitable and the jungles were infested with malaria, which did not stop Jayavarman VII from erecting this magnificent site. The temple complex covers 7.5 miles (12 kilometers) and includes 119 acres (48 hectares).

Until recently this temple and some other areas were under the control of the Khmer Rouge soldiers, which meant that nobody else had access to it. Access to the temple was forbidden not only to the tourists and the local administration but to the military as well. Some people say that the Khmer Rouge, who practically did not damage the temples, were the best protectors of Banteay Chmar. Similarly, another site—Kbal Spean, which was also under the Khmer Rouge soldiers until a few years ago—was damaged by the looters as soon as it became accessible. The numerous stone carvings, created on the stones in the River of 1,000 Lingha and its waterfall have suffered from looters who chiseled out the faces and even managed to take out one of the stones. Even after the Khmer Rouge soldiers had left and the main roads had been cleared of mines, the temple still

MAP 6: TEMPLE DE BANTEAY CHMAR (Jesus del Rio Luelmo)

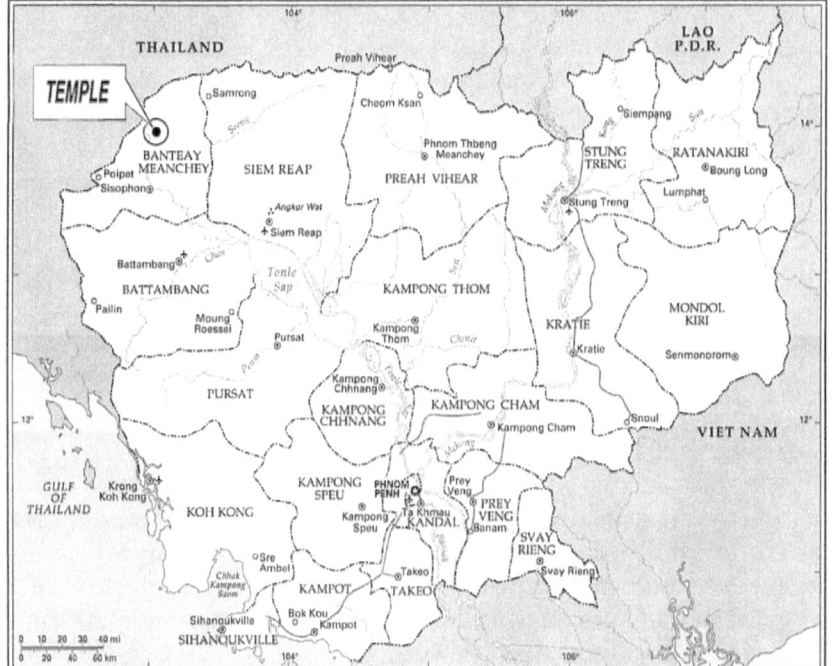

remained almost inaccessible because of banditry, bad roads, mines, and the malaria-infested jungles.

As soon as the Khmer Rouge left Banteay Chmar, the temple was looted on several occasions. The artifacts from Banteay Chmar were openly sold at the River City Market in Bangkok. In December 1998, Claude Jacques, a scholar who worked in Cambodia for years, saw a thirteenth-century stella from Banteay Chmar that he had examined in the temple on a number of occasions in the past. It was offered for sale in one of the shops for ten thousand dollars. The involvement of the Thai authorities and the international organizations has helped to return stella back to Cambodia. Thai dealers learned of the free access to the temple immediately, and no doubt commissioned soldiers to steal the pieces. One can assume that any of the participants in the trade who could access the temple would have done so.

Nothing was done by the local or central authorities at the time to introduce measures that would protect the temple, which was so evidently in danger of being looted. Such a lack of action from the authorities is, however, too easily explained by financial difficulties and by the temple's isolation. During the discussions on the inclusion of Angkor on the World

Heritage List, some of the UNESCO representatives were against the inclusion of Banteay Chmar because it was too far away (47.5 miles [70 kilometers]) from Angkor and tourists would not go there.[42]

UNESCO specialists and French scholars in Angkor who worked in the temple and visited it from time to time noticed that a few sculptures had disappeared from the temple between their visits to the site. A UNESCO report gives the following description of the damage done to the temple by the looters.

"There are only 4 steles of inscriptions carved on the doors of the different galleries. One is the east gallery of the northern section. The upper part of the inscription in the east gallery of the southern section of the wall was stolen at the end of 1998. For the west gallery of the southern section, there is a stele of an inscription which was cut out and left on the spot at the end of 1998. And there is also an inscription of the inner wall near the central tower, but the upper part is stolen.

In particular, the sculptures of each wall of the third gallery were cut out. As for the sculptures on the lintels and pediments they were almost ruined. In addition, the statues of good spirits and evil spirits supporting the Naga balustrade of all the causeways of four entrances were nearly all stolen."

The most devastating and daring theft that ever happened in Cambodia took place in the temple in 1998. The military stole a 98.4-foot (30-meter) section from the southern wall of the temple, which is altogether about 1,312 feet (400) meters long. According to Claude Jacques, the stolen part was engraved with six-foot images of Lokeshvara[43] and carved reliefs of Apsaras. The villagers say that the military arrived one day at sunrise and completely blocked access to the temple without providing any explanations to the local people, who were not allowed to be in the area of the temple that they had been used to going to every day.

They were the only witnesses of the incident and say that the soldiers were from the military division responsible for their area. The local village is situated a mere 984 feet (300 meters) away from the temple. The villagers, who live only 9.3 miles (15 kilometers) away from the Thai border, know all the dealers who come from Thailand, know what they are looking for and the rest of the details of the trafficking, and know the market prices for different objects of art—even the children have this knowledge.[44] Local people hardly ever interfere with the military, partly due to fear of being killed and partly due to tradition. One of the few cases known when the villagers alerted police happened at Prei Khmeng in the Angkor area, when the armed group of soldiers threatened the whole village and forced the people and children to help them to pillage the temple. One of the children alerted police.

The soldiers worked in a group of about twenty, but judging by the size of the destruction their number could have been twice as many. They arrived armed with AK-47s and with many various instruments to dismantle the wall, including road drills, pneumatic drills and trucks to transport part of the wall. The part destined for transportation was more than 1,312 feet (400 square meters) and weighed several tons.

The soldiers obviously worked in a hurry and left evidence behind them, such as two chisels that were discovered near the temple by the UNESCO team.[45] The part of the wall that was to be dismantled was marked in advance, judging by the traces of red paint left on the nearby stones by the thieves. They worked for two weeks, loading thirty tons into six trucks that left the temple one by one heading toward the Thai border. The trucks probably crossed the border at San Ro Changan, north of Arnyaprathet, and probably were met there by Thai dealers.

Some time after the incident, on January 5th, 1999, a truck that contained 113 stones and 37.8 feet (11.5 meters) of the wall carved with Apsaras was stopped in Thailand in Sa Kaew province. The truck stopped by the Thai police was a 10-wheel cattle truck, which normally goes to Thailand with cattle and comes back empty. This one gave the impression of going to Thailand empty and for that reason attracted the attention of the officials. The officials working on the border wanted to show their zeal, although one never knows whether the officials knew what was in the truck.

According to some sources, the truck was reported by the officials only because the Cambodians who accompanied the vehicle did not want to pay the local police, who eventually reported them. One could easily imagine the scale of the trade by the number of trucks that passed on a daily basis and the number of objects being looted over the border. This report, of course, could have been an accident if the officials were not really aware of the fact that the truck was transporting a part of the wall from the Banteay Chmar temple.

The story was much discussed in the media and at an intergovernmental level because of its unprecedented scale of looting. The piece was most probably privately ordered by one of the collectors and destined for a private collection in somebody's house or a garden.

The theft has never been investigated. Nobody took responsibility for the incident, apart from two people who drove the truck. One of the cattle truck drivers said that he was hired for three hundred dollars as a driver the day before his arrest and did not know what was in the truck until he was stopped by the police. Both are serving three-year sentences which were reduced to eighteen months. Neither of them gave any other lead. Police could not make a serious case based on their evidence.[46]

No one—not the administration of the province, the local military, the local police, the Ministry of Culture, the APSARA authority, or the central administration of Phnom Penh—accepted the responsibility for what had happened. The wall disappeared and the participants in the operation, although probably known, remained free to continue looting the temples.

In government and diplomatic circles it is said that the names of the main participants are known but diplomatically nobody wants to discuss it. Most logically, one could accuse the local military authority of the province; however, there is no evidence leading to them. The report of the Cambodian Embassy in Thailand to the Ministries of Defense, Culture and Foreign Affairs mentioned two generals and was confirmed by the vice governor of the province, but it was not followed up by any action against these generals.[47]

The part of the wall found in the truck, which consisted of 113 pieces, is now exhibited in the National Museum of Phnom Penh, while the rest of the wall has disappeared. Now, after the incident, the Temple of Banteay Chmar is protected by the police assigned by the local authority and UNESCO. Japan, UNESCO, and other international organizations have provided money for installing police forces and providing some other measures of protection for the temple. It is planned to put the temple on the World Heritage List, which will mean the development of the area, the attraction of tourists and, therefore, more people on the site causing a potential reduction of the danger of theft in the future.

This incident is not the only one. Similar cases took place in other remote temples like Koh Ker. In February 1997, the Thai border police stopped a military truck transporting ten tons of sculptures, among them nineteen Naga statues and nine large Apsaras that were coming from the temple Koh Ker, situated eighty-five kilometers from Angkor. The truck was guarded by seventeen soldiers under the command of the general and a commander of a military region, who later claimed that he did not know the soldiers. However, the military insisted that none of the soldiers should be arrested because they just wanted to make some money and were not aware of the consequences of their activities. This incident has been discussed on a number of occasions in the media and in the literature.[48]

International Crime Community

A powerful crime community that was organized in Cambodia and links the country with the rest of the world was created after Cambodia found itself free from invaders and the Khmer Rouge but destroyed after wars and the Pol Pot regime. As in all countries going though this period of social and economic restructuring, the crime syndicate is directly connected with the economic situation and the sharp differences between Cambodia and Thailand and Western countries. Such a situation provides nourishing ground for organized crime. For example, one of the reasons for the looting activities in the northwest of Cambodia is clearly the instability in the region.

Transnational organized crime is a rather recent phenomenon and has not yet been sufficiently studied. From Cambodia the trade net spreads its web all over the world. Participants in different illegal activities may often unite the trafficking of various goods. On a few occasions drugs have been found in antique sculptures or, vice versa, rare objects of art were found in drugs.

The River City Complex in Bangkok is one of the main trading centers for looted objects. At least half of the Khmer objects of art found on the international market come from Thailand. There are no statistics available to tell exactly how many objects cross the border. At the beginning of 1999, the Thai police found 399 Khmer artifacts stored in Ayuthaya, an ancient Thai capital located fifty miles (eighty kilometers) from Bangkok. Accidental findings like that reflect the daily trafficking of hundreds of pieces of art. When pieces are sold, the buyer receives the relevant certificates and the objects can leave the country.

It is often hard to tell where objects come from. There are some Cambodian sites in the northeast and southeast of Thailand because it used to be one large empire. Recently, more and more objects have gone from Bangkok to Hong Kong, Malaysia and Singapore. Because trade via Thailand is getting more and more complicated for the participants, it is said that many objects find their way to Singapore, which is becoming a new marketplace. It is also possible that many of the artifacts are shipped to Singapore and from there to Thailand, where the market is wider and more flexible.[49] A UNESCO report of the mission examined the antique boutiques in Singapore and mentioned galleries of Khmer art situated in the shopping plazas and hotels. The owners of the galleries insisted that the objects were bought at least fifteen years ago, belonged to private collections, and were not for sale.

The dealer is usually the first person contacted after any finding. Many of the Thai dealers, for example, often communicate with Thais who live abroad, who own boutiques in the River City district and whose family members are also in the antique trade. The owners of one of the galleries in River City, for example, have relatives living in Lugano, Switzerland, who also are in the antique gallery business. Collectors who arrive in Lugano may choose objects of art from available photos and they will be delivered promptly from Bangkok.[50] Dealers are usually very discreet; they do not ask for the provenance or disclose information. They usually have knowledge and appreciation of the objects they see and know who to offer them to. In most of the countries the dealers are united in associations that protect their interests.

After leaving Thailand—mostly by plane—the objects may go just about anywhere in the world. The areas that come first to mind are the United States and Europe; one should not, however, forget Japan. It is hard to say what quantities of objects of art are bought and sold in Asia and what percentage goes to the United States, Japan or Europe. Museum curators and private collectors from Japan are very fond of Khmer art and it is valued very highly on the market in the Far East. The element of Cambodian art that is very popular in this region is Lingha, the sacred phallic symbol, which is bought by Asian collectors for its religious and theological significance.

Prices for such objects of art can often be higher in Japan than in the West. The Japanese are known to operate locally, within Japan, and not to turn the trade of art into an international auction. The main trade cities in Japan are Tokyo and Osaka. The biggest market, no doubt, is situated in the United States, followed by Europe. The price for Khmer objects of art, depending on their quality, may reach five hundred thousand dollars. One can assume that all objects of Khmer art sold or exhibited outside Cambodia are acquired illegally. The provenance can be easily changed or hidden, proving that a particular object was exported from Cambodia years ago. Often if an object is publicly displayed in a museum or a gallery, the etiquette says "Khmer Style," which means that the provenance is not known.

In the United States the key entry points for illicit objects of art from Southeast Asia are New York, Los Angeles and San Francisco. It is estimated that over eighty percent of the objects of art sold in the United States enter the country illegally. There are dozens of other cities in the world that can be considered as first rank for the art trade. In Europe most of the antiquities often pass through Belgium before being offered for sale in any other country.

Once the art objects are out of Asia with an easily acquired false export certificate, often bought in Thailand, they are transported by plane to the art dealers. They are often resold several times before they find their way to a collection or a museum. On some occasions the objects are stored for some time before being sold to the public. The curators in the museums usually say that the object was not bought in Cambodia. The own-

MAP 7: MAIN CAMBODIAN ART TRADE ROUTES (Jesus del Rio Luelmo)

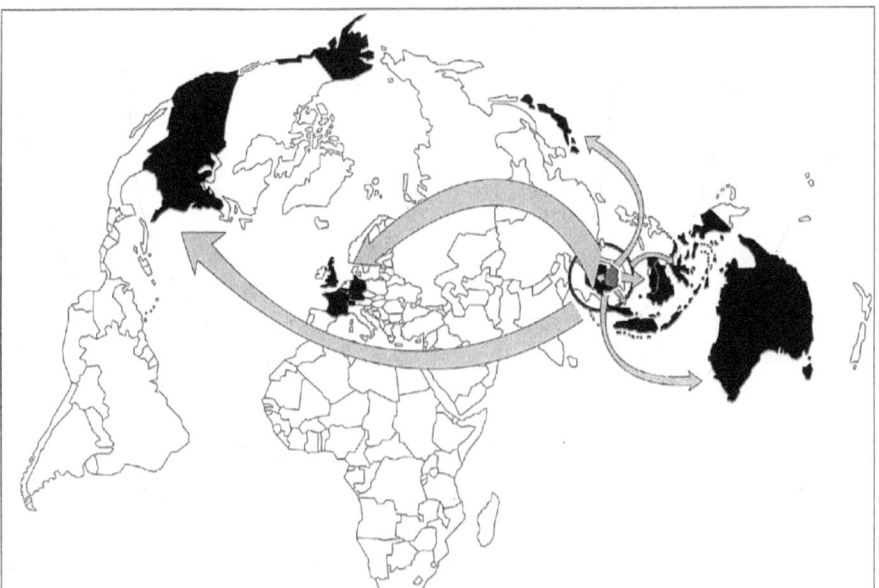

ers of the antique galleries may ask the collectors they know to say that the object had been in the family collection for decades. The auction house catalogs for Khmer art mention most of the time that the object is from a private collection. There is hardly ever any archaeological provenance or specific location cited.

Most of the curators, collectors, owners of galleries and employees of auction houses know each other and often exchange references and information. Many of the specific orders for objects of art mentioned above come not only from private collections but also from museums. The collections of many American, European and Japanese museums, such as the Metropolitan Museum or Museum in Tokyo, have been greatly enriched in the last ten years by their curators.

Forgeries

The forgery of art is hardly a new problem and certainly is not restricted to the Southeast Asian market. It is hard to say what percentage of fakes is circulating on the market; however, forged Khmer objects of art could easily exceed seventy percent.

The best fakes are produced from ancient stones without carvings, which are bought in Cambodia by weight and are as much in demand as the rest of the objects of art. The price for one kilogram of such stone is approximately a hundred bhat (Thai currency; approximately three dollars). The stones are carved by very skillful artisans who are both Cambodian and Thai nationals. The majority of the fakes, however, are made in Thailand. According to the experts, most of the objects of Khmer art that are sold in Thailand are fakes. According to Stan Sesser, the observer of *The Asian Wall Street Journal*, "Attempting to buy a Khmer relic is as much a minefield as Cambodia itself."[51]

The turnover of the market for fake art is estimated at millions of dollars per year. For example, scholars insist that the majority of objects of art in Thai galleries are fakes. Often even the most professional critics cannot differentiate fraud Khmer sculptures. Many defects that give away the forgery may be often found at the back of the statue, which usually remains poorly finished. Sometimes fakes can be determined by the price. For example, if the price offered in one of the boutiques in River City is too low, the piece is a fake. Most of the forgeries, however, are sold at the prices of the real pieces.

One of the problems of fixing the size of the art market is that copying the art can be legitimate and even necessary. The National Museum in Phnom Penh makes some of its money by selling copies of the most well known objects of art. For that reason they have founded a workshop in the museum with artisans who are first taught how to make copies and then end up working either in the Phnom Penh Museum or in the other workshops in Cambodia.

The creation of this kind of workshop is very useful in countries like Cambodia. Not only do they help develop and reintroduce new or forgotten skills but they also create jobs. This kind of production makes profit for the museum, where copies are sold between twenty and ninety dollars. In terms of profit this is not enormous, but it is nevertheless important for a Cambodian-scale budget. Not surprisingly, many of the artisans make copies for sale and it is impossible to control this industry.

To be good at this job a forger needs to address the same factors that were addressed in the earlier works in the different periods. An ideal forgery has to be made with knowledge of art and techniques. The forger also needs to know the market to succeed. According to the art dealers, the most well-known restorer and craftsman who "repairs" Khmer and Thai pieces of art and creates new ones is a man who lives in Ayutthaya. He is considered to have the most skillful techniques for creating fake antiquities that cannot be identified by the most experienced dealers.

The problem of fakes has a big impact on the international market. Many of the museums and collections display forgeries instead of originals. Fakes also make it difficult for scholars and archaeologists to know how many statues were created or had been stolen and from what site and to analyze the various historical developments, such as the production possibilities in the ancient Khmer civilization.

The stories of experts coming across fakes are numerous. Two anecdotes will suffice. Pich Keo, the ex-Director of the National Museum in Phnom Penh, said that once in an art gallery in San Francisco he saw eight objects of Khmer art, three of which were fakes, carved from ancient stones. On another occasion, an American couple who had bought a Khmer statue and believed that it was stolen from Cambodia decided to offer it back to the country. The statue was identified by Pich Keo as fake.[52]

Participants

The aim of this section is to describe the participants, analyze their goals, and see how they behave and relate to the rest of society. There is great diversity among those who participate in the trafficking of art. Even though quite a lot is known about the main participants, precise and detailed information about their background, values and behavior is sketchy and contradictory. Most of the information is provided by journalists, whose work covers only some parts of this field. There are also some official reports that provide an insight into the personality of the participants.

One can say that their most generalized characteristic is their lack of respect for the country's legal system. This characteristic is increasingly widespread in Cambodia, where it should be said that the legal system is far from perfect. (Laws and sub-decrees are only now beginning to be adopted in many areas.) However, the actors in the stolen art trade appear to be more advanced than most Cambodians in their disrespect for the country's institutions. They feel fewer moral constraints upon their actions, and they are willing to use any means to achieve their nefarious goals.

Many of the participants have military backgrounds. The majority of the trucks that have been stopped by the police and contain objects of stolen art belong to the military. The military generals have been mentioned in all reports written to the government regarding the looting of temples. It is interesting to note that the Khmer Rouge soldiers rarely participate in art trafficking and prefer to make money trading other things like gems and lumber.[53] One can assume that the people who are involved in trafficking do not feel as if they are doing something bad. That is true of most of the soldiers who loot the temples under the command of the generals and most of the other participants of the trade.

Their main reason for participating in these activities is to make a little money that might help their families to survive and their children to receive an education. One may also assume that the fact that they are making money makes their activities easier and legitimizes them. In making this money legitimate, the participants legitimize their status in society, obtain more wealth and power, and are more respected by their friends and neighbors.

A participant in trafficking usually might not break any other laws in the country, such as failing to pay taxes. They can be good family men and even good people. Sociologically, their average educational level is very low. Most of them have only an elementary education. Also, most of them are quite young: twenty to thirty-five years old. Their friends, some of them politicians and military men, do not think of them as criminals and society does not condemn their activity. Some of them come from social groups with connections to the elite and have social recognition.

The involvement of the army, however, is evident. The military that participates in the trafficking of art is involved in other illicit activities as well. One can assume that the whole of the Cambodian military uses its influence to make money in the different spheres previously mentioned, such as drugs, arms, and cars.

Other categories of participants are numerous and include just about all social sectors of the society, such as municipal officials who are known to participate in the looting. However, this kind of incident is rarely exposed because these officials have good ways of protecting themselves from accusations.

On one occasion, the governor of the Russey Keo district was accused of removing the images from Wat Santepheap Pagoda on Yukuntor Island. Witnesses said that the Buddha images were removed at night; however, the governor insisted that the Pagoda was blocking the view of the Royal Palace and needed to be destroyed, that the removal of the images was announced three or four months before it happened, and that the images were stored in the local museum. The case could not be followed up because all the officials and police in the district gave evidence in favor of the governor.[54] Another governor was known to decorate his office with art from the temples in his province. He explained, however, that in this way he was protecting the art from being stolen.

Much of the work is done by peasants, who evidently try to gain some money and cannot be blamed when their monthly income often does not exceed a few dollars. In Cambodia the population is about eighty-five percent rural. The illiteracy rate among men is about forty-two percent and among women is about seventy-nine percent.[55] It is clear that they often find pieces of art while they are working on the rice fields and rarely specifically look for art. It would be wrong to assume that Cambodian peasants specifically search for objects of art, as is done in many other countries. In China, Italy or Turkey local people look for art systematically, either organized in groups or villages or individually. In each village there is at least one metal detector machine bought by the village for this purpose. In Cambodia, however, it is not in the mentality of the people to do so. They take pieces of art only if they find them by chance, if there is an archaeological site next to the village, or if they know in advance that they may find something on the spot. However, there is never an organized systematic attempt made by groups of peasants or by the village to dig the site.

The government has, however, recorded a few cases and has even intervened on a number of occasions, in instances such as the Temple of Angkor Borey in 1996, when the peasants found so many objects of art in the area that they started their own excavations. "Four-meter high brick walls surrounded the three square kilometer site...and ministry officials have uncovered monasteries, a Royal Palace and villages within its walls. Thousands of antiquities, including pots, pans silver necklaces, golden bracelets, Buddhist statues and ancient weapons were discovered at the site...and some of them are now on sale in Phnom Penh and exported to Thailand and Vietnam as a large number of local people in the area are discovering antiquities every day, and there have been no tough measures taken by provincial authorities to stop them."[56]

Unfortunately, interventions by the government are very rare. Often before the archaeologists know about the site, it can be completely destroyed by the locals, thus depriving the scientists of the possibility of researching the old urban structures of the cities, looking for clues to the roots of Khmer civilization, and studying how people lived before the influx of Indian and other cultures.

On another occasion, villagers who were excavating and completely destroying one of the pre-Angkorienne cemeteries in Banteay Meanchey province said that they needed to eat. They explained that it was their ancestors who lived there and who provided them with the possibility of making some money by selling what belonged to them to survive the difficult times.[57] As soon as they find objects of art, they inform the buyers, whose whereabouts are obviously known to the locals. The buyers in turn, come to pick up the objects. Such an attitude, however, is possible to understand in a country that is not only poor but has suffered four years of terror, during which all educated and professional people were killed in an attempt to build a peasant-dominated society. Most, if not all, of the peasants do not have any understanding of the notion of cultural heritage or why and how it should be protected.

According to Bruno Dagens, who has worked for many years in Angkor, at the beginning of the 1980s an Angkorienne head could have been exchanged for a bowl of rice.[58] In this case, can one really blame or accuse the Cambodian people of looting? The local people may often help the army by other means; for example, fishermen participate by transporting the statues to the cargo ships in their nets.[59]

A small part of the looting may be done by the monks themselves, individually or even by the whole temple committee (each village in Cambodia has a temple and each temple has a committee). The committee could decide to sell part or all of the objects from the temple to the traffickers or the military. Because the monks cannot touch money or get involved in any financial transactions, they often hire somebody from the village to proceed with the financial operation.[60] Stories of monks coming to archaeological sites at night to look for gold or objects of art or, similarly, starting their own excavations next to the site discovered by the archaeologists are not unknown, either. Not all monks, however, participate in the trafficking; they themselves often get attacked by armed gangs who steal sculptures from the isolated temples.

Among other categories of art traffickers, one can always name tourists, many of whom often try to take out stones just out of curiosity. In general, foreigners (non-Cambodians), particularly those in the diplomatic service, are often used to transport the objects of art. Many tourists come to Cambodia because they know that one can buy art here, and the idea of it being illegal makes it more attractive and romantic. Many of the French writers who visited Cambodia wrote in their diaries that they took a small stone as a memory.

French writer Jules Roy notes in his diary "Les années Déchirement 1925–1965," "*Pour elle, j'ai volé, à l'autel le plus élevé, une banderille de prière devant le Bouddha le plus solennel. J'en avais le cœur qui battait. Jusqu'au retour à l hôtel, je gardai la banderille bien cachée sous ma chemisette, comme un oiseau qui m eut picoté le flanc de ses griffes et de son bec, et je me hâtai de la sortir dans ma chambre. Mais là, elle avait perdu tout son mystère.*"[61]

Thai dealers or businessmen themselves are known to operate in Cambodia. On many occasions the arrested looters say they were hired by Thai nationals to pillage the temples. This type of job may cost a few hundred (one hundred to three hundred) dollars, and when they are caught the looters never give out the names of the people who hired them. Other people involved may include customs officials or employees of the various ministries, such as the Ministry of Culture or Transportation, whose salary varies between ten and twenty dollars per month. Some ministry officials who often travel abroad may have the authority to issue certificates for export.

Another category includes the diplomats, foreigners and expatriates working in Cambodia in IGOs and NGOs. The stories of these people who, after living and working in Cambodia, acquire pieces of art, pottery, bronze, papyruses, etc., and then use their political connections to take them out of the country to Europe, often to France where they are kept in private collections or sold at auction houses, are numerous. Rarely do any of them get caught; however, on a number of occasions the employees of IGOs and NGOs may be questioned by the Ministry of Culture and customs officials in Phnom Penh.

On one occasion an Italian NGO worker was arrested for trying to sell a few ancient Khmer objects of art, including Shiva Linga.[62] Being an irrigation engineer he claimed to have found the object while working in the field. He was freed after spending a few days at the police station. He claimed that he wanted to return the object to the National Museum but was too busy.[63]

It is interesting that Cambodians themselves are rarely, if ever, interested in Khmer art. Most of the time they find ancient objects of art old and uninteresting. This is one of the reasons why the peasants may sell the statues in the temple. The only reported case of a Cambodian who had a collection of Khmer art was in 1999. Ta Mok, one of the most cruel generals of Pol Pot and one of the leaders of the guerilla movement until 1997, had a collection of sixty-one stones in his house that was officially seized only before his arrest in May 1999.[64]

One can see the great diversity in social backgrounds and goals of participants in the trade of illicit trafficking of art. What most of the participants have in common is the lack of respect for the legal system of the country. At the same time many of the participants have political connections; most of the top military officers are active members of the political parties in Cambodia. The same is true, for example, for the diplomats or the expatriates who travel without their luggage being checked and who have connections in the government. The people who participate in it, the various strategies used by participants, and the loose structure of the trade make it difficult for the government to put a stop to or slow down the trade. Participation does not meet any negative response from society; on the contrary, one can say that all of the participants are well integrated and even respected in society, where power and wealth bring respect and a better possibility of survival within the highly hierarchical structure of the country.

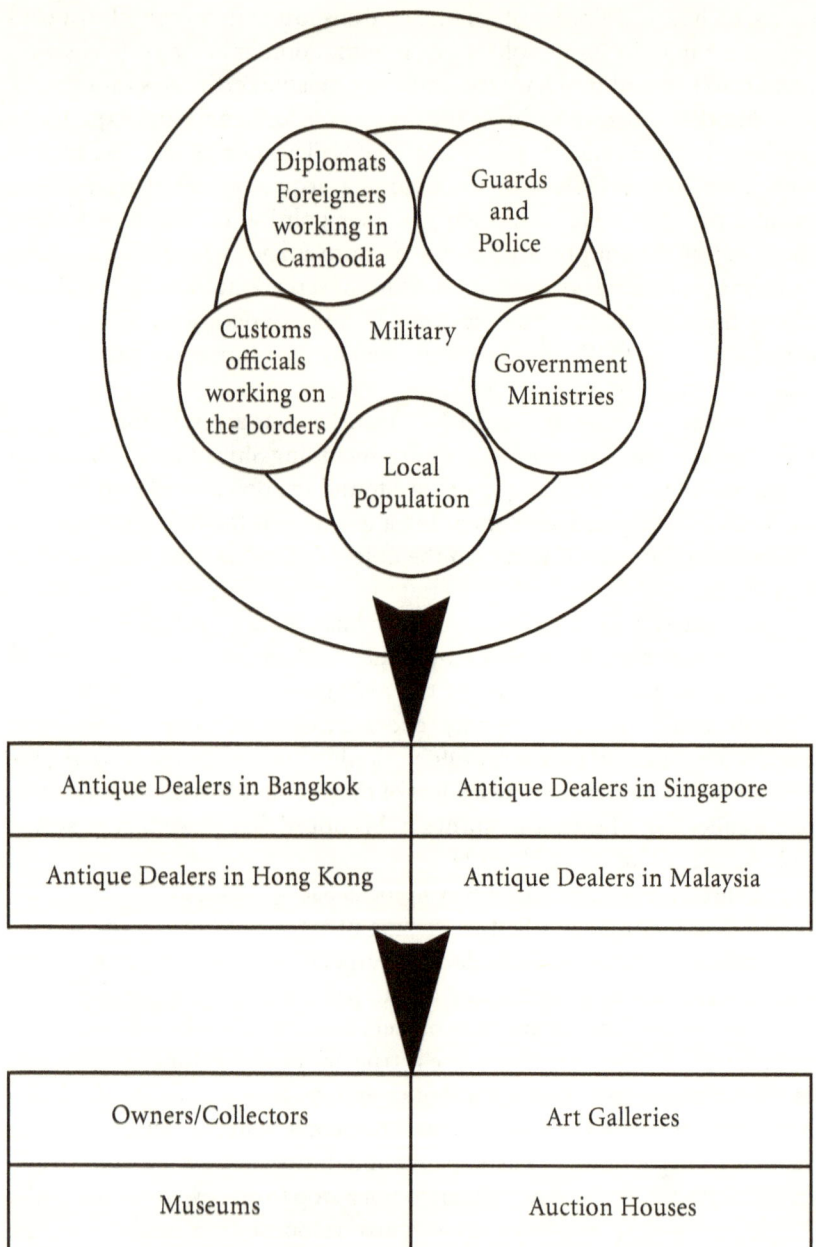

Figure 2: Trade Infrastructure

The Dimensions of Illegal Trafficking/Profit Margins

Determining the dimensions of illegal trafficking is vital to understanding its impact on the cultural heritage, but that is a difficult task. The most obvious problem is the lack of data. Most available data are weak and were obtained indirectly, and various data sources have used different and, at times, unclear methodologies. Not surprisingly, the resulting estimates must be interpreted and used with great caution, and authors who have tried to measure the size of trafficking warn readers about the "science-fiction" nature and weakness of their estimates. Nevertheless, size must be addressed if the trade is to be understood.

As noted above, the main objects of art stolen from Cambodia are sculptures made out of stone. Smuggling these presents certain difficulties because of the weight of the stones. For this reason, soldiers would break the statue into pieces or behead it, often taking just the head of the statue or the torso, or chisel relief carvings from their settings. The pieces are dismantled with jackhammers and circular saws and then taken away in trucks.

Most of the reports that have attempted to describe the trade focus on these pieces of art. Other objects of art that are looted include uncarved ancient stones, bronze, wood, and papyruses. Also, because the precise volume of the art trade is unknown, one of the ways to estimate the size of the trade and the revenues received by the participants is to look at the galleries and auction houses; however, this method underestimates the size of the trade.

The size of the trade is determined by the number of artifacts in the country and by the revenues received at each stage of the trade. There are over one thousand temples registered in the country by French scholars during the years of protectorate. It is estimated that up to ninety-eight percent of the temples in Cambodia are destroyed either partially or entirely. Another estimate is that at least one temple is looted per day in Cambodia; however, the real figures are much higher than that.[65] Altogether the illicit trafficking of art is estimated at one billion dollars a year, second after the drug trade. It is estimated that in the last twenty-five years Cambodia has lost ten times more statues than in the past twelve centuries. Cambodian authorities assume that since 1986 more than half of the nation's heritage has been stolen from the country.[66]

Determining the prices of the artifacts at each stage is another difficult problem. As one may expect there are no official price lists. Following are the average prices obtained on the market by the participants, which give an approximate idea about the financial side of the trade. On the border with Thailand the objects usually cost between two and three thousand

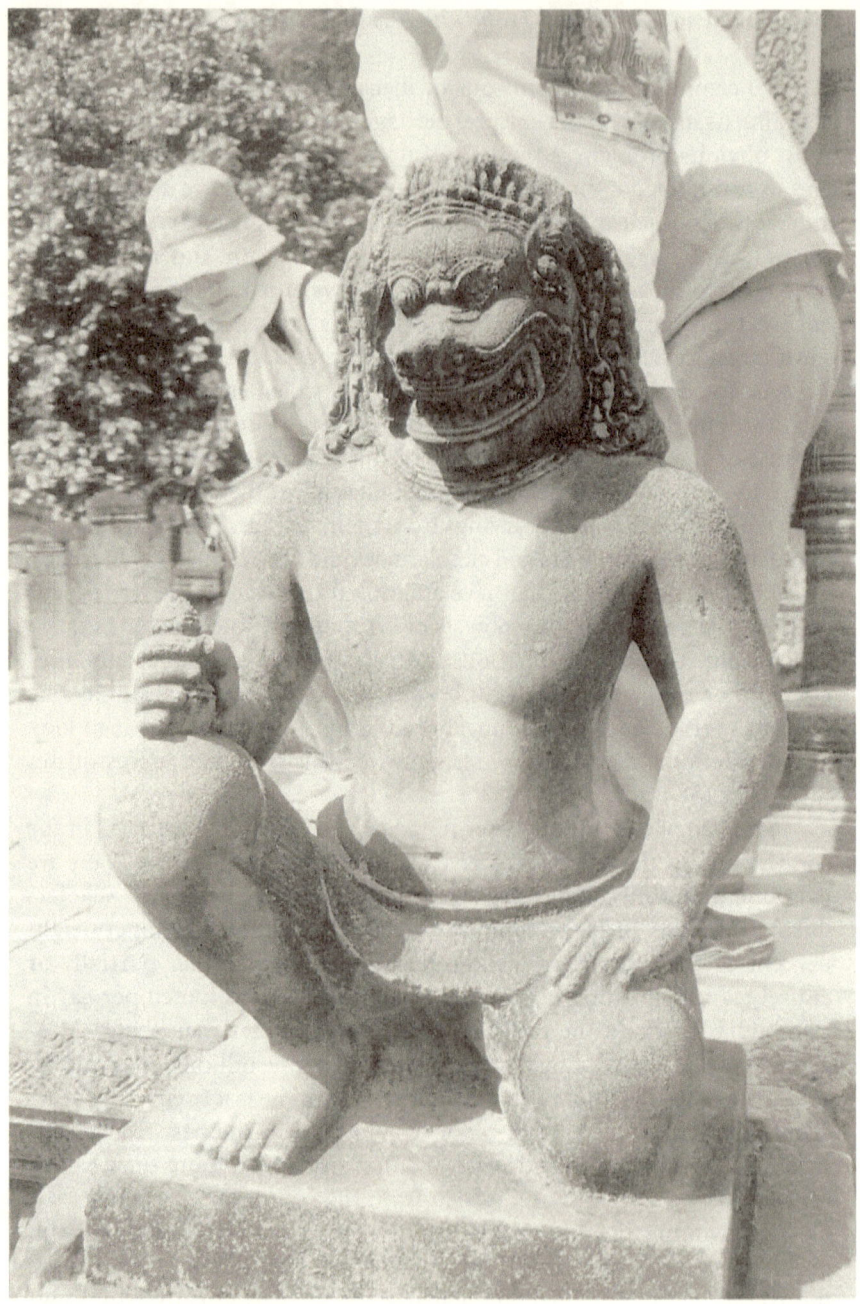

A giant statue in Banteay Srei; end of the tenth to beginning of the eleventh century; built by Jayavarman V.

dollars for an average piece from a neighboring temple. From each one thousand dollars received from the item sold, the group of soldiers that usually consists of four to five people gives two hundred dollars to the officials on the border, about five hundred dollars to the general or the head of the group, and the rest goes to the soldiers. The amount may, of course, be reduced due to unexpected fees that may be paid as bribes or for other services.

The guard working in the territory of the Temples of Angkor gets between twenty and thirty dollars for permitting the object to be taken outside of the Angkor area. In the case of a particularly good piece, each soldier may make over one thousand dollars, but these cases are rare. For these people whose salary does not exceed fifteen dollars per month, it is a significant addition to their monthly income.

To determine the actual potential influence of the trade, one would also need to obtain estimates of the income acquired by the military or the amount invested and spent both inside and outside Cambodia. It is estimated that the government loses about two million dollars per month because of all kinds of smuggling. In other words, this is money lost officially for the economy. However, traffickers use their profits to acquire consumer goods, which means that there is an inflow or investment of the capital into the country. What is also evident in Cambodia is the growth of the real estate business, which may serve as money laundering for those who want to legitimize their capital.

Once the objects get to Bangkok, the price may increase up to tenfold and rise much higher again outside of Bangkok, once the objects are transported to their final destinations in Europe, America, Japan and elsewhere. A twelfth century statue from Angkor can easily fetch one hundred thousand dollars.[67] Prices of about two hundred seventy thousand dollars for a good piece of art are rare but also not uncommon. Each Southeast Asian auction of the most prominent auction houses sells about ten items of the best Khmer sculptures. Analysis of the Asian museums in the United States, Europe and Japan often reveals magnificent collections of Khmer art that did not exist until about ten years ago.

In Angkor Wat, the biggest temple in the territory of Angkor, almost all the Buddhist statues have been beheaded. Looters and dealers prefer to take mainly heads because they are smaller than torsos or other items and easier to deal with. Free-standing statues that survived looting were taken away into storage. In Angkor the site of all the empty bases that once contained statues gives a shocking impression. Out of thousands of statues that once stood at Angkor Wat, only twenty-six are left.

In small isolated temples in Cambodian provinces, there may be just

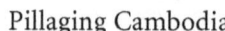

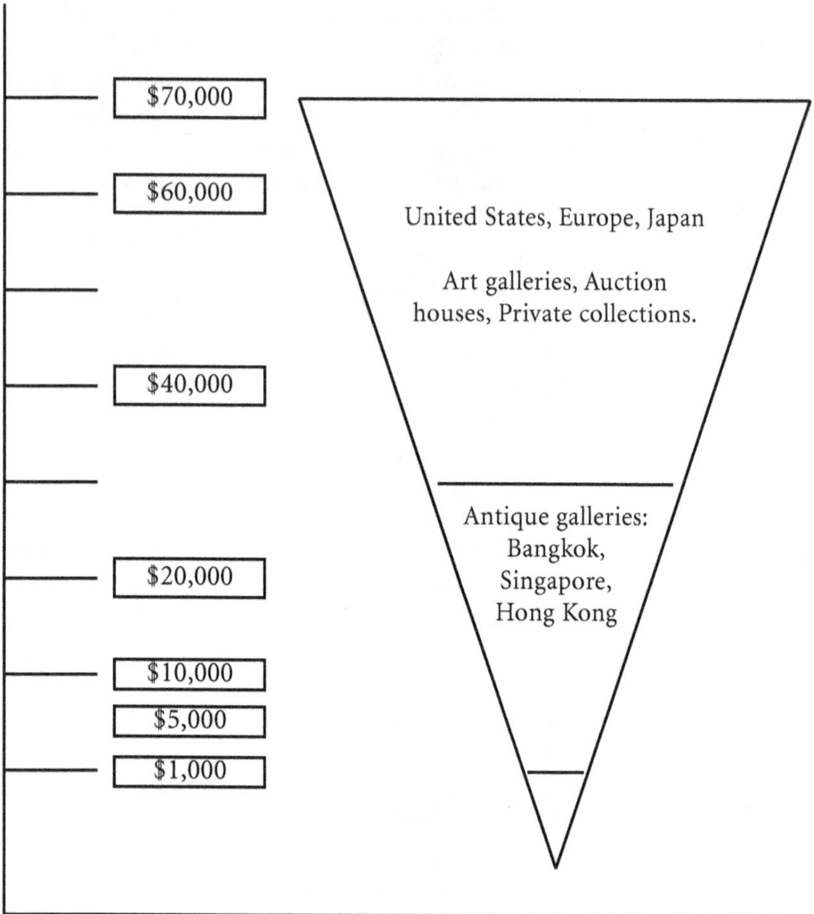

$70,000

$60,000

United States, Europe, Japan

Art galleries, Auction
houses, Private collections.

$40,000

Antique galleries:
Bangkok,
Singapore,
Hong Kong

$20,000

$10,000

$5,000

$1,000

Sources: Interviews, catalogs of Drouot 1960–2000, Sotheby's catalogs 1997–2000.

Figure 3: Profit Margins

one small statue of Buddha made out of bronze or wood standing in the
center of the monument. Once the statue is taken, the temple is entirely
destroyed. Other sculptures that are very much in demand are Apsaras
and Garudas, whose faces and heads are often chiseled out by the looters.
In one of the most beautiful temples of Angkor, Preah Khan, all the statues of Buddhas and Apsaras are beheaded.[68] From the rare recordings and
available statistics, we know that in 1991—1992, sixty sculptures were
beheaded at Pheah Khan and Ta Phnom, and over a dozen sculptures were
stolen and defaced in Banteay Srei.[69] On June 9, 1999, five heads of Apsaras

disappeared from another temple in the territory of Angkor—Banteay Kdei. In the temple of Banteay Kdei, twenty-five Apsara heads were chiseled out within a five-month period.

The figures (see Figure 3) provide an insight into the size of the trade, which touches every part of the country, and show the scale of looting in the temples.

2

The "Demand" Side of the Story

The growing worth of heritage aggravates conflicts over whose it is, what it means, and how to use it. Heritage builds collective pride and purpose, but in so doing stresses distinctions between good guys (us) and bad guys (them). Heritage faith, heritage commodities, and heritage rhetoric inflame enmity, notably when our unique legacy seems at risk. Entrenched myopia foments strife; ignorance inhibits reciprocity. Besotted by our heritage, blind to that of others, we not only eschew comparison but forfeit its benefits.1

The analysis of what is called here "the demand side" for Khmer art is very important for this book. Its understanding and estimation are as important as the knowledge about the illicit trafficking of art from Cambodia and the structure of the trade. The availability of correct information on both sides of the issue may help to evaluate the problem correctly and realistically as well as to find the right approach to solve the problem. It is hard to say which analysis is more complicated or more important: demand or supply. Both are equally significant for the problem. The proper analysis of both is nearly impossible due to the lack of information that is necessary to analyze the issues, tendencies, structures, scale of the matter, and participants—that is to say, all of the issues mentioned in the previous chapter, which made an attempt to study the supply side of the story.

I think that the demand side is the main reason for art trafficking from Cambodia. Study of the demand includes a variety of questions that compose and coordinate this matter. They include issues of fashion, economy, politics, and various psychological theories. Undoubtedly, the issue of demand is difficult to analyze because it includes many different components and patterns that cannot be predicted or are difficult to analyze. Auction houses, antique dealers and private collectors are among the main buying forces. How many people are interested in acquiring objects of Khmer art, how often, and on what basis are the issues that cannot easily be predicted. Another matter is market changes. The demand for objects of Khmer art is constantly changing and the prices may rise and fall depending on the income of the buyers, sometimes on the economic situation in the country, on fashion, or on the number of collectors and their potential.

On the other side, the question of collecting and buying objects of art involves psychological aspects that are very complex in nature. The love for art, its collection, and its appropriation when often everything else does not matter is one of such issues. The drive to collect has existed in the history of humankind since its beginning and it is not something that can be stopped or prevented. The participants of the art trade have their own arguments, their own laws, and their own rules that are proved legally, may be correct politically, and confirm the correctness of these arguments. Even though we know that most of the objects of art that are found outside of Cambodia were illegally smuggled from the country, can we say that people buying this art are wrong, or can they be accused of committing a criminal offense?

It is difficult to answer this question by simply yes or no. The answer raises such issues as the role of the museum in the modern world and how new tendencies introduced by globalization may change the classical idea of a museum. There are also many other ambiguous questions about this issue. For example, in the case of Cambodia there are questions of colonial heritage and of the objects that left the country during the period of the French protectorate. All of these questions are very complicated, need a lot of research, and have different angles of approach; the answers to them are very subjective.

For example, the question of art restitution that is so important for Cambodia is as old as the world. Since ancient times conquerors have taken objects of art from occupied lands. Debates over the restitution of art exist all over the world. It is even difficult to say who in the history of mankind was the first to face the question. The ancient world is full of examples when the army of the country that won the war took home objects of art. There are cases when this art was returned.

It is known that Cicero had to pay forty-five million sesterces to the

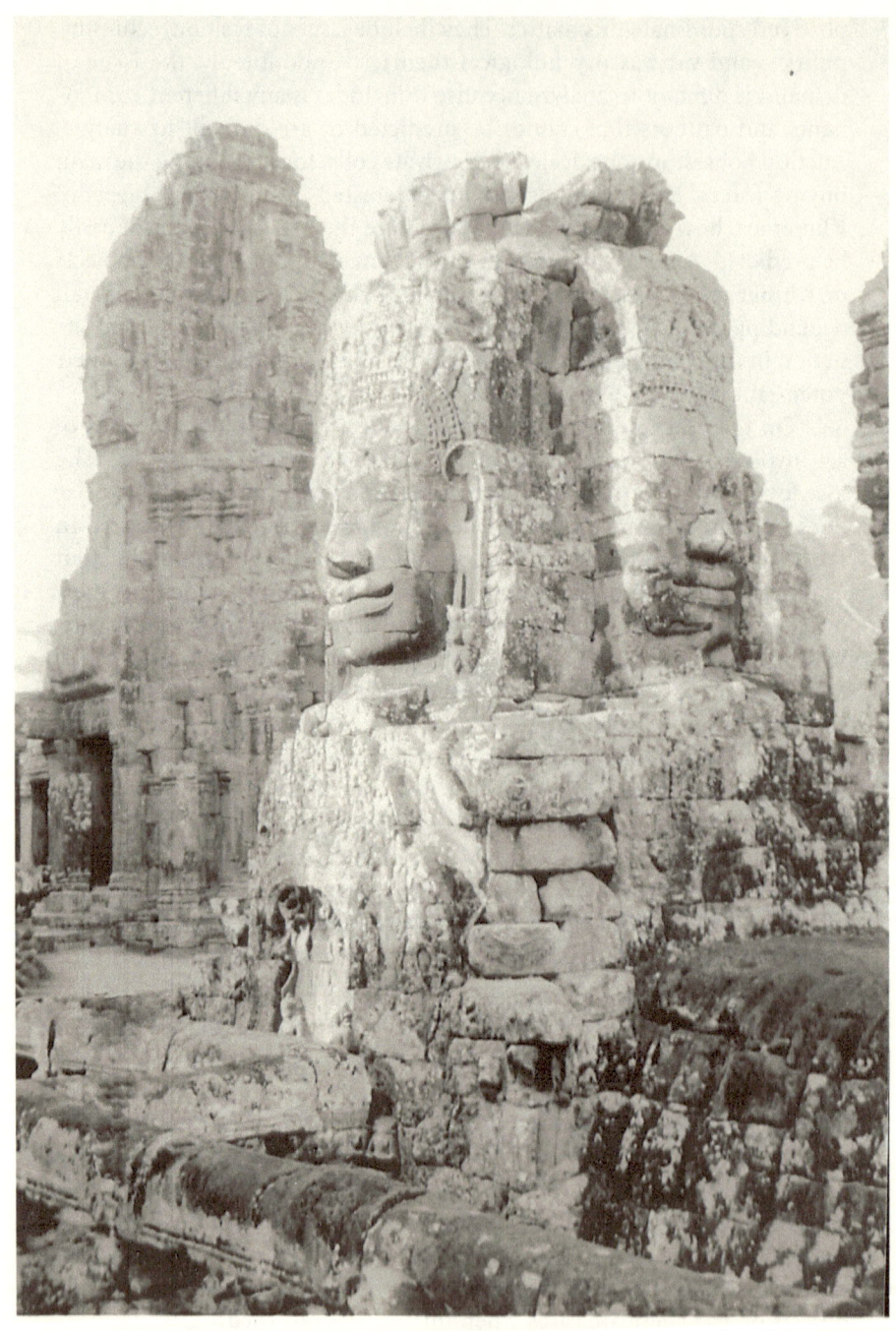

Temple of Bayon; 12th century; built during the reign of Jayavarman VII.

Sicilians as part of the restitution for plundered art. It also known that Richelieu, Mazarin, Cobert and Louvois were praised in history and by their contemporaries for not taking objects of art from the countries that were conquered by the French army at the époque.[2] The first large case of art acquisition during the war and subsequent restitution involved Napoleon. The Congress of Vienna in 1815 made the decision of restitution of art to its countries of origin. It is not the task of this chapter to provide the historical details of art plunder and restitution, which are not relevant to the topic of this book. However, it is important to stress the idea that art plunder and collection is not a new phenomenon faced by Cambodia and other modern states, but that it has existed for centuries.

The first National Museum was opened by Napoleon in the Louvre and the collections consisted largely of pieces of art whose acquisition took place during his wars of conquest. More and more museums opened during the nineteenth century. The collections consisted often of objects of art brought from the colonies and from the wars. The twentieth century has changed the scale of art plunder. We saw in Chapter I that the objects of Khmer art taken from Cambodia by visitors before the 1970s were already quite numerous, but of course there is no comparison with the plunder of the last three decades.

Antique Dealers

> We fully accept the need of countries to protect national treasures, but we do not believe that all objects must remain in their country of origin, any more than we believe that all Georgian brass candlesticks should remain in the United Kingdom.[3]

The antique dealer is the first person to get contacted when antiquities are traded. In the case of Khmer art it is often the Thai dealers. On rare occasions Western dealers come directly to Cambodia or to Thailand to organize a deal themselves. It does not mean that all dealers trade illicit objects of art. Many of the dealers in Cambodia and Thailand, though, take orders from clients they know or contact local thieves to receive the art, which cannot leave the country on legal grounds. Dealers usually have all the necessary contacts all over the world. They know the curators of museums, private collectors, and the employees of auction houses.

The nature of the job, however, is by definition very discreet and requires a lot of knowledge about the subject. The dealer will never reveal his contact and is rarely inquisitive about the provenance of the object.

Naturally, an experienced dealer will usually know much more about the origin of the object.

In most countries dealers belong to associations that protect their interests and establish rules and regulations of the trade. For example, the IADAA is in the United Kingdom. Formed about twenty years ago, it includes many members, some of which are overseas. Auction houses and dealers may also be members of this association. The association has a code of ethics that normally prohibits trade of objects of doubtful origin. Article twelve of this code reads: "The members of IADAA undertake to the best of their ability to make their purchases in good faith; they undertake not to purchase or sell objects until they have established to the best of their ability that such objects were not stolen from excavations, architectural monuments, public institutions or private property."[4]

Similar associations exist in the United States and other European and non-European countries. It is true that in recent years many dealers have shown an interest and concern for the protection of art trade. Also, the trade in Khmer art was much damaged by the number of fakes traded on the market. Often even the most experienced dealers find it hard to distinguish a fake from an authentic statue.

The code of conduct, however, is often not followed and dealers pass on objects of art that they know were acquired illegally. On a number of occasions one could see magnificent Khmer statues in the Asian galleries in New York sold for over a hundred thousand dollars stating: "This statue comes from a known family, which is going through difficult times and desires to remain anonymous."[5] Another example is provided by the case of the statue that was returned to Cambodia. It was bought by Mme. L. at Sotheby's. Before arriving at Sotheby's it had passed through two New York dealers: The Doris Wiener gallery and a dealer called Maurice Pinto. Each time its price was nearly doubled. Acquired for a few thousand dollars in Bangkok, it was finally sold at Sotheby's for about one hundred and twenty thousand dollars.[6]

The dealers were the first to address the question of whether art should remain in the country of origin or, on the contrary, should travel. Is it more important for an object of art to be of historical value and constitute the cultural heritage of the country, or is its aesthetic value more important and does its presence in other countries serve a better purpose than when it stays at home? The arguments presented by art dealers are numerous.

They insist, for example, that all objects of art cannot stay in the country of origin because there simply would not be enough places for them. In many cases with Khmer art it was true that it was better preserved in the West rather than in the Conservation d'Angkor during the Pol Pot regime. Literal examples of such situations have been sadly seen recently in Afghanistan, where Taliban soldiers have destroyed unique Buddhist statues. Whether it is important to make art known, visible and accessible to the public and what actually helps the preservation of its artistic values more—remaining in Cambodia or in Western museums and collections—are arguments that will be discussed later in this chapter.[7]

In many cases the history or the provenance of the objects may be very complicated. They may be sold and resold many times and one cannot accuse dealers of trying to make some money on the deal. One of the opinions of the dealers is that the problem of illicit trafficking should be solved by the countries that suffer from the problem. They should rearrange their administrative system better in order to reduce corruption and bribery. "Only those countries rich in archaeological treasures can solve the problems of clandestine excavation and the black market in antiquities. They must replace the bribery and corruption surrounding the underground trade in antiquities with an enlightened, practical and realistic policy of national self-interest; a liberal control export policy for duplicate objects already excavated and fair compensation to local finders. The establishment of an open and legal market is the only way to begin a new era of partnership and cooperation between source countries and the international art market and to preserve what is still in the ground."[8]

This statement from Peter Marks, the President of the National Association of Dealers in Ancient, Oriental and Primitive Art in New York, shows the accepted attitude—that the art should not leave Cambodia in the first place. Second, there should be a difference between legal and illegal trade in art. Art trade cannot be completely prohibited. Legal trade in art is a different domain and has its own rights. Much argument was caused by the U.S. government imposing import restrictions on some of the Khmer objects of art (issued by the Cultural Property Advisory Committee) and the agreement concluded between Cambodia and the United States on nontrade of any items of Khmer objects of art.

The dealers argue that the trade is thus pushed more and more underground; it becomes illegal. The American market suffers while Canadian, European or Japanese markets continue to trade Khmer art without any barriers because they did not join the United States in this agreement.[9] The agreement was effective in the United States; however, the absence of such a treaty in other countries makes it much less effective. The agreement, which ended in 2001, is likely not to be renewed because of the influence of the American art dealers who argue that it contradicts the law as well as the trade in the country.

However, it is true that dealers often trade objects of art even if they know about their doubtful provenance. In fact the good or "reputable" dealer is a dealer who can just guarantee that the object is authentic and not a fake. The rest is of secondary importance.[10] Many objects of art sold in Singapore are acquired illicitly. UNESCO visits to the boutiques in Singapore, for example, showed that many of the boutiques openly display Cambodian art. This is also true for the reports from the boutiques from Bangkok. Many of the items were actually identified by scholars from the EFEO as coming from particular temples in Angkor.

There is no proof about these objects of art. No one can say when exactly they left Cambodia, whether they were brought into the country legally or whether they were most probably looted within the last decade, lost for a few years and have now resurfaced with an American dealer. The prices for these objects, providing they are real, are high. The Cambodian government cannot sue the dealer for their return because it does not have any legal proof. Therefore, the dealer is not responsible before the law. The objects of art, clearly presenting an important cultural value to Cambodia, have lost their historical and archaeological significance, which again brings up the discussion between the academic and aesthetic values.

The dealer obviously knows exactly what he is doing. The provenance of the objects will never be proved and he will be able to make a significant profit; because Khmer art is fashionable and is in demand many people will have it in mind to purchase it. The dealer will not try to establish its provenance because if any of the dealers start questioning the provenance of an item the truth hidden behind the object will come out.

The trade of antiquities is estimated at several billion each year. Khmer art has a large share in it. Khmer antiquities, which have been in fashion for the last decade, attract numerous buyers with their unusual style and sense of mystery. Neither the dealers nor the buyers are interested in knowing their provenance; they buy objects of Khmer art to satisfy their aesthetic tastes and values. Many of them will not be interested in the illicit acquisition of a piece. Many of the antique dealers, like James Ede, think that the aesthetic value is more important than any other prerogatives or categories that may characterize the statue. In the defense of antiquity dealers, James Ede writes: "Aesthetic considerations weigh more heavily with us than contextual information. If contextual information is the only important consideration as has been stated again and again by archaeologists, once established and recorded why should not all objects come to the market?... We do care deeply about the subject and spend a great deal of time conserving and researching the pieces."[11]

Dealers like James Ede are obviously right in their own way. It is true that the Cambodian government is being excessive by prohibiting the trade of all objects of Khmer art prohibiting everything altogether is a measure that is very Asian in nature. Many of them are duplicates and, in fact, should be allowed to leave the country, which will permit legal trade. Moreover, the museums of Cambodia probably cannot even keep all the pieces of Khmer art found there, not to mention the pre-Angkorean vases. The information about them, however, has to be recorded and researched by scholars to provide an idea about the civilization, its tendencies and development. The issue will be discussed in more detail in the next chapter, "Impact of the Illicit Trafficking of Art on the Cultural and Socio-Economic Systems in Cambodia."

In cases where the object is recorded and then sold, the collector, dealer or a museum can provide fuller and better details of the object. Jerome Eisenberg, however, argues even this point. He says that archaeologists exaggerate the loss of historical significance of objects of art due to illicit excavations or illicit trafficking. He insists that the illicitly acquired material can provide just as much information for scholars and art historians as the properly excavated material. This does not mean, of course, that he supports illicit trafficking or excavations of the materials.[12]

One must admit that the position of the dealer in art-importing countries is very difficult and even delicate. The profit margin for the objects of Khmer art varies between moderate to high. Often the middlemen who bring them into the importing country may already charge the largest part of the profit margin. The dealer also must safeguard himself from smuggled goods.[13] In many countries the responsibility of the object lies with the person who possesses it; therefore, once the dealer has sold it to a collector he is no longer responsible for the piece of art.

The Collectors

> I spent between $15 million and $16 million over the last two years on Asian Art, and most of it was smuggled. (Norton Simon, a California tycoon and collector.)[14]

Collectors and the idea of collecting precious objects of art (Khmer art in this case) are relatively easy to understand. The drive of collecting, which includes searching for the objects, knowing the right people, and spending fortunes on the objects of art for which the collector has longed, can be understood and explained. The collecting of the first objects of

Khmer art started at the end of the nineteenth century, when Angkor Wat was first discovered. The drawing made by Mouhot that showed a practically unreal world that still continued to exist somewhere fascinated the French public. The first moulages of the Angkor temples were shown at The Great Exhibition where the reaction of the public, however, was mixed.

In fact, Khmer art was one of the last Oriental cultures discovered by Europeans, who had been collecting art from colonies from the sixteenth century (Netherlands-Indonesia). It had always been prestigious and aristocratic, such as collecting Indian art in England, the tradition of which goes back to the seventeenth century.[15] The discoveries of the new world have always fascinated Europeans; the Americas, Japan or China offered new possibilities of understanding the world, provided new dimensions, and offered new opportunities to Europe throughout the centuries.[16]

The first tourists were starting to bring the objects back from their trips to Angkor. Such trips were often aimed to complete the classical education of the young gentry before they were released into society and many bought back souvenirs of their journey, including vast amounts of antiquities.

The view of such activities was greatly different in this era; antiquities were as much a commodity as any other goods. The example of Lord Elgin and the Parthenon Marbles shows how perceptions have changed toward the sale of cultural property. However, Khmer art was not really appreciated by the French public. The first changes happened after World War II, when more Cambodian art arrived in Paris. Many of the items that arrived at that time went to private collections.

Most collectors acquire their taste for collecting over a lifetime. Oriental art requires more knowledge and understanding than many other fields of collecting.[17] The desire to collect Khmer objects of art is linked with a desire to possess authentic objects of art—real masterpieces—to own the best of what mankind has produced.

The argument about collecting objects of art has been discussed on a number of occasions—whether collecting is good for society and for cultures. It is true that private collectors usually keep the most valuable pieces of art, depriving people from access to them. All of the objects of Khmer art found in private collections were acquired illegally. Many of them were stolen from the sites and from illicit archaeological excavations.

Cambodia and other countries such as Iran and Afghanistan have lost the basis of their cultural heritage to vandals. In fact, the pillaging in Cambodia cannot have many comparisons. Much is written, for example, about illicit excavations in Italy, but the deserted places left instead of the

Khmer temples cannot be compared to the illicit digging in Italy.[18] In recent years, collecting Khmer art has become an obsession rather than a simple fashion, which is evident from the scale of destruction of the Cambodian monuments.

At the same time, even the most fanatical protectors of any cultural heritage cannot prohibit collecting. There are many objective reasons as well as many philosophical and cultural reasons that do not necessarily have to be accepted by all the participants in this discussion. By collecting, collectors undoubtedly protect the items. In most of the private collections, the items may be kept in much better conditions than in the best museums of the world or in the place of origin. Collectors have the time and means to pay more attention to the objects of art they have. Also in the case of Cambodia, one may argue that if the objects of art had not been found in collections, they could have been broken, kept in unacceptable conditions, or stored away from the eyes of the public just as much as if they had been kept in private collections.[19]

Again the question is more complicated than it seems. There is a question of morality and ethics. Some of the pieces of art stolen from Cambodia come from the temples and some were used for worshipping; in many cases this meaning has become inseparable as happens in all other countries where Hinduism or Buddhism is practiced. As we know from the previous chapter, many pieces are often stolen to order. Many collectors are attracted by the possibility of owning an object of art that had been cherished by the whole nation for centuries, while others respond to a psychological demand for the best pieces of art. In these cases provenance does not matter. Werner Meunsterberger wrote in his book:[20] "Powerful emotional experience of owning an object that was cherished a millennium ago, by an appreciative Sicilian or Roman citizen. It serves as evidence of continuity and symbolic communication with a distant past."[21]

Speaking from a moral point of view, is it ethical to remove objects of worship and deprive people of their religious practices? The question is answered negatively by most of the scholars and by me. However, it is evident that many collectors have differing points of view on this subject. It also seems obvious from the material analyzed in the previous chapter that collectors indirectly encourage and even finance looting because most of the objects are either specifically ordered by private individuals or are bought by interested clients.

If we look at any of the collections of art, it will be evident that most of the items in the collection do not give the provenance and were never published or studied by scholars. Another question that may be raised here is whether private collections should be displayed in museums so that the public may have access to them and, if they are, is it ethical to do that? Museums like to do this because it is prestigious and because some time in the future a part of the collection may be presented to this museum.

From one side, the public has access to very rare objects of Khmer art; from the other, the public does know that all of it was illicitly taken out of Cambodia and resold.[22] Many people come to Cambodia with the idea of buying an object of Khmer art. Most of them are prepared to obtain pieces at any price and some of them, as we saw, get fakes and do not even know it. There is also a romantic idea of the temples lost in the jungles, of the mysterious country lost in time; here is the interest, even necessity, to bring back something mysterious and prohibited.

Auction House

> *Two-thirds of any auction house catalog of antiquities is smuggled goods.*[23]

Auction houses are different from all of the categories mentioned here because they sell goods that do not belong to them. They sell objects of art on behalf of people who own them and who place them in their trust. According to their code of rules, auction houses are not responsible for the provenance of the materials they sell at their auctions. At the same time the catalogs, particularly those of New York, portray the finest pieces of Khmer art available on the market. Auctions such as Sotheby's Indian and Southeast Asian Art take place on average twice a year.

Up to a dozen of the most magnificent pieces may be presented at the auction. Hardly any of them will state the provenance (on average about twenty percent of the objects display the present owner, and very rarely is there an object with full provenance). The question of what liability auction houses have toward the goods they sell on behalf of their clients is rather complicated. Naturally, they do not have the right to disclose the identity of the owner. At the same time, the question of whether they should inquire into the provenance of the object of art cannot easily be answered.

When talking about Khmer art the word "provenance" does not mean a classical or a very detailed description of the history of a particular object that traces all of its owners back to the origins of the object. Just a mentioning of the previous owner and of the origin of the statue is more than sufficient. Indeed, Khmer art is one of the areas in antiquities where the display of the provenance is rare. Also, to avoid explanations to the Cambodian government or international organizations protecting cultural heritage, the origin of the object mentions something like "Angkor Wat Style" or "Bayon Style" instead of saying exactly which temple it came from. This erases the possibility of any inquiry on the legitimacy of the provenance.

Khmer objects of art are presented in each auction. Most of them are very exclusive or "important" as the catalog description says. On some occasions these are objects that have recently disappeared from Cambodia. Many of them have an inventory number, meaning that they are actually registered in Cambodia and that there is proof that they belong to the cultural heritage of the country, such as the object with inventory number DCA 1664, which was sold in Sotheby's, London, in 1985 and was found in the Honolulu Academy of Arts.[24]

The analysis of the restitution of objects of art that were returned to Cambodia will be presented in the Appendix. It shows that the majority of objects of Khmer art that were traced went through auction houses and that a much smaller portion went through antique dealers in Thailand and in Hong Kong. However, what can the Cambodian government or UNESCO or any other concerned organization do? They do not have the money to buy the object of art and the auction house will not disclose the identity of the seller, which means that the object is sold at the auction.

What impresses people in the catalogs is the initial price attached to the item. Starting from a few thousand dollars, most of the items go up to hundreds thousand of dollars. Most of the items are sold during the sales and the prices are often double the estimate. "Offices and academics from the Fine Arts Department conducted further studies into the age and estimated value of antiquities. These indicated that a work from Banteay Chmar Shrine in Cambodia's Mienjeui Province could fetch at least one hundred million bhat in the open market. This case alone makes future probes worthwhile into smuggling methods used at this site."[25]

Auction houses were accused of misconduct for selling a large amount of art without mention of its provenance. Sotheby's faced this problem in 1996. Sotheby's had introduced a policy whereby clients who did not want to disclose the provenance of an article were to be held responsible for the items they presented for auction. In this way no laws were broken by presenting the items at the auction. The U.K. Department of Indian Art was closed with the explanation that New York is "already the largest marketplace in this field" and that the concentration of sale in one place would actually help to control the sales. The two employees working in this department in London have since left the company.

The scandal continued recently when a former chairman of Sotheby's was accused of conspiring to fix commission fees for more than 130,000 customers over six years. In April 2001 the judge approved a $537 million settlement against the auction houses brought by these 130,000 customers who claimed that they were cheated by the auction houses. This meant serious damage to the reputation of Sotheby's and Christie's.[26]

These statistics show a certain improvement because about twenty percent of the objects of Khmer art sold in Sotheby's have a given provenance. The percentage, however, is still very low and evidently serves as a source of worry for the Cambodian government and international organizations. However, what auction houses, just as antique dealers, continue to do is to put all the responsibility on the buyers or the sellers. In case of an inquiry, they do not have the right to disclose the identity of the seller; they may pass an inquiry about the object on to him. From there it is up to the individual to decide what he or she wants to do.

A rare example here is presented by the case of Christina Tanewska-Elliot, who inherited a Khmer Brahma head of a rare quality and learned that it was stolen from Angkor when she gave it for sale to Sotheby's and it was identified there by UNESCO officials.[27] Auction houses should take more direct responsibility for the objects of art they sell at auction.

Museums

> The chase and the capture of a great work of art is one of the most exciting endeavors in life—as dramatic, emotional, and fulfilling as a love affair.[28]

The notion of museums is relatively recent when compared, for example, with private collections. The Louvre and the British Museum were among the first examples of public museums. In fact, before 1753, when the British Museum first opened its collections for show, public access to the collections of art was highly restricted.[29] One of the main topics of discussion now between scholars is what is the purpose and main idea of the museum in the twenty-first century and how should it be different from precedent times. At the same time practically all the most well known museums are constantly accused of buying objects of art, some of which are clearly acquired illicitly by middlemen, without knowing the provenance.

In the past ten or so years, the collections of Khmer art in many museums have significantly increased in size. I have talked to many people in Phnom Penh—some of them in the government, some working with Khmer art—who mentioned how surprised they were to see the glamorous collections of objects of Khmer art in many of the museums they visited outside of Cambodia in the last twenty years. They pointed out that only a decade ago some of these museums did not even have such departments. Examples included the display of beautiful bronzes that had not been there during previous visits and a display of Khmer art that consisted of about forty pieces, mainly statues, most of which were dated by 1939. The guide insisted that the pieces were not bought in Cambodia.

At the same time, one of the best places in the world to see the most outstanding pieces of Khmer art is the Guimet Museum in Paris, which is an exception among other museums that contain Khmer art. "Phnom Penh, the capital, is one of two places to go if you're looking for the cream of Cambodian art. The other is France's Museum National des Arts Asiatique–Guimet, the Guimet Museum for short."[30]

The National Museum of Arts in Phnom Penh of course has a very rich collection of Khmer art. It cannot be otherwise. It is also true that the museum is in very bad condition and keeps struggling for survival. More precise conditions of the museum and the problems faced by the staff will be described in the last part of this research in the discussion of government policies. In brief, however, it lacks the most basic things, including security, locks, telephone lines, resources etc., as well as poor displays. On one occasion an exceptional statue was returned to Cambodia and then stolen again. Since then it has completely disappeared from view, most probably into somebody's collection.

Some examples are nearly comic. The roof of the museum needs urgent repair. However, a very rare species of bat, found only in this place, lives under the roof of the National Museum. The disturbance of these bats, according to the Australian scientist who discovered them, may cause unexpected effects that may even lead to the extinction of this species. For this particular reason they cannot be disturbed. The museum needs urgent fundraising, professional help and investment.

There are also some museums in the provinces. The museum in Battambang, already mentioned in the previous chapter, had an incredible collection until practically all of it was stolen during the 1980s. In fact, many provinces could have good museums that could also attract visitors; however, for reasons of finance and security this is hardly possible. Also, many of the objects are already in the museums of Europe, Japan or America. One can say that the museum of Phnom Penh is lucky to have such an astonishing collection.

In some African countries, the situation is much worse. Most of the museums do not even have acceptable objects for display.[31] The same is true in some of the regions of Latin America.[32] The argument presented

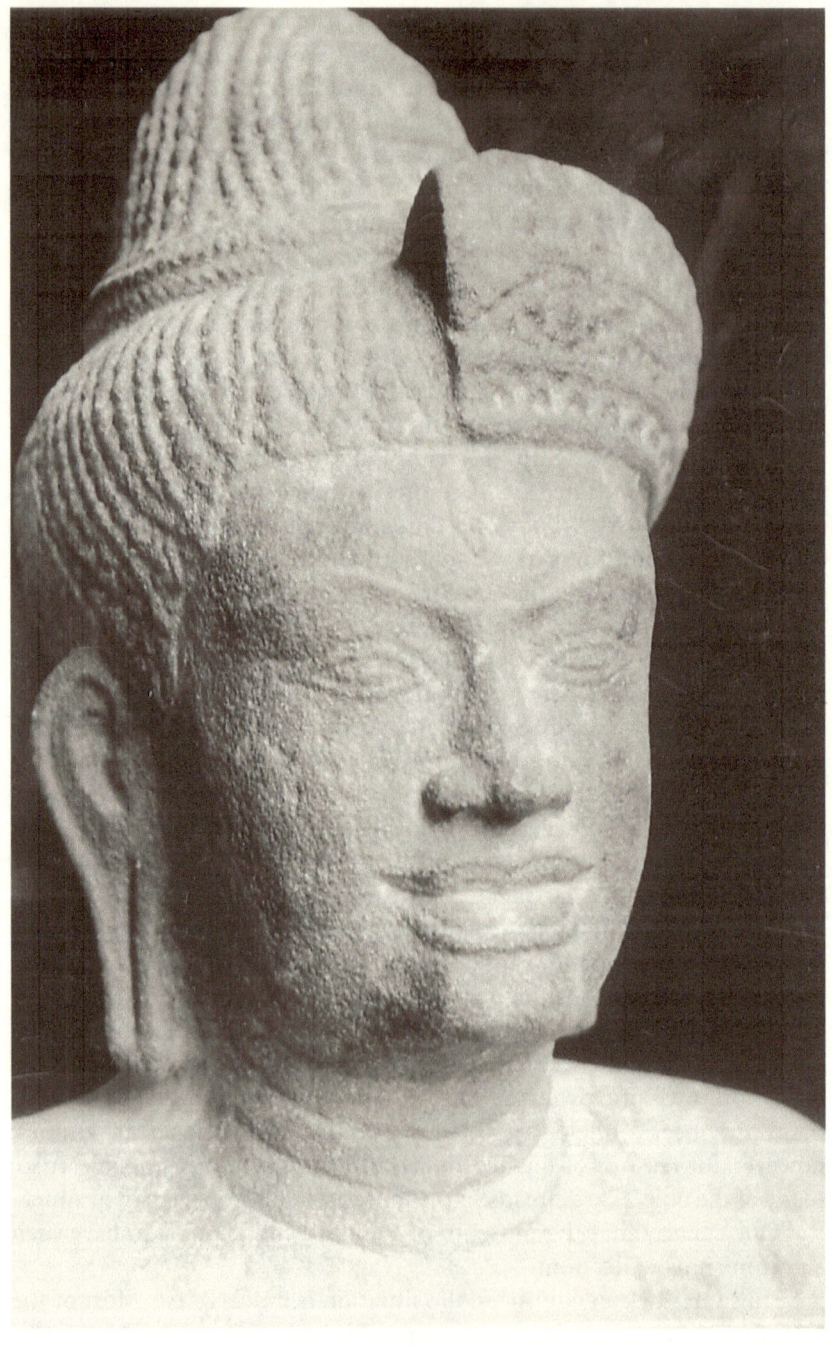

From the display of the Museum of Phnom Penh.

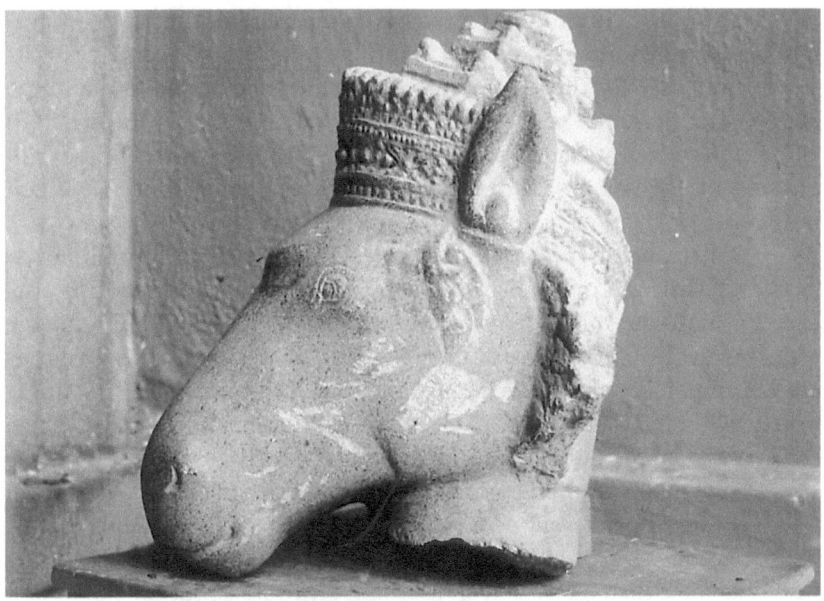

From the display of the Museum of Phnom Penh.

by the protectors of the Cambodian cultural heritage is clear. Practically all of the objects of Khmer art found abroad were smuggled out of the country. The objects of art the museum acquired in recent years clearly state that they have an unknown origin, that is, they were most probably acquired illegally. The technique used by museums is similar to that of the auction houses. The descriptive labels say that the objects were presented or donated by someone and then state that it is a "Style of Bayon" or any other temple, thus avoiding the statement that it comes from Cambodia.

Museums, however, have another point of view. Many of the objects bought could indeed be acquired by licit means. The curator of the Metropolitan Museum of Fine Arts says that as soon as the media hear about smuggled objects of Khmer art they become hysterical and, in fact, not all objects of art appearing on the market are stolen. For example, he insists that a Cambodian farmer who comes across a piece of art while farming and sells it is only trying to help his family to survive, which cannot in any way be considered as illicit trafficking of stolen art. "Not every piece of Khmer art on sale in auctions or antique shops is stolen and a great deal of the pieces are patent fakes.... It's absolutely inaccurate to say all these works are stolen.... If a farmer digs up a bronze piece and that will pay for his children to go to school for two years and sells it to some soldier who slips it across the border, that's not stolen stuff."[33]

Many of the curators and directors of the museums insist that Cambodian art is better protected and that more people have access to it outside Cambodia. Tourism in Cambodia is still very limited. Many more people visit museums in the United States and Europe. In the epoch of globalization, art belongs to mankind. Museums serve a very important purpose of education. Visitors may learn about past civilizations, which in the case of Cambodia is not well known.

The British museum, for example, receives more than six million visitors each year, and more than half of them are foreign tourists. It is possible for thousands of students to study there every year.[34] Prohibiting the export of art, and in the case of Cambodia of all objects of art even if they are not important and have duplicates, reduces this possibility of education, which can also be argued as legally and morally unacceptable. It also limits any possible publications and research work.

Many items acquired by countries during the epoch of colonization were acquired by different means. This was not seen as pillaging but, on the contrary, was accepted as a "highly civilized and legal process."[35] It is true that since then many perceptions and attitudes about the policy and laws have changed. In general, however, the arguments of the museum employees, who have continued to improve their collections, for the preservation of the items of other nations that were acquired by museums often in the eighteenth century due to colonialism and wars, present a wide spectrum. They start from the most usual arguments that in most of the Third World countries the security is not adequate and there is too much pollution or political instability. They further grow into arguments that have a more universal basis such as that many museums in Europe and America are the biggest museums in the world and have a significant universal and historic mission. They also consider it their duty to represent art from all over the world.

The main task of the museum is to collect the best pieces of art. In fact, it is the main task of the curators. Curators constantly keep looking for new pieces of art to enrich and improve the collections in their departments. The actual process of acquisition of objects of art is complicated. The piece has to go through a commission that should approve it. There are constant problems with funding.

Before the 1970 UNESCO Convention on the Means of Prohibiting and Preventing the Illicit Import, Export and Transfer of Ownership of Cultural Property, museums could acquire all sorts of objects of art, no matter what their provenance was. The adoption of the 1970 convention has changed these rules and was accepted by many museums such as the British Museum, which does not acquire recently smuggled objects of art no matter what they are.[36] The same is true for the Berlin and Paul Getty museums. This might have negative effects on the museums and for art itself. Museums collect less and buy only from collections with proof of provenance.[37]

Many museums have recently faced so much pressure from archaeologists, international organizations, and the mass media that they have had to refuse many objects of art, which have then disappeared from public view. Such an attitude cannot be considered as acceptable, and clearly the protectors of cultural heritage should rethink their policies. In some cases, one can say these objects of art could be rescued by the museums if they bought them.[38] Indeed many museums have changed their policies and adjusted them to the 1970 UNESCO Convention. However, no help was offered to the museums to change their policies on object acquisition. The museums that are members of ICOM follow the code of ethics that dates from 1986.[39]

As mentioned at the beginning, the Guimet Museum in Paris occupies a separate place in this situation. The EFEO and French scholars have done much for the development and research of Angkor. It has often been said that the main positive impact of the French protectorate in France was the discovery and study of Angkor.

Public Opinion

> It is shaping up as the issue of the decade. The growing debate over the international trade in cultural property—who owns and has the right to exhibit humanity's artistic and archaeological treasures—is rapidly becoming the art world's newest cause célèbre, affecting everyone and everything from collectors and museums to Third World "source" nations and the people who live in them.[40]

The issues that are important when talking about public opinion is what the general public thinks about these matters and who presents the interests of the public. The archaeologists and the Cambodian government say that they are the ones who represent the interests of the public and protect the cultural heritage of the country, which is the national heritage of Cambodia. The museum curators think that they represent the interests of the public because the presentation of Khmer art in exhibits is important to the millions of visitors who come to European and American museums every year. It seems that both groups represent the interests of the public, which does not help to solve the problems of illicit trafficking and of who actually has more rights in these issues.[41]

It would be wrong to say that the priority and interests of archaeologists are of more importance than the interests of collectors or dealers, who are also a part of the public, or the interests of museums and auctions. It is clear that the public has the right of access to objects of Khmer art and to the information available about it as well as the right to see it and know about it. The destruction of Khmer objects of art or information about them is against the interests of mankind.[42] This issue, however, is complicated as it continues to be based mainly on moral grounds rather than on grounds of law or specific rules and regulations.

It is true that not only Khmer art is in such a difficult situation. In many countries such as Greece, Italy, Egypt, India, Thailand and many others the illicit trade of arts is in a bad situation. Each heritage is unique for its country and for mankind. In Cambodia, however, it is made more complicated by widespread economic and political instability and by nearly complete destruction through the social passivity of the population, who do not think that selling their past is a bad thing or is against the law. Instead they thank their ancestors who have helped them to survive in hard times. At the end it becomes an economic issue rather than a cultural one.

At the same time, Khmer art became popular and fashionable in the West not only among private collectors and a few individuals but among the general public as well. The Western public and purchasers of art like Khmer art. Many say that it is up to Cambodians themselves to sell their art; they also insist that in this way Khmer art becomes accessible to everybody. Apart from the fact that it is fashionable at the moment, it is a rare and unique art that should be known and appreciated by everyone all over the world. The only possible way to do this is to exhibit it for the general public in museums.

Indeed, the Guimet Museum, which has one of the best collections acquired during the epoch of the French protectorate, has just opened after many years of reconstruction. It presents a beautiful display of the best pieces of Khmer art that it has complemented by numerous publications, photos and catalogs sold in the museum shop. In the end, does one blame the Cambodian government, system and even the public for being corrupt and not protective enough or the Western dealers and buyers for offering to buy it? Or both?

The Cambodian government and UNESCO from their side undertake many steps to expose the problem. A few films were made recently by French, American, and Cambodian teams to attract the attention of the general public to this matter. In Cambodia there are brochures and booklets available on this issue. Many sides participate in these issues and have their own opinions, often fully explained and protected. It is hard to imagine that it will be possible to find an agreement on the issue that will be acceptable to all. It also means that the discussion of cultural heritage will continue for some time.[43] Of course, everybody is against illicit trafficking and stolen art.

Conclusion

This chapter shows that Khmer art is very much in demand by Western and Asian collectors, art dealers and auction houses. Such collections are very much appreciated by the museums. The illicit trafficking of Khmer art from Cambodia may be considered one of the country's main social problems; however, this is not the way it is reflected in current government policies. It is clear that there are many other problems more pressing than that of cultural heritage. Economic and financial issues remain, by far, more important for the country.

At the same time, on the demand side there is much interest other than financial that creates an overwhelmingly strong pressure and keeps the market of Khmer art very animated. Khmer art remains in fashion and the aura surrounding it remains mysterious and unusual. There are many different parties participating in this issue. All of them have their interests and their ideas "for" and "against" the problem. The main arguments presented by museums, collectors and antique dealers were mentioned earlier. Many of them are well-argued and focused issues that have a political and legal right to exist.

All categories of participants interested in buying Khmer art actually compete among themselves and create an antiquities market. None of them is interested in acquiring information on whether the object of art was obtained illegally or whether it has a recognized provenance. All of them, however, have a policy that explains the rightness of their motives and does not connect them with the illicit market or destruction of the Cambodian cultural heritage.

Therefore, there is a certain tension among the protectors of cultural heritage, historical and academic values and the representatives of commercial interests. And therefore, realistically speaking, it is hard to imagine that an amicable solution to the problem will be found in the near future that will suit all sides.

Logically speaking, the provenance gives more value to the item in the eyes of collectors and proves its authenticity, which is important in

Khmer art, and increases its value. Therefore, both dealers and auction houses should be interested in knowing it. It could also help to solve the problem between the two sides: the side of the archaeologists and scholars and the side of the commercial dealers. However, this solution is not an issue at the moment.

3

Impact of Illicit Trafficking on the Cultural and Socio-Economic Systems in Cambodia

Illicit traffic results in the Third World countries being systematically deprived of their cultural heritage and being economically exploited at the same time. Under many guises (for example disseminating information about mankind by showing cultural artifacts from every nook and corner of the world in London and New York) we find objects of veneration removed from their spiritual homes to adorn museum showcases and private homes.[1]

The question of the impact of illicit trafficking of art on the cultural and socio-economic systems in Cambodia is very complex. It is obvious to anyone that the loss of cultural heritage is unacceptable and painful for any country. Although the effects of trafficking are difficult to quantify, one sees the damage done in various areas such as political and economic, cultural identity, nationalism, ideology, legitimacy, psychological factors, and the deterioration of architectural and historical values. The combined effects of these factors, the scale of illicit trade and the illegal nature of this trade have had a complex and dramatic impact on Cambodian society. The scale of illicit trafficking has exceeded all imaginable dimensions. According to archaeologists in Siem Reap, up to ninety-eight percent of the temples in the country were destroyed by looters.

The illegality of the trade has many negative effects. They arise from the increased violence, corruption, underground activities, and economic instability that illegal trade spawns. It should be noted, however, that this trade creates extra income for the people who participate in it. Most of them no doubt need it for their most basic needs; thus, one can argue that it brings a higher revenue, better lives, and increased consumerism to certain groups of the population. It is arguable, however, that illicit trafficking may have positive effects. The scale of trafficking and illegality are also highly related since illegality is the main reason for the industry's high profits.

The complex impact of the illegal trade on the country has frequently been underestimated and omitted from the official reports and publications. In the first chapter, I made an attempt to estimate the size of the industry and proved that the scale of this trade is relatively large for the country in question. Here we'll try to look at the impact of the trade on the country and society. The variables mentioned here do not pretend to make an exhaustive list but only identify some of the primary effects of this trade and evaluate the evidence available.

Legal Issues

One of the main effects of the illegal trafficking of art is the worsening of the delegitimation process that occurs in Cambodia. The continuation of trafficking affects certain variables within the social system of the country. For example, it contributes to the establishment of an underground economy. Another factor of illegal trafficking is the lack of respect for the legal system. It has always been an issue and certainly remains a big problem that will not disappear as the trafficking of art continues.

Laws on the protection of cultural heritage are practically nonexistent. The first attempts to introduce a law to protect cultural heritage started in 1992. The attempt was made by international organizations present in Cambodia, mainly UNESCO, that tried to stabilize the dramatic situation that existed in the field of arts. It was evident that laws were absolutely necessary to provide for the legal side of the protection of cultural heritage; that is to say that without laws on the protection of cultural heritage one cannot even start preventing illicit trafficking of art from the country. The very first law on the protection of the monuments was written during the epoch of the French protectorate by the Government of Indochina in 1925, "*Législation relative au classement, à la protec-*

tion et à la conservation des monuments historiques et des objets d'art de l'Indochine Française." It was rewritten in 1965 after Cambodia became an independent country. During the Pol Pot regime and Year Zero all legislation was annulled. By the beginning of the 1990s, when objects of art were stolen from the country on a daily basis, there were no legal rules and regulations that could help to regulate the issue.

The only law that exists at the moment was written by Swiss lawyer Ridha Fraoua, who was invited to Cambodia by UNESCO in 1996 for this purpose. After the trip to Cambodia he wrote in his report to UNESCO: "*Les instruments juridiques en matière de gestion, de promotion et de protection du patrimoine culturel adoptés jusqu'à présent ne sont guère appliqués. Ainsi, les prescriptions de la loi sur la protection du patrimoine culturel ne sont pas observées.*"[2]

As I have already mentioned, there are not many competent lawyers in the country and any legal intervention requires the participation of outside specialists, often provided by UNESCO. Although written and adopted by the administrative system of the country in 1992, the Law on the Protection of Cultural Heritage has never been put into practice. Its Section 9 focuses on the export of cultural property. Article 51 states that "The export of any cultural objects from Cambodia is prohibited, unless the competent authority had granted a special export license for the purpose." Article 53 specifies that "The export of cultural objects shall be subject to duties and fees. The amount of those export duties and fees shall be set by law."

Article 54 describes which objects of art may get an export license. However, there are no sub-decrees for this law. It means that even if there are provisions for import or export, as in Article 51, there are no clear written administrative procedures or regulations for the import or export of objects of art from the country. Therefore, if anybody buys an object of art, no matter whether it is an important piece or not, nobody knows what to do or under what conditions or according to what legislation one can or cannot export art. Therefore, most of the articles of this legislation require logical development.

The same is true for the excavations and other problems related to the protection of cultural heritage. The absence of such criteria leads to the systematic export of art from the country, which is not approved by law but also is not disapproved by it. As a result, any foreigner who buys Cambodian art and wants to take it out of the country finds his or her solution personally with the responsible ministry, usually the Ministry of Culture. The Cambodian government does not give the impression of being in a hurry to introduce the sub-decrees. It seems that the implementation of these laws would be against the interests of certain people or groups of people. Considering the research made in the first chapter, this group appears to be the military, which is powerful enough to slow the process of legislation establishment in the country. Ridha Fraoua further writes in his report: "*Le cadre institutionnel mis en place pour assurer la gestion et la protection du patrimoine national cambodgien n'est pas non plus opérationnel. Le manque de volonté politique, de personnel qualifié et de moyens financiers suffisants sont certainement à l'origine de cette situation précaire.*"[3]

The absence of law on the protection of cultural heritage is certainly due to many factors such as the absence of political will, the lack of financial resources necessary to implement the law, and the lack of trained personnel in the concerned areas. The responsibility for the protection of cultural heritage is also divided among at least five ministries whose tasks are not clearly identified. The legislative texts usually adopted by the National Assembly and officially published are not implemented or discussed by the organizations concerned. Furthermore, they are not brought to the attention of the administration or public.

Cambodia has many faults in its legal system that are eventually used by the traffickers. It is true that implementation of legal measures will not stop the looting of art, but it will create order within the system and definitely ameliorate the problem. One of the faults mentioned in the previous paragraph is the visible lack of action from the national authorities, who do not even take the minimal required steps toward the necessary measures to prevent trafficking. Another negative aspect also discussed is a legislation of 1996 (The Law on the Protection of Cultural Heritage), where the decrees must be adopted. In general the country needs to work on the gaps within the legislation.

Cambodia also needs to put more stress on work in the field of regional cooperation. One of the problems we saw in the first chapter was the issue with the Thai border. Thai authorities could return hundreds of objects of art to the Cambodian authorities if the right approach were accepted. A similar problem exists with all neighboring countries; however, the most urgent issue is Thailand. Dozens of objects of art that are discovered in Thailand on a daily basis are not returned to Cambodia, partly because of the absence of necessary agreements.

The situation with Thailand is not only legal but also political and economic in nature and will be discussed in the next part of this chapter. It is necessary to say, however, that there is a border agreement between the two countries that will work for Cambodia only if the country itself adopts the necessary action. In the case of the temple of Banteay Chmar

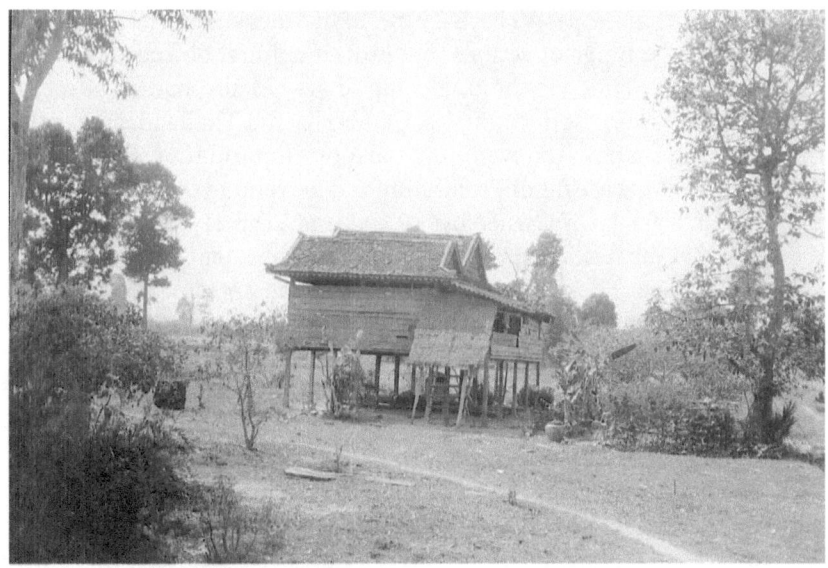

A Cambodian house; the road between Banteay Srei and Angkor.

(when the Thais agreed to return to Cambodia eleven-and-a-half meters of the temple wall that was found on the border), the Thais have shown that they are ready to cooperate. It must be noted that in the case of Banteay Chmar it was UNESCO that provided all the technical assistance, such as the preparation of the relevant requests and dossiers, because Cambodian lawyers did not have the necessary knowledge to do that. No doubt similar work should be done with other countries such as Singapore and Hong Kong.

Cambodia still has not ratified some of the international conventions that are very important in this field. Among them is the Diplomatic Conference in Rome, which took place in 1995. It was attended by Vann Molyvann (Director of APSARA, the most important figure in Cambodia associated with its cultural heritage). What is more important among other international instruments that have been adopted especially to fight the illicit trafficking is the UNIDROIT convention, which focuses on private law. In 1962 Cambodia did sign and ratify The Convention for the Protection of Cultural Property in the Event of Armed Conflict (The Hague, 1954) and its Protocol, which protects all types of cultural property. It is the state that is responsible for its protection in time of peace and two states in the time of armed conflict (both states participating in the war.) Cambodia also ratified in 1972 The Convention on the Means of Prohibiting and Preventing the Illicit Import, Export and Transfer of Ownership of Cultural Property (Paris, 1970). It provides an international legal framework for a range of actions that protect cultural objects of art.

To be more concrete the trafficking of art has also had an effect on the following issues. Both countries, Cambodia and Thailand, are parties to various international conventions, the most important of which is The Convention on the Means of Prohibiting and Preventing the Illicit Import, Export and Transfer of Ownership of Cultural Property (Paris, 1970). It mentions that the states may conclude bilateral agreements to protect their cultural heritage. The non-conclusion of such an agreement pushes the delegitimation process even further and reduces the achievements made by the countries on an international level. Because both states are parties to this convention, they should negotiate the agreement that will allow them to improve the situation.

On the national level the countries receive the necessary assistance with legislation. An intervention of UNESCO from 1992 with legislation, customs training, or the establishment of a special police force in Angkor was a direct result of the 1970 Convention, which also facilitates the return and restitution of objects of art if they are registered in the inventory. What makes things difficult is that Cambodia does not have a proper inventory. A few inventories were drawn up by the French in Angkor before 1970. Many papers disappeared during the Pol Pot regime. What Cambodia needs at the moment is a new inventory on the national level, particularly in the remote regions, that will help to control art trafficking and identify objects of art. For example, such an inventory could have saved the temple of Banteay Chmar from looting.

Another convention ratified by Cambodia in 1991 is The Convention Concerning the Protection of the World Cultural and Natural Heritage (World Heritage Convention, Paris, 1972). It helped to put Angkor recently on the World Heritage List, which helps this particular monument to get more international assistance and attracts attention to it.[4] Cambodia is required to protect Angkor, "make every effort and employ every means and resource to ensure the application of legislation for protection…," but the absence of legislation in Cambodia makes this difficult to follow. There is also a new international convention, the UNIDROIT Convention on the International Return of Stolen or Illegally Exported Cultural Objects, which has not been ratified by Cambodia. In general it could help Cambodia to reinforce its legal framework and extend the rules and regulations on the restitution of objects of art.

Considering Cambodia's difficult legal, political and economic situation, much has already been done in the country since 1992. However, Cambodia is still not efficient enough in adopting all the legal

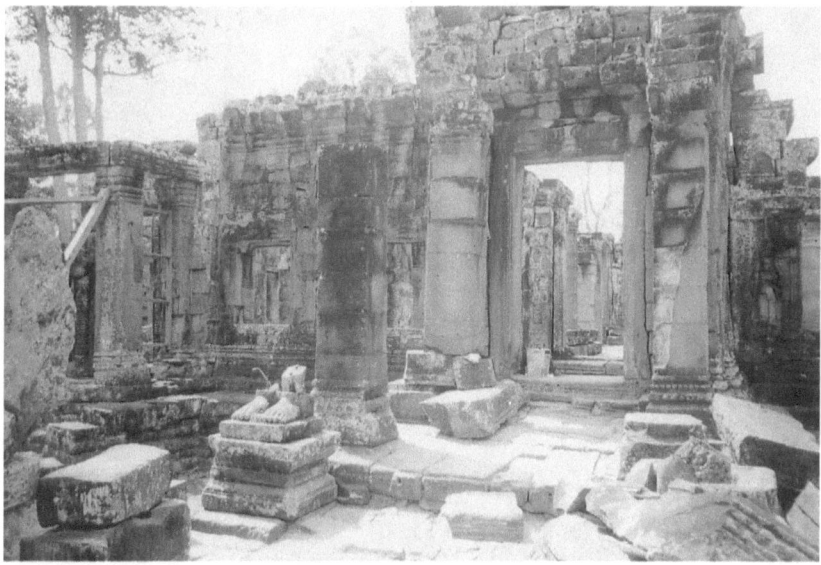

Temple of Banteay Kdei; end of the twelfth century; built during the reign of Jayavarman VII.

instruments that could permit a much more efficient protection of its cultural heritage.

Political and Economic Issues

The illicit trafficking of art directly affects political and economic issues in the country. Among many factors, the trafficking of art worsens the system of corruption and bribery in the government. As a result of multiple sales of objects of art, the participants in illicit trafficking are used to making quick profits (36.1 percent of the population live below the poverty line).[5] The relatively large (in terms of Cambodian lifestyle) sums of money can be earned quickly and may help to solve the most basic problems. The word "participants" here does not mean a few hundred soldiers who participate in the trafficking itself, but primarily the local population that tries to make a living and needs this money often just to survive.

It is true, however, that most Cambodians do not have a clear understanding of the law, its functions or implications, or even the notion of cultural heritage. All of these issues have received much attention in jour-

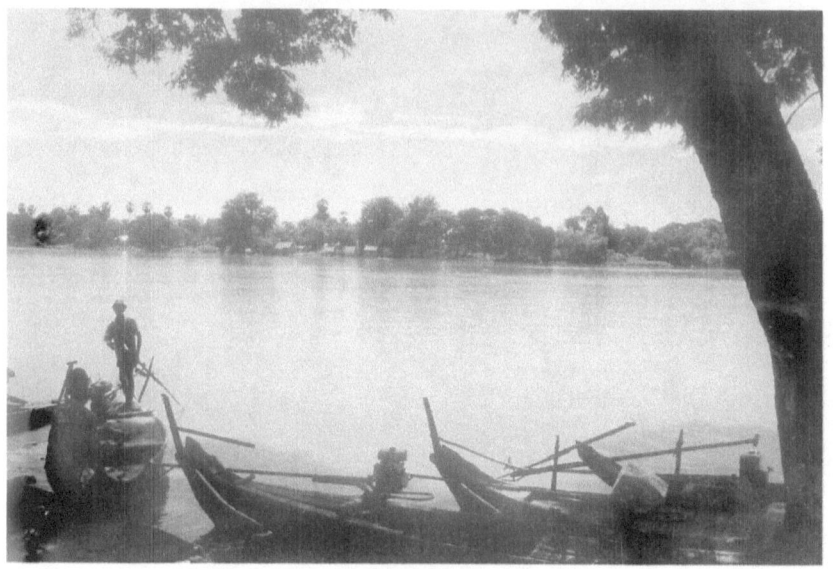

On the river.

nalistic publications. Each of the factors mentioned above, which do not constitute a complete list of the problems caused by illegal trafficking, worsens the situation within the country. Continuous trafficking increases the gap between what exists in reality and what should be socially accepted in a legitimate society. Not only does it fasten the process of delegitimation but it also weakens the state.

Clearly it is not the illicit trafficking of art that started the delegitimation process or corruption of the administrative system in Cambodia. It was already there and the existence of trafficking only accelerates it. Also it is not only the trafficking of art that has effects; many other types of trafficking, such as arms, drugs, gems, cars, and oil, were mentioned in the first chapter. The administrative system of the country should also be taken into account. Trade in art no doubt helps to promote the existing situation.

The issue of art smuggling has an impact on the political relations among the countries in the region. It has an immediate and long-term impact on the relations of Cambodia, first with Thailand and then with other countries such as Singapore or Vietnam. Even if art trafficking may be of lesser importance than the rest of the economic and financial problems or types of contraband that exist between the countries, its impact may be surprisingly powerful. In many cases, the questions of smuggling and restitution of art may become highly important diplomatic issues, involving a few states. It is widely known that Cambodia did not want to bring up an issue about certain objects of art kept in the Metropolitan Museum of New York because political and economic relations between the two countries were improving.

The most visible and important impact of art smuggling on the destabilization and aggravation of already existing political and economic problems between the two countries is presented by Thailand and Cambodia. Because the government has no control over smuggling, certain issues become further destabilized. For example, the question of illicit trafficking of art is closely linked with Thai border problems, discussed in the first Chapter. It further complicates the relations between the two countries and brings in political instability. "We agreed that there shall be a meeting of the general border committee soon to look into cooperation to bring peace, stability and understanding."[6]

As violence increases, the governments of both countries are trying to reach an agreement on the main problem—the checkpoints on the border. An official attempt to regulate the problem was made recently. In December 1999 the defense ministers of both countries established checkpoints on the border.[7] The problem is more complicated than it seems because illicit trafficking of art cannot be separated from other illicit activities. Many cars are stolen from Thailand and sold in Cambodia, thus creating another type of cross-border trafficking. The Thais agree to cooperate on the issue of artifacts only if the Cambodians will agree to cooperate on the problem of the stolen cars, which is one of the biggest issues facing the relations between the countries. The representatives of both countries say that the 807-mile (1,300-kilometer) border is not well defined and needs to be surveyed and marked.[8] Similar border problems exist with Laos and Vietnam.[9]

The smuggling of all kinds of goods in general and of artifacts in particular and the illicit income received by the participants of the smuggling costs the government about two million dollars each month. One of the categories of losses is tax revenues. Each year the government collects only about half of what it expects in tax revenues, particularly in customs.[10] According to recent reports, though, the smuggling has significantly decreased and the situation on the Thai border is much more regulated than it was because there are more checkpoints and more border inspectors. It is clear that trafficking remains a daily issue in politics and economics. The illicit trafficking has an impact not only on political and economic issues but on historical and interethnic issues. The conclusion of a bilateral agreement may easily solve these issues because the countries are aware of each other's problems and could solve them rather smoothly.

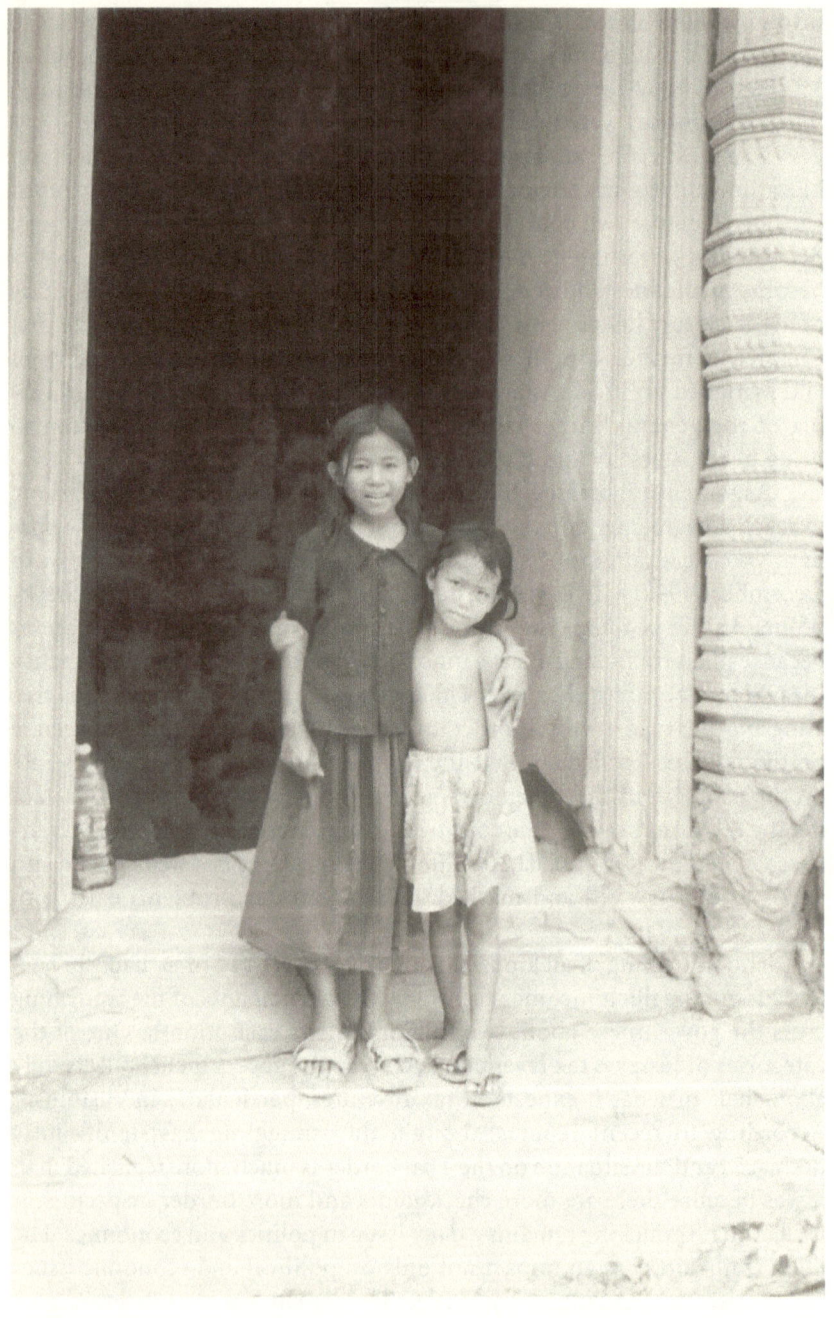

Two girls selling souvenirs in the Temple of Pre Rup; tenth century; built by Rajendravarman II.

It is obvious that all types of smuggling and contraband have a significant impact on the official and black markets and many economic variables such as GDP growth (4.5 percent in 1999); GNP per capita (two hundred sixty dollars at present); employment; and legal and illegal capital inflows, which are complex categories and can hardly be analyzed here. Estimating the actual impact of art smuggling on the economy is quite difficult. In the case of Cambodia, one can assume that most of the money stays in the country. Thus, in this particular case, we are talking about the internal changes rather than influence at the international level. Also the financial impact of trafficking of art is not as strong as, for example, that of fuel or other products that have an impact on the industry of the country. However, these issues are still interrelated and should be mentioned here.

It is obvious that illicit trafficking of art contributes to the economic decline of the country. Often people, talent and capital are attracted to the higher rates of return in illicit activity and, thus, abandon the agricultural and manufacturing sectors. Among many problematic issues, this trade contributes to inflation. The impact of art trafficking is, however, too small to be determined here. One of the industries that have progressed in Cambodia recently is construction. Many hotels and villas were built all over the country, particularly in areas that may become resort areas such as southern towns on the ocean like Kampot and Sihanoukville. Construction is often financed with illegal capital and permits money laundering.

Another issue is that the environment for direct foreign investment has greatly deteriorated.[11] Many potential investors may be discouraged by the near absence of a judicial system and the existence of an underground economy and corruption. It is clear that the smuggling and corruption that exist on the governmental level reduce the potential financial help that could be enjoyed by Cambodia.[12] The financial stability of the country is directly affected by the above issues, which create undesirable effects and uncertainty. The question of smuggling should be resolved, at least to a certain extent, before Cambodia can be admitted into the international world of politics. However, the issue of illicit trafficking of art is not the most important factor contributing to this problem. The situation of political instability in general lowers the possibilities of foreign investment. However, the issue of art smuggling is much discussed in the media and diplomatic circles, and it is the indirect effects of trafficking that have been negative for investment.

"Mr. Customs have to stop disturbing investors.... Customs is the king of corruption." said the Cambodian Prime Minister Hun Sen during a meeting with potential investors.[13] The impact of art smuggling or, in

other words, the inability to understand the importance of cultural heritage, has a direct impact on the lack of financial resources, which can be
seen just about anywhere, for example in the most urgent field—protection of objects of art from smuggling. The Police Heritage Forces were created with the help of the French government in the territory of Angkor.
Four hundred police soldiers are there to protect the monuments from
trafficking, and many temples suffer on a daily basis because of the absence
of trained soldiers in other areas of the country.

There is a desperate need to increase police expenditures, which are
just consumption costs and do not contribute to revenue or growth. The
existing police force needs money, cars and equipment to perform their
work in the Territory of Angkor. The government does not have enough
money for the Ministry of Culture or APSARA or for training the administrative staff, customs or employees of the ministries, whose salary does not
exceed twenty dollars. There is a lack of resources to make a simple inventory of the temples in the regions or to improve the conditions of access.

Art smuggling is evidently one of the obstacles standing in the way
of the country's development. It adds to instability in the society. At the
same time it is conducted by the military, which is gaining strength in the
country, dictating their politics and introducing their values. It introduces
its web of trafficking into the social system of the country and eventually
into the government. It includes the regulated functioning of the groups
of looters, the raids on the temples, the transportation of the goods and
the protection of the participants from the legal system.

One of the country's biggest problems is that the administrative system has not changed much throughout the history of the country. Its main
elements, discussed in the first chapter, have not evolved sufficiently. Many
of the features that existed during the reign of Jayavarman VII and then
during the French protectorate are still visible now. These features, most
of which date back to a feudal system and are definitely precapitalistic in
their essence, are the root of many of the country's problems. In Cambodia, once these networks are established they cover the whole society and
make every member of this society vulnerable to the actions or propos-
als of the participants of trafficking. Apart from corrupting and intimi-
dating the administrative system, they also recruit new members for the
performance of their activities.

Even though Cambodia is developing economically faster than before,
the existence of an underground economy and corruption lower the possibility of economic growth and implementation of the legal system. The
negative impact of illicit trafficking of art affects the otherwise possible
political and economic development of the country.

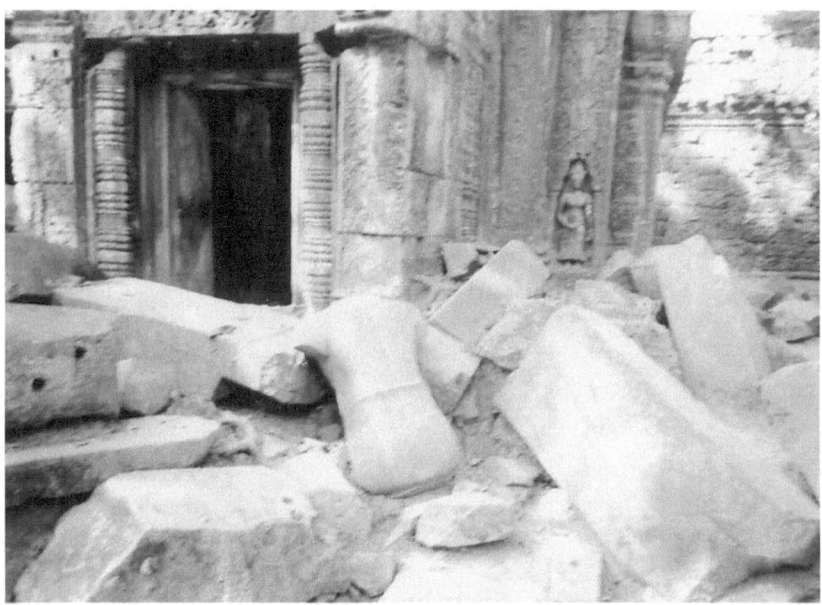

Temple of Ta Prohm; end of the eleventh to beginning of the twelfth century; built during the reign of Jayavarman VII.

Architectural and Historical Values

> *The looting of archaeological heritage has become what is probably the world's most serious threat to our archaeological heritage.*[14]

The most visible effect of the growth of illicit trafficking of art has been on the cultural heritage of Cambodia itself. The devastating effect of art smuggling is clearly visible in all parts of the country. The results of the growth of the illicit trade, its changes and cycles can be observed in each temple, particularly in the temples of Angkor, which possess the most interesting and beautiful objects of art. The growth of the trade, discussed in the previous chapter, shows that the majority of the statues disappeared between 1986 and the late 1990s, when Cambodia became more accessible to the international trade syndicate.

The illicit trafficking erases the historical and architectural heritage of the country. The looting of every new statue robs historians of another small chance to reconstruct the evidence of pre-history. Hundreds of pre-angkorean vases can be found in the local markets, used at home as vases for flowers or occupying places as part of collections. Not many, however,

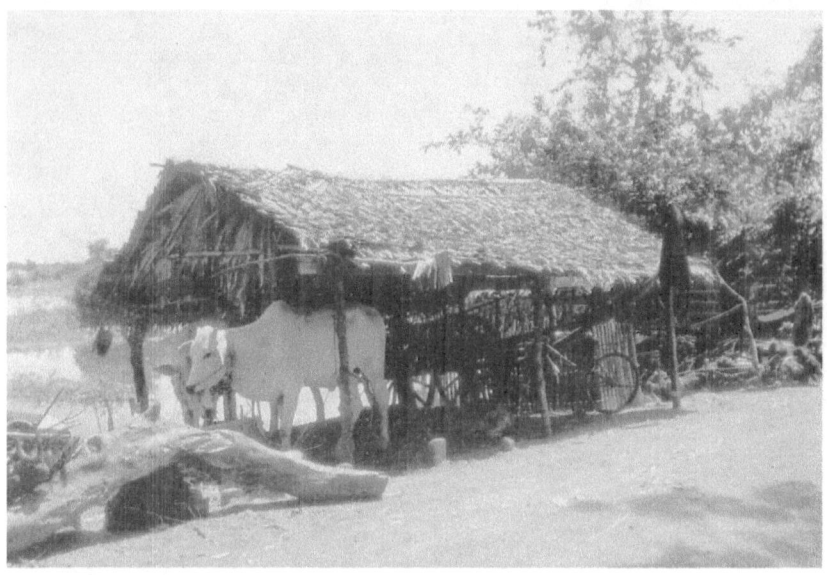

Cambodian village.

are available in the museums. It is true that the museums do not need to keep all these vases, and most of them in any case may be sold or kept by private collectors. What is very important, however, for the knowledge of history—and these data are probably lost forever—is the information that could be obtained concerning these pieces, such as how many vases were found on a particular site, in what regions they were produced, and how they were found. This kind of information could help researchers to make an analysis of the urban civilization, the production methods, the materials that were used, and the use of the vases. All of the above could help to reconstruct the detailed infrastructure of the society, its development and industrial capacity at different periods of time. Similarly the destruction of archaeological sites destroys the evidence, which is already very rare, about the construction patterns and lifestyle of the people at that time.

The loss of objects of art is evident in the deterioration of the structure and symbolism of the temples. Each monument in Angkor symbolizes the universe, and the usual elements include raised terraces representing Mt. Meru[15] and other structures representing oceans, mountains and continents. The astrological and cosmological meanings lie in the foundation of every temple because the four walls of the temples are oriented according to geographical coordination. The entrance door usually faces east. The predominance of this location toward the east is connected with the sunrise.

This description of the symbolic architectural layout explains why the destruction of the architectural plan of the temples destroys the meaning of the culture and religion. The sacred temples lose their primary purpose and significance and turn into beautiful but meaningless ruins. The ruins lose their value not only for the people but also for science. Many secrets of the ancient Khmer civilization are lost forever with the objects of art that have disappeared from their places of origin. The pieces of a most complicated composition containing unique theological and philosophical meaning are disconnected and lose their meaning. Even when statues are found and returned to the government they have lost their historical value. Usually there are no traces of the origins of the statues. Only in rare cases may the scholars who have worked on the site clearly indicate where the statue came from. In other situations it is practically impossible to distinguish when and where a statue was made, and, what is more important, what temple it came from and where it was placed in this temple.

No doubt, the statues in the leading world museums are still astonishing in their beauty. The museums also buy and display the most exquisite pieces of Khmer art. However, something else is missing. The most important component of these statues has disappeared, leaving only external beauty, which does not tell everything. Many more statues are not even displayed but remain in private collections. Many others were broken into pieces during transportation or were divided into smaller parts to facilitate transportation from the temples.

Damage is done when objects are taken from the foundation of the temple and the whole structure collapses. Looting objects from the foundations of the temples cause the structure to fall, and many other pieces of art that could have been valuable to the researchers are lost. One of the first such cases happened as early as 1986 near the temple of Banteay Chmar when a group of soldiers caused the collapse of a few structures in the territory of the temple.

In Figure 4, the arrows indicate the parts of the temple that are usually stolen and cause the collapse of the structure.

Very often the looters do not know anything about the statues or the materials used to make them, which also causes damage. Sandstone, the material often used for the construction of certain parts of the temples such as the carvings on the frieze, does not hold together if it is separated from the structure. The looters who do not know this try to chisel the frieze out only to see it crumble on the spot.[16] Many sites and temples have been destroyed in this way. In many instances, looters destroy the sacred places while looking for gold. Some objects may be fragile and usually need professional intervention for them to survive.

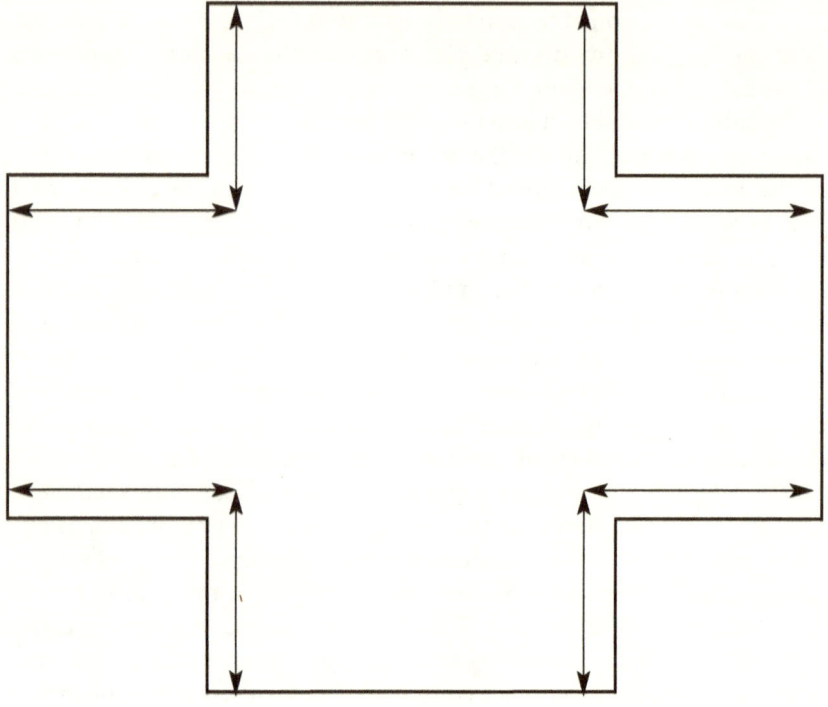

Figure 4: Perspective of the Temple from the Ground

In Figure 5, the arrows indicate the parts of the temples that are being removed. The black figures on the second drawing show the parts that were removed and what the temple may look like afterward, which explains why the structure collapses.

The most dangerous element of the illicit trafficking in Cambodia is its dimensions. Even now, with all the security measures, theft continues in Angkor. In 1999, within a period of six months, twenty-five Apsara heads were chiseled out from the carving in the temple of Pre Khan.[17] The art that was illegally stolen from Cambodia and remains now in circulation presented an enormous amount of information that is lost for study and analysis. The objects that are found and sometimes returned to the country are always valuable, but in this case they lack the necessary chronological information that could allow them to be placed correctly into the system of studies. "A work of art is a metaphor or constellation of metaphors crafted as an instrument of communication and information storage. The artist or craftsman necessarily revealed himself as a communicator within a 'consuming' community by tapping a larger ideological repertory shared with that community."[18]

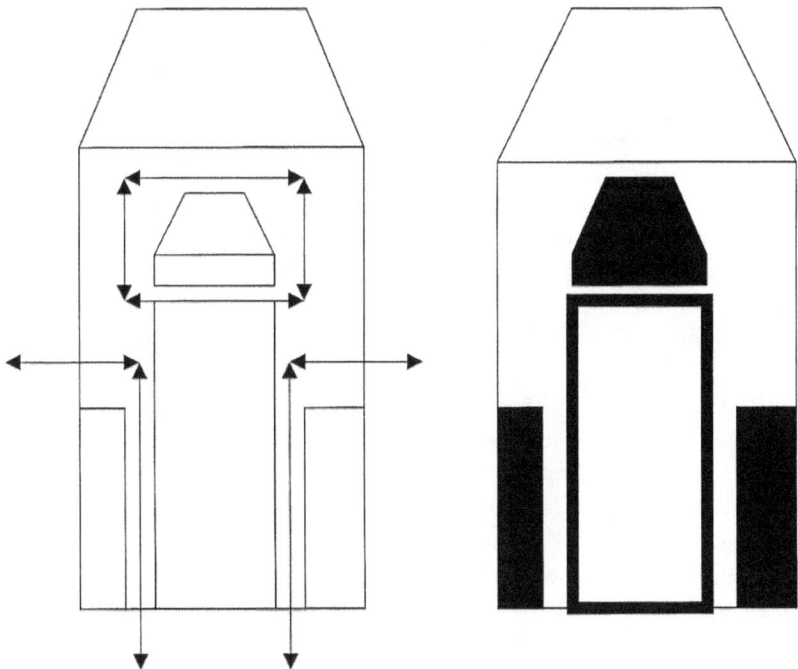

Figure 5: Perspective of the Temple from the Facade

No matter whether it is a simple piece of pottery or a complex object that contains many symbols, its context buries a lot of important information for the archaeologists. Objects found on the site provide information about the industrial, social or economic life of the society at the time. For a country like Cambodia, which does not have many written sources or oral traditions, all objects found on a site are very important and provide the possibility of discovering more facts and making comparisons and logical deductions that may lead to new discoveries.

For example, there are still many debates on the location of the seventh century capital of Yatpure, the City of the Hunters. Many recently discovered prehistoric sites are still under question. Excavations are going on in Angkor Borei, which was considered a capital; in Kompong Cham province; in Sambor Prei Kuk; and in other places. Every little piece discovered is very valuable, but objects disappear from the site every day. The archaeologists say that something is missing every morning they come to the site. The local population is poor and does not understand the value of the objects of art.

Archaeologists from the University of Hawaii who worked in Angkor

Borei tried to talk to the local population and educate them, but the illicit excavations continued. In 1997 archaeologists found out about a prehistoric site in Kandal, which is about 17 miles away from Phnom Penh, after it had already been excavated by the local population and practically everything had disappeared. They are still trying to do a survey there and hope to discover something on the site or with the local population. Prehistoric sites like Sambor Prei Kuk are beautiful areas dating back to the seventh century but are not well known. Places like these could easily become tourist attractions, which could raise money for their protection and for the local population. At the same time the organization of mass tourism in Cambodia is still very difficult and sites need more work and less unnecessary attention.

It is evident that nothing is more important for an archaeologist than a possibility to see these objects as a whole in order to have a perspective of the past culture, everyday life, religion and beliefs. It is for this reason that knowledge of exact details is important. In order to achieve this the objects have to be kept in their place and properly dated, described, and recorded from the time they were discovered. "A piece of art taken from the ground without record made of the associated archaeological stratum becomes a chronological orphan."[19]

For many years the areas of Phnom Kulen and Kbal Spean were out of reach for archaeologists. The beautiful mountain is considered the most sacred in the country and has been for centuries a place of pilgrimage. It is from the mountain Phnom Kulen that Jayavarman II proclaimed independence from Java and gave birth to modern-day Cambodia. Excavations on the site could provide much information about the beliefs and cults practiced there at one time. It is situated with the waterfall Kbal Spean about 17 miles from Angkor near the River of a Thousand Linghas.

Kbal Spean reveals rare riverbed carvings that depict meditating Vishnu as well as images of Rama, Lakshmi, and linghas carved by Khmer ancestors between the ninth and thirteenth centuries.[20] The monument was discovered in 1968 and has never been thoroughly studied by scholars, who still do not have access to the site. It was controlled by the Khmer Rouge until recently and was opened for tourists only a few years ago. At the moment, the Khmer Rouge is no longer there, but the military is in charge.

A tourist fee of twenty dollars (only one dollar goes to the official institution concerned; the rest goes to private individuals) is paid by visitors. The carvings started to disappear right away. Two stones were stolen, faces were chipped away from the carvings and one of stones shows the

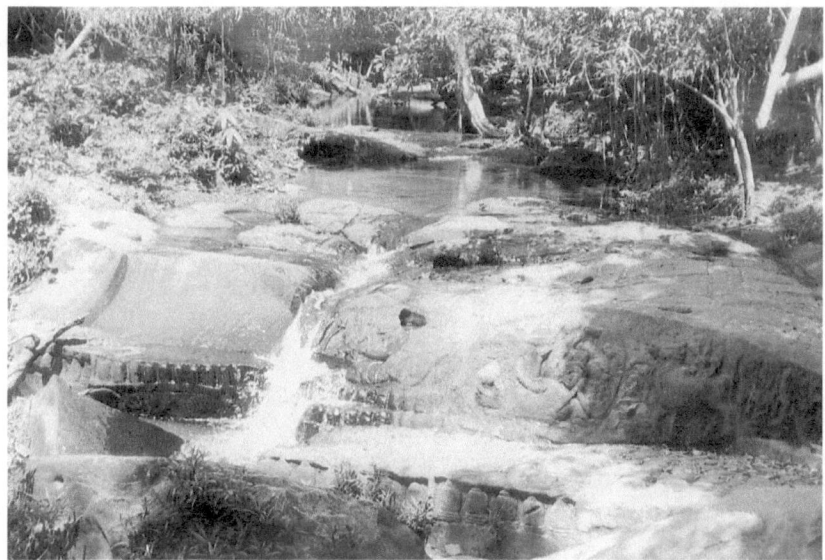

Carvings of Kbal Spean.

marks of a drill. The looter wanted to fill the holes with acid and rip the carving off. The military was blamed for the looting.[21]

The situation remains virtually the same, and archaeologists still cannot get access to the area to proceed with excavation. Considering the historical importance of the site—particularly because the site was practically untouched until recently—its study could provide unique information on religion, practices, and beliefs from the eighth century onward, which are so hard to discover in Cambodia. The objects need to be examined and identified, their condition needs to be diagnosed, and they need to be put into historical context. Only by making a correct scientific and technological excavation from the beginning can the whole picture be made of the site.

It is evident that the scale of illicit trafficking in Cambodia produces enormous damage to archaeological, cultural and historical knowledge, which remains at its preliminary period. Much information has already been lost and will never be re-created even if the objects of art are returned to Cambodia.

Religious Aspect

The aim of this section is to explain the effects of illicit trafficking of art on religion and its practices in Cambodia. I will explain and discuss

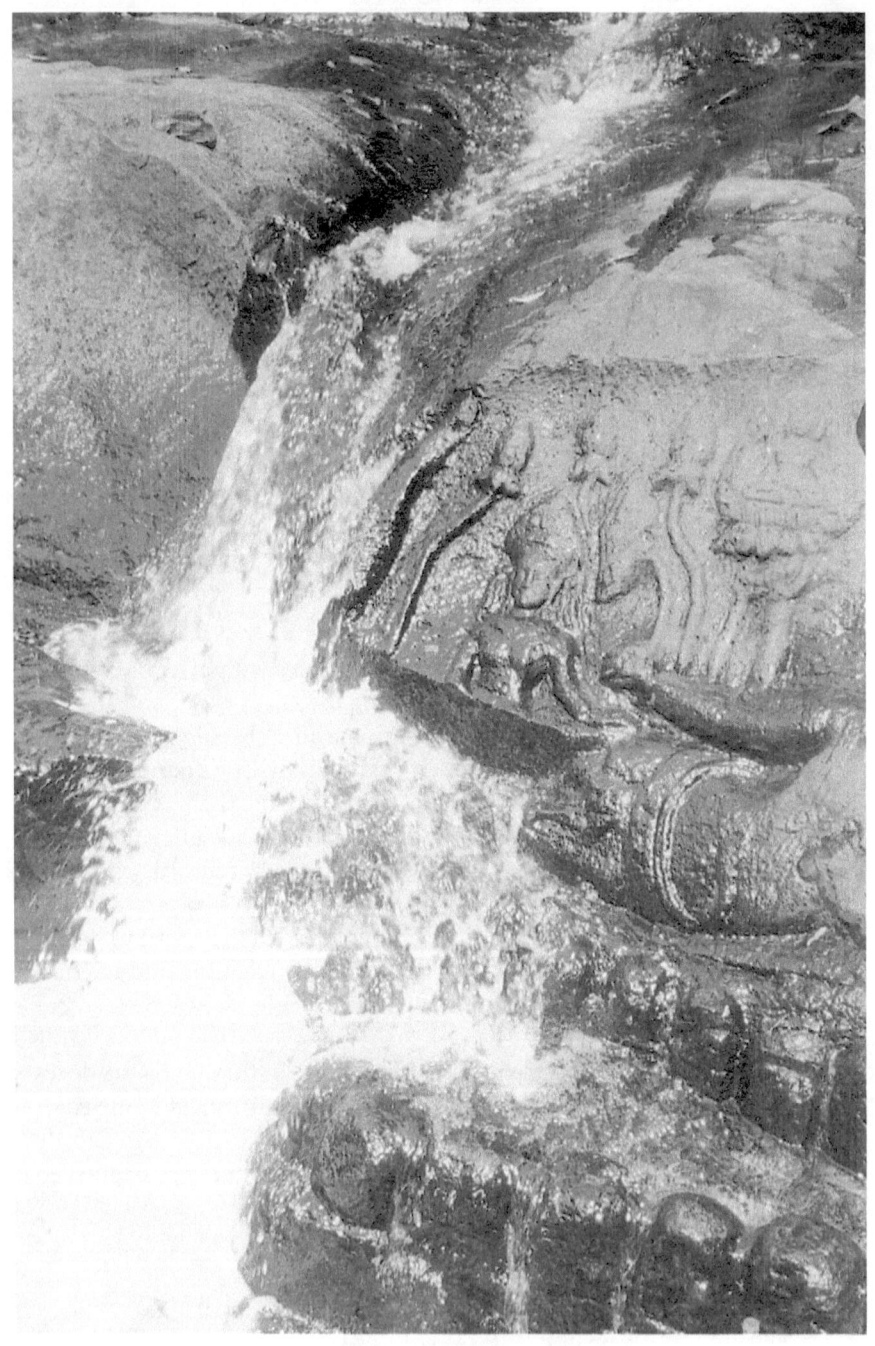

Carvings of Kbal Spean.

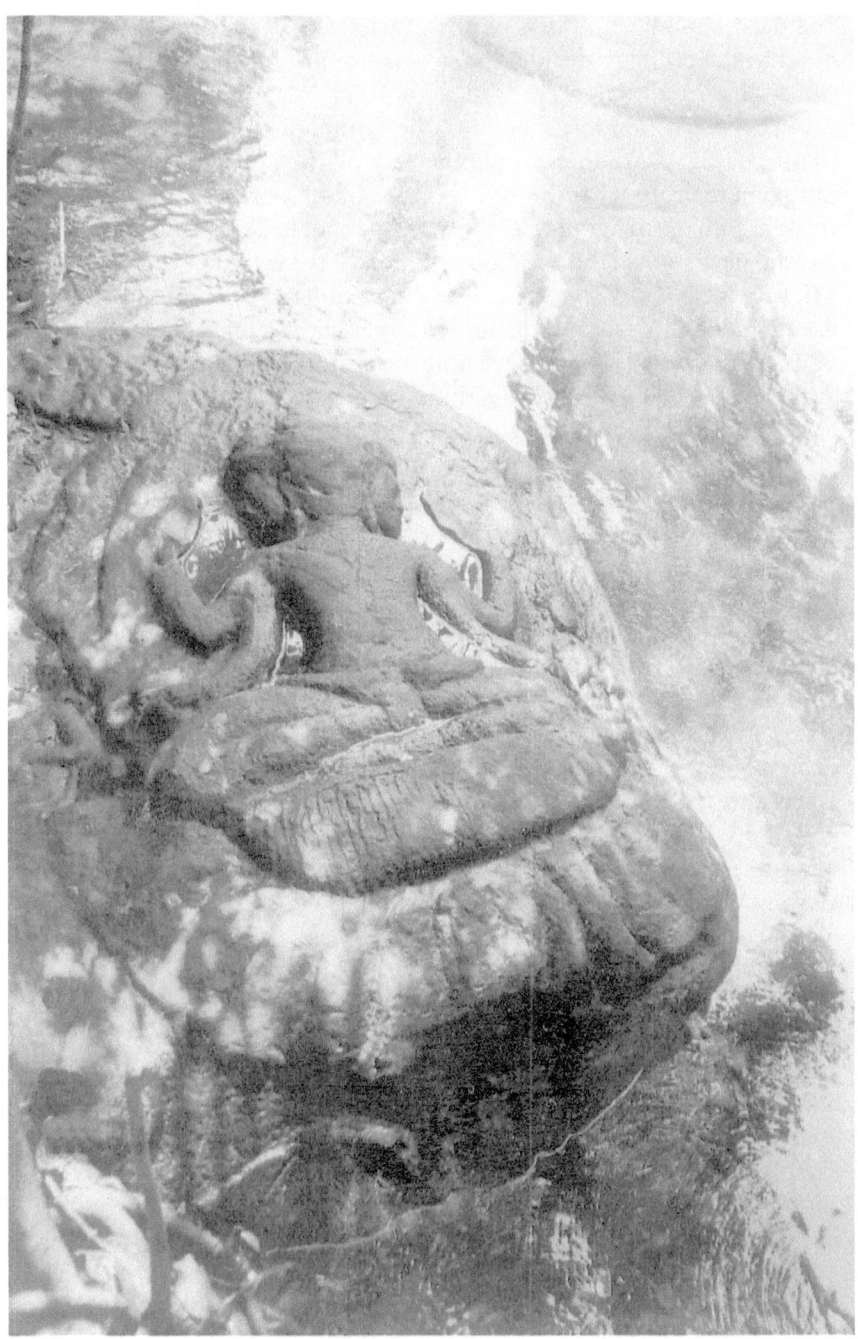

Carvings of Kbal Spean.

Theravada Buddhism, the way it is practiced in Cambodia and under-stood by the ordinary people, and how the trafficking of art destroys reli-gious values in the country.

Theravada Buddhism entered the Cambodian society in the thir-teenth century. Until then Cambodia had followed Hinduism, which had existed in the country from the beginning of the Christian era. This con-version from one religion to another still has not been explained by schol-ars who have studied the question. As a part of the conversion, Jayavarman VII, who introduced Theravada Buddhism, ordered all Hindu symbols in the temples destroyed and substituted with Buddhist ones. On many occa-sions the craftsmen did not have time to substitute the statues or carvings by the time people left Angkor in the middle of the fifteenth century. Many places in the temples of Angkor still hold the marks of destruction from the thirteenth century.

This religion is also practiced in Thailand, Vietnam, Laos and Burma. In Cambodia, which has followed the teachings of Theravada Buddhism for seven centuries, traces of Hinduism are still visible in the way religion is practiced.

Buddhism started from the teachings of Buddha, who was born in the sixth century B.C. Born the son of a prince, Siddhartha Gautama left his father's palace at the age of nineteen and became a monk. After seven years of spiritual search and travel, he reached enlightenment while sit-ting under the sacred tree, where after understanding four sacred wisdoms he became the Buddha. Buddhism has always had many different inter-pretations. The existence of Buddha or Prince Gautama has never been questioned, for example, as has the existence of Zoroaster or Jesus Christ. However, it has always had different schools and sects. Theravada Bud-dhism is one of the branches of Buddhism. It has a few concepts, such as its concepts of heaven and hell, that differ from the main teaching of Buddhism.

Religion entered all parts of cambodian society. The wats, or tem-ples, occupy an important place in religion, education and politics. Wats reflect the stability in the country. When the economy is stable, wats are built everywhere. Every village has at least one temple, and they are also constructed in the palaces. They may serve as a meeting place for the com-munity, a village committee, and as a center for different artistic activities such as architecture, painting, mural painting, theatre and dance. Often during the holidays and festivities, the temple ground may serve as a stage for the performance of Ramayana, which is presented by dancers. The temples are usually decorated with paintings that retell the life-story of Buddha so that people are able to follow it and learn from it. The paint-ings also serve as beautiful decorations for the temple.

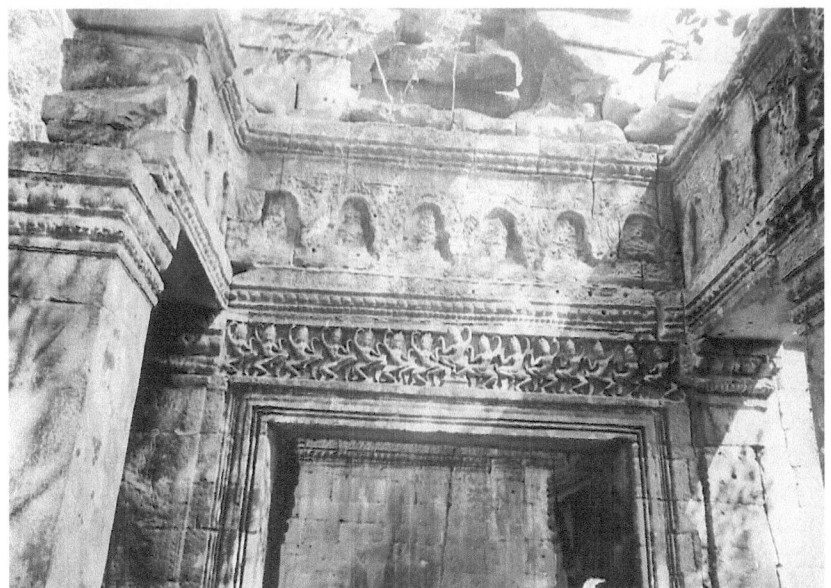

The images of Hindu gods chiseled out in the epoch of Jayavarman VII.

Therefore a wat in the religion of Theravada Buddhism is not only a place for prayer and moral recreation but also a center of the village that is highly important for the whole community. It serves as an educational, cultural and social center. It may often be a place for a school or a library, where learning and culture are kept and transformed from generation to generation. The temple may also serve as a place for the poor or needy; the monks offer food, shelter and medical help. Until the 1970s, all young men had to be ordained as monks at least once in their lives. The first ordination is usually done as a ritual for young man entering adulthood and society.

People go to the temple, often on a daily basis, to pray. Each month there are also days on which every Buddhist must go to the temple. These days are marked on all the calendars published in Southeast Asia. The usual offerings made to the Buddha include flowers such as orchids and lotus and sometimes food. The offerings may be made to the statues of Buddha, Shiva and Vishnu, and the cult of Lingha is still very widespread. Both religions, Buddhism and Hinduism, have forms and traditions of representing their gods. Buddha may be seated or lying meditating, and he is often depicted in the shape of a multiheaded snake, Naga. Shiva may be presented with six hands. Lingha is another form of Shiva.

The practice of making statues of the gods as human beings—even with many heads and hands—and placing them in the temples started in India. It made it easier for ordinary people to visualize their gods and understand religion. In Hinduism, which is still followed in Cambodia, such a representation of a god is understood by everybody. The image of each god, its attributes, and the animals that are associated with it are also well known to people and also explain the focus and possibilities of each particular image of the god. Many myths and legends explain these images, attributes, and animals. Knowing this "biography" of the god, people go to different temples depending on their needs. The practice of sacrifice or offering to the gods has also been practiced from the beginning of the religion. The cult of Shiva represents strength in life and a masculine power. The latter found its depiction in the form of respect for Lingha. Linghas made out of stone may be found in the temples and homes of people and symbolize strength and Shiva's potential. The cult of Lingha is very widespread and the temples or parts of temples that contain Linghas attract many people who come there to pray—often women who want children. The cult is also very philosophical because lingha is the highest achievement of knowledge and is considered a unique representation of the power of the god.

In Buddhism the idea that God was born as a human was interpreted as a great event. It is considered that Buddhas possess a unique strength and force, both psychological by understanding the thoughts, minds and karma of people and physical because Buddha can fly, walk on water, and become invisible. Apart from Buddha, Theravada Buddhism also praises Bodhisatva, a Buddhist monk who nearly reached Nirvana. One of the most sacred and popular Bodhisatvas is Avalokiteshvara. The most famous temple in Angkor and in Cambodia—Bayon, also built by Jayavarman VII in the thirteenth century—is a temple of Avalokiteshvara. He is considered a universal savior and is the one who protects those who suffer. The tradition of representing Buddhas as human beings in sculptures makes the religion understandable for simple people. They may come to the temple every day and address Buddha, Bodhisatva or Lingha and converse with them, asking for help or advice. Buddhist temples usually guard various relics, such as the imprint of Buddha's foot, which may often be made of gold, or his tooth, which is also very important.

Numerous festivities and rituals present a very important part of this religion. All of them take place in or around the temple. Many of them take place on particular days defined by the lunar calendar and are spectacular. They make take the form of a demonstration, pilgrimage or a theatre—Ramayana. There are also many family rituals connected with marriage, the birth of a child, ordination or a new house. The family usually invites a

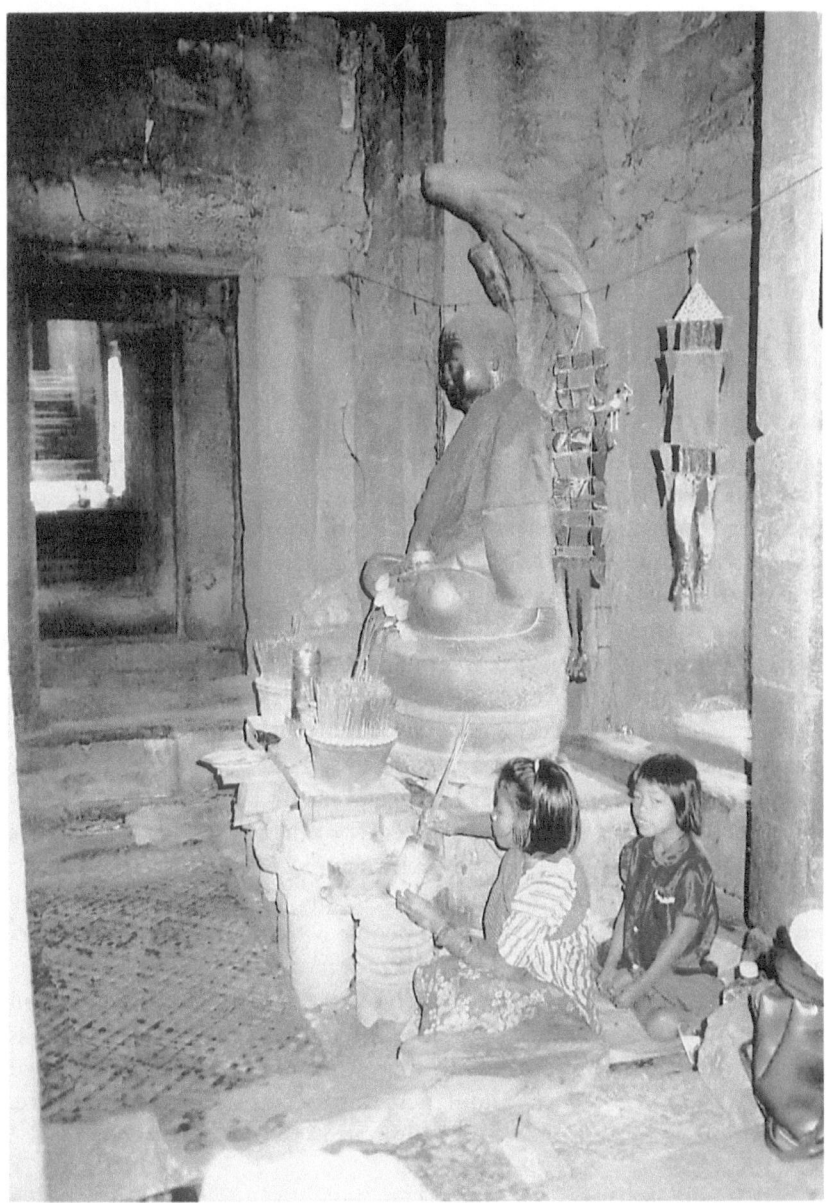

Two girls praying in the Temple of Bayon.

monk to their house to conduct a ritual and make offerings to the Buddha. All of the above show to what extent the religion and, more important for this topic a wat and the statues in the wat, occupies all parts of the society.

Another example that explains the importance of the visual image of God in the life of the people is the small spirit houses that are kept in every house or home. It is a very small re-creation of the temple where people burn incense and put food, (bananas or cakes) and flowers. It is considered that a house like this keeps the bad spirits away and it is a must to have one. The above explains the importance of wats and the sculptures and relics in the wats. In many villages the wat may be just a small temple with one statue. Once the statue is gone, the temple loses its meaning for the people, who are left without the means of communicating with the gods.

Cambodia is, in fact, a special case because of the Pol Pot regime, which changed many social structures in the society including attitudes toward Buddhism. From the beginning of the civil war in 1970 many traditions like ordination were abandoned. During the Pol Pot regime religion was forbidden, practically all monks were killed and many religious texts were burned. Such a trauma, which lasted for nearly five years, could not pass without leaving its effect on the population in general. The number of religious people in towns is very low.

It is also true that many people do not much like these old and ancient objects. Many prefer to have new temples and statues rather than old ones. They find new ones more beautiful. It was mentioned in Chapter I that Cambodians do not collect Khmer statues. That is why in many villages the committee of the village may decide to sell the statues; they think the objects are old and unnecessary and prefer just to keep the temple building, which continues to be used as a center of the village. Peasants always sell the objects of art they find in their region.

At the same time, many statues in the temples situated in the provinces are still very sacred to the people, who know about the looters and do not want to lose the statues. On a few occasions, archaeologists came across writings made on the temple walls by the local population asking potential looters not to remove the statues. One such writing was found in the temple of Banteay Chmar. After many statues disappeared from this temple, the local population was too scared to lose any more. The temple is important in the region and is visited every day by the Khmers who live in this area.

It is evident that the looting of the sacred statues has had a devastating effect on religion. The presence of the statues in the temple is very important for many of the people. Those people whose lives are very sad and full of misfortunes and whose only happiness and possibility to keep faith in life may often be a festivity in the temple or just a visit to the temple.

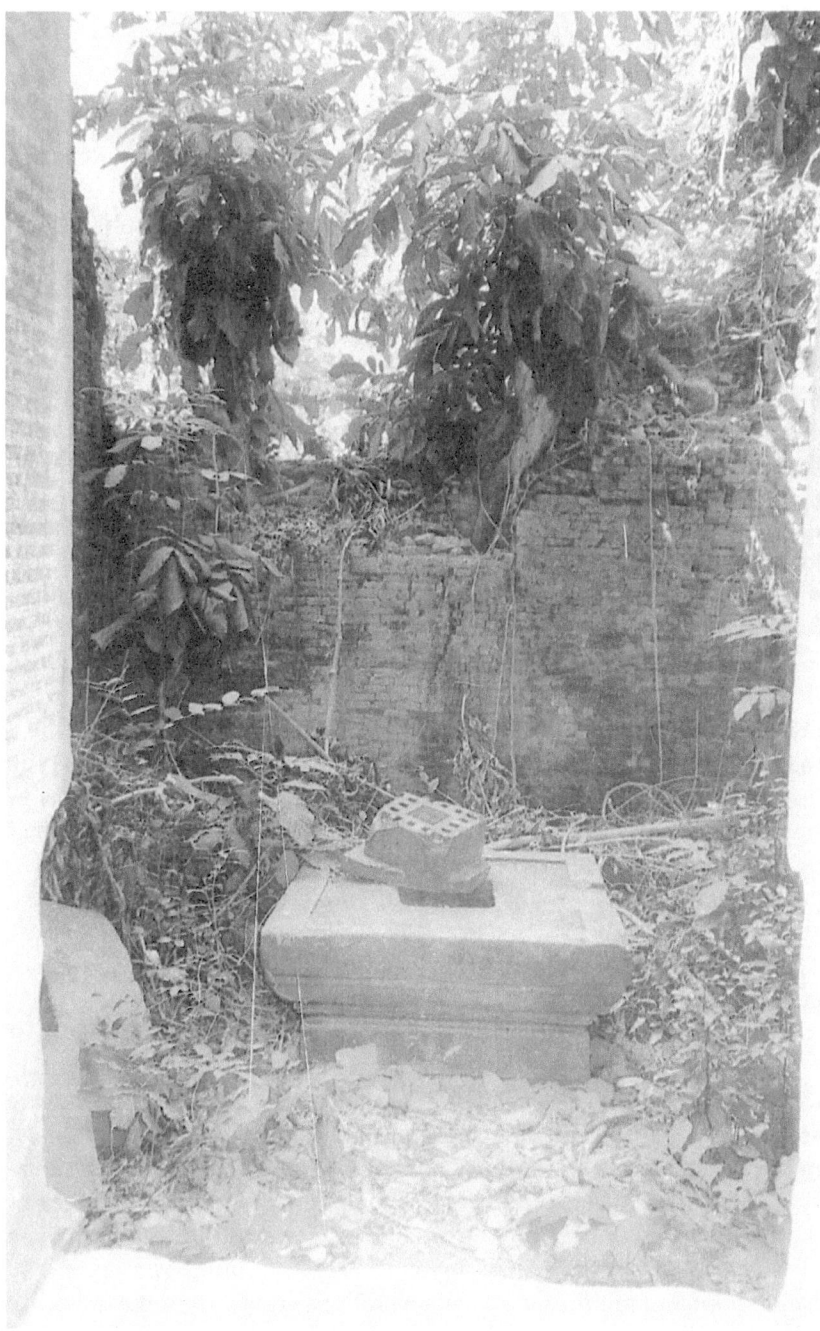

Temple of Lolei; ninth century; built by Yasovarman I.

Issue of Cultural Identity

The psychological value of cultural heritage is very significant. It assists in an appreciation of the past and provides inspiration for current endeavors and future inspirations. A well-understood and valued cultural heritage serves as a foundation on which a modern and functional society can be built.[22]

In this section, I'll try to analyze the connection between art trafficking and the way it influences and changes modern culture as well as the problems it presents for the society and the country. Culture is an epicenter of human existence. When we look at the culture created by each nation, we can judge the achievements made by this nation and see the highs and the lows of the development of each particular culture. The nation continues its existence and has a possibility to develop further only if it preserves and further renovates its cultural identity throughout its history. The Khmer civilization has created a very unique and unusual culture that needs to be preserved. This preservation is highly important and has a direct impact on the present and the future existence of the nation.

Culture delivers to us traces of the past. It also presents the past so that we can research, analyze and discover. Therefore, it is very important to understand the civilization and culture of our ancestors. In order to do that, we have to study their past, which still remains accessible to us. Its importance cannot be underestimated for the future. One of the ways to stay in touch with culture is to keep up with all types of behavior created by our ancestors, for example, those that regulate the relations between people in the society—traditions. Tradition is one of the ways to preserve culture. It shows the experience and level of development of the society. The deterioration of and forgetting traditions causes the disintegration of culture that, in other words, means disintegration of the nation.

Khmer culture is currently in deep crisis. The years of the Pol Pot regime, when culture was burned and erased from the earth, followed by the absence of financial support to revive the remaining traces of culture are just a few of the reasons for cultural deterioration. One of the most important of them is the recent relationship between culture and the market of demand. The most wanted pieces of art are in demand, which leaves the country with only the poorest examples. This leads in turn to the loss of culture and the absence of any cultural background and makes the nation poor and unprotected. New generations grow up without any sense of their traditions or cultural belonging, which is one of the main reasons for economic, political and ecological catastrophes. It increases crime and

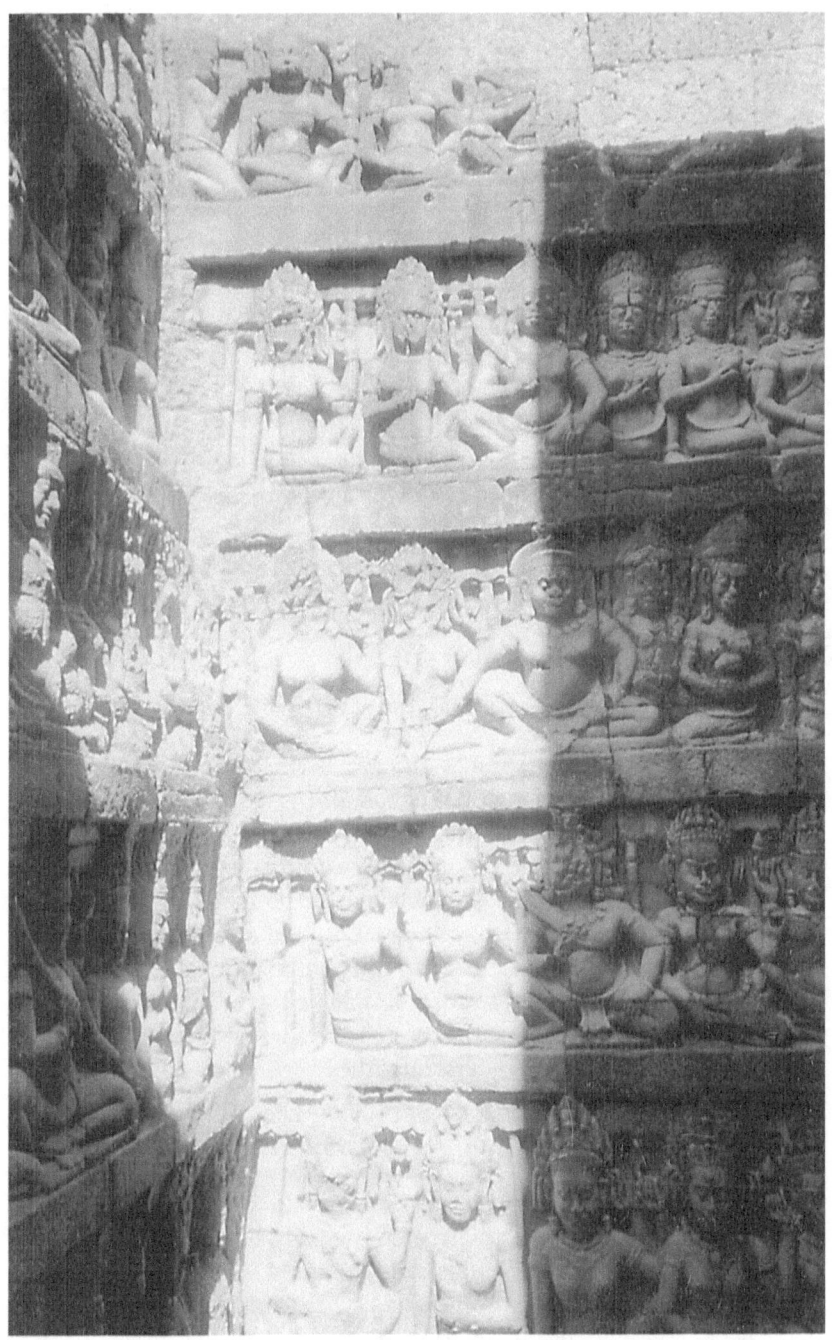

Terrace of the Leper King; end of the twelfth century.

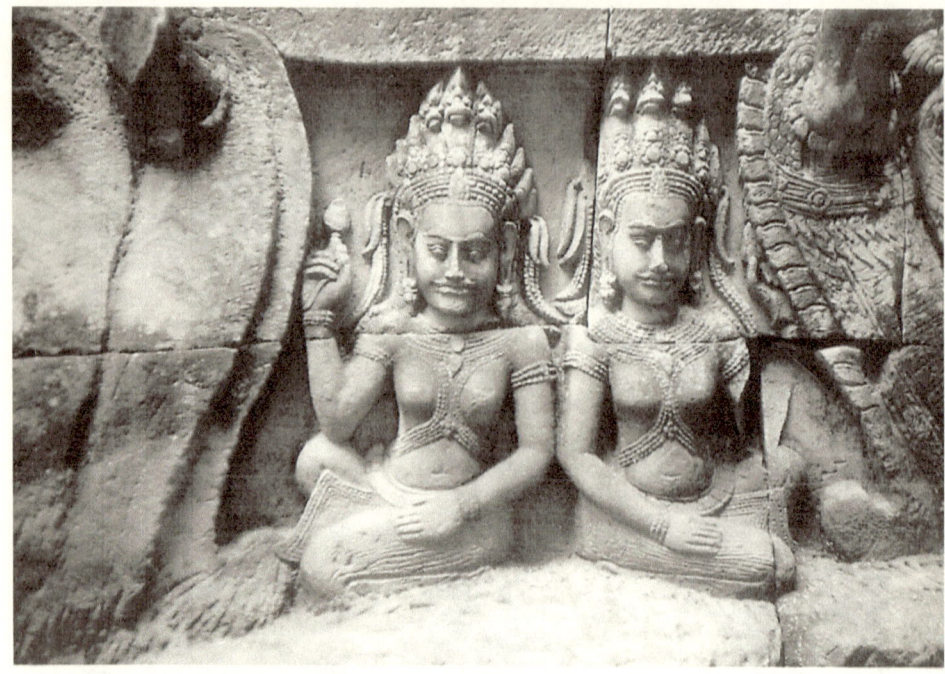

Terrace of the Leper King; end of the twelfth century.

violence, causes a decrease in morality and is closely connected with the future development of science and education.

The modern generation, brought up in the aftermath of the 1970s and the 1980s, sees in objects of art only their commercial value just as they see any other industry whose products may be bought and sold or bring the quick profit so desirable to modern Cambodian society. Such commercialization of culture brings out in people the lowest values, desires and tastes; it forms another type of a human being interested only in certain economic values. Such a crisis of cultural identity causes psychological deterioration because it deteriorates the connection of a human being with his real cultural values. Culture cannot exist without such connections. In Cambodia the ideal of these real cultural values has changed a lot. It has become a culture that is falling apart and that cannot be preserved and retained. Therefore it cannot give birth to the changes, the new revival of culture within the country. Only a truly strong national culture can provide the future development of the nation.

Unfortunately, modern Cambodia is going through radical changes that have a great tendency to deteriorate the past, and all this is done only to achieve a small profit for a few individuals. Cambodia is not alone here.

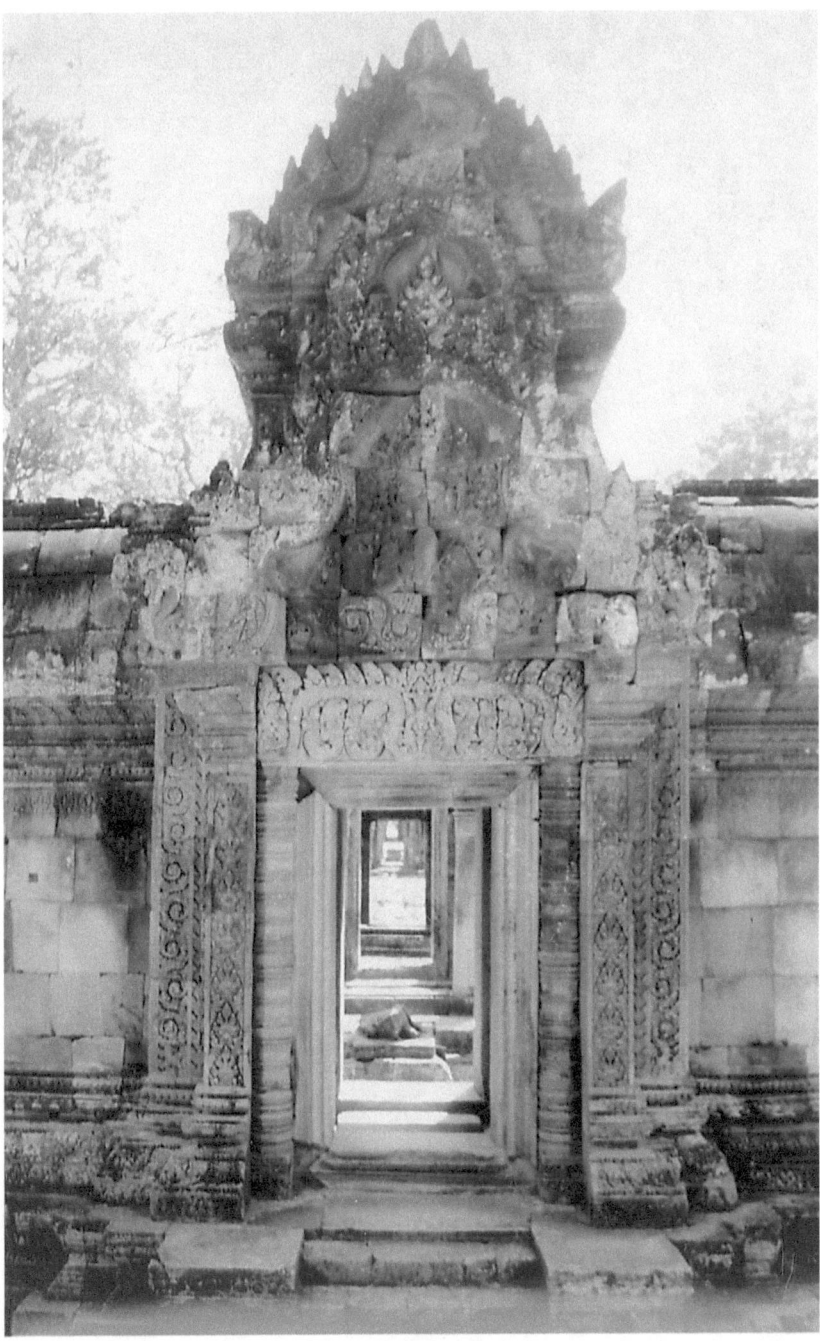

Temple of Banteay Srei; tenth century; built by Jayavarman V.

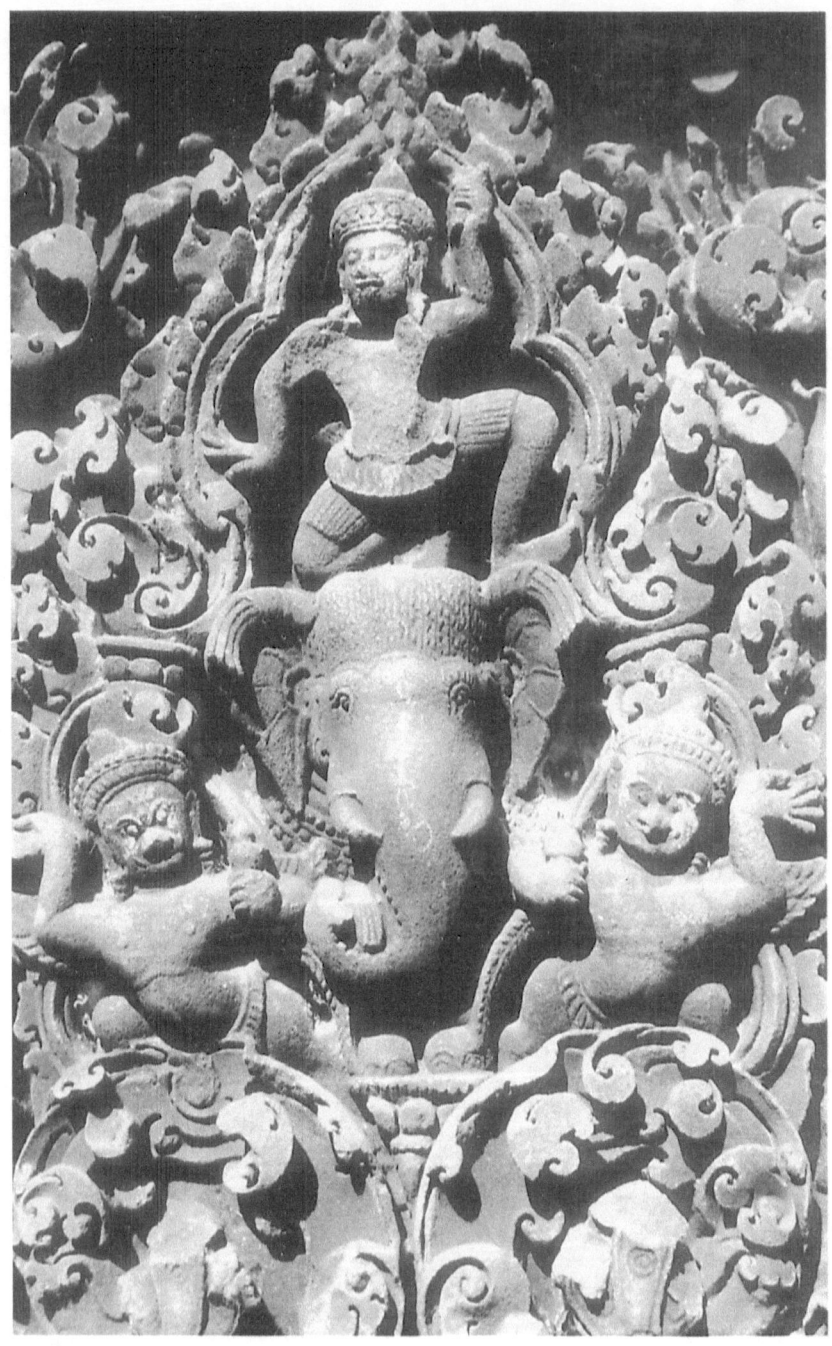

Temple of Banteay Srei; tenth century; built by Jayavarman V.

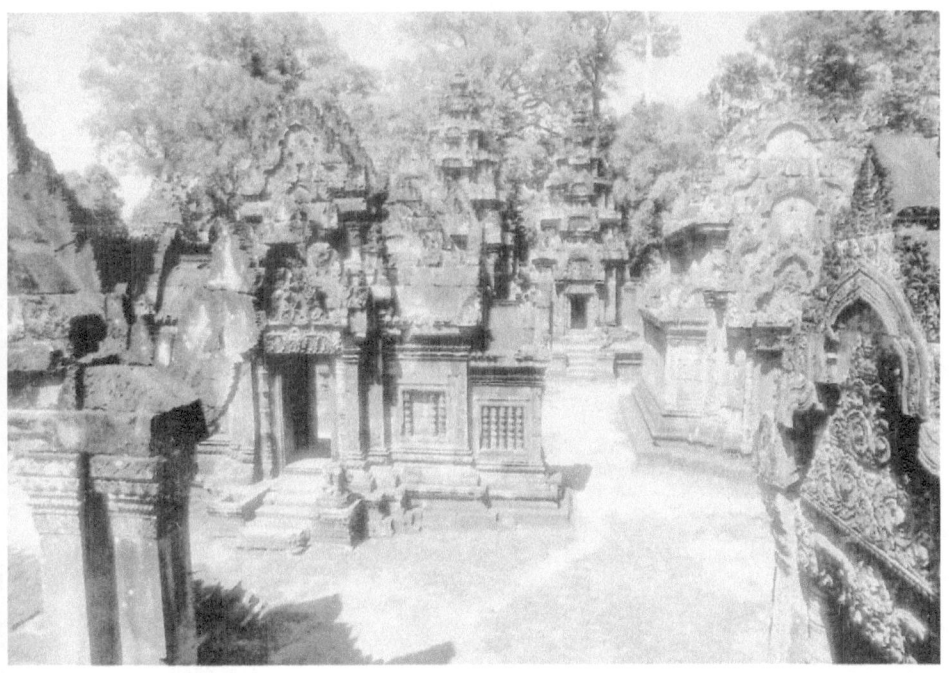

Temple of Banteay Srei; tenth century; built by Jayavarman V.

It joins many other countries that are in the same condition—countries that are so eager to join the new society that they deteriorate their past without stopping for one minute to look back. They do not realize to what extent national culture creates the background for the only real, long-term positive development. Analysis of the condition of modern Cambodian culture shows the absence or weakness of stable cultural forms. Cambodia has lost many structures and definitions that existed in its previous culture. It has been stressed by all historians who studied the history of Cambodian society, such as David Chandler and Michael Vickery, that Angkor and its monuments have remained the center of Khmer cultural identity even during the Pol Pot regime.

The Cambodian dictator stressed on many occasions in his speeches the importance of the monuments to the country as the main representation of the achievement of the nation. However, it is not known whether Pol Pot planned to continue his policy toward Angkor or just used it as a partial measure and planned to drop it when it would no longer be useful.

Culture is a world of objects that surround us that were created by human beings and reflect the level of development of the society. These

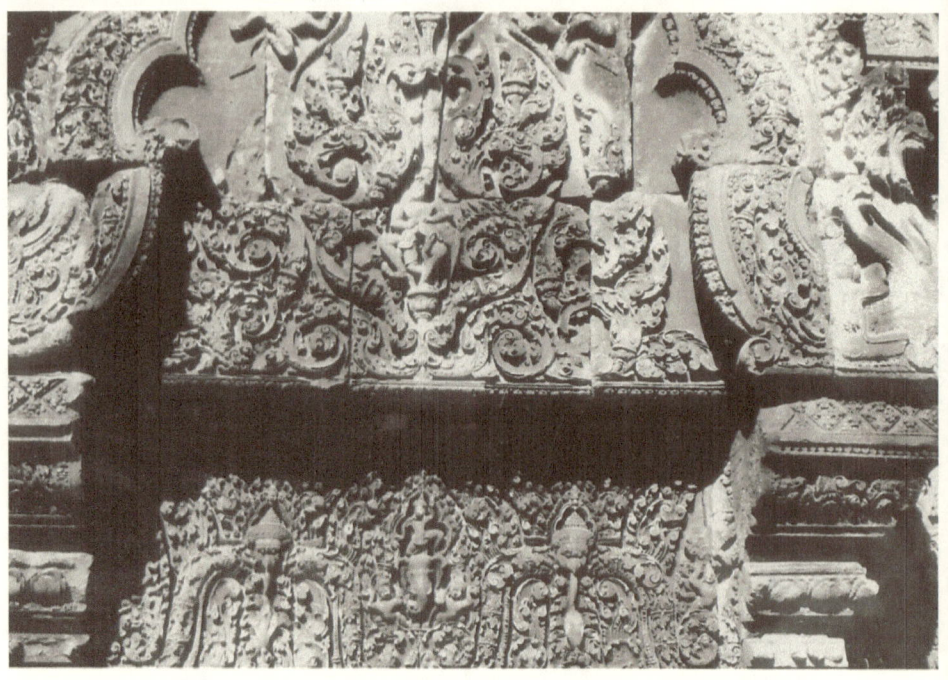

Temple of Banteay Srei; tenth century; built by Jayavarman V.

objects present efforts of human beings—their knowledge, norms, traditions, tastes and values transferred by a creator onto the object of creation. The mere creation of such objects corresponds to a certain cultural
tradition. The objects give us ideas about the social system that existed
(its uniqueness, social levels, groups and institutions, and religious or
bureaucratic systems). Therefore, culture always renovates during the
process of human activity and this process of renovation is as important
as its creation. It gives culture a new strength and power, a new and fresh
stream for development. There is a difference, however, between renovation and deterioration.

Buddhism, as all religions, has acquired new features that were connected with a cultural and national identity and previous cultural traditions throughout its existence. It changes in time and forms different
people. Theravada Buddhism was introduced after centuries of Hinduism,
the traces of which—as well as the traces of previous beliefs in spirits—
still remain visible in the daily lives of the people. A part of these beliefs
is that the life of the person on earth is considered an episode, one of the
links in a chain of many different lives. This means that spiritual strength
and religious behavior are more important than the material life.

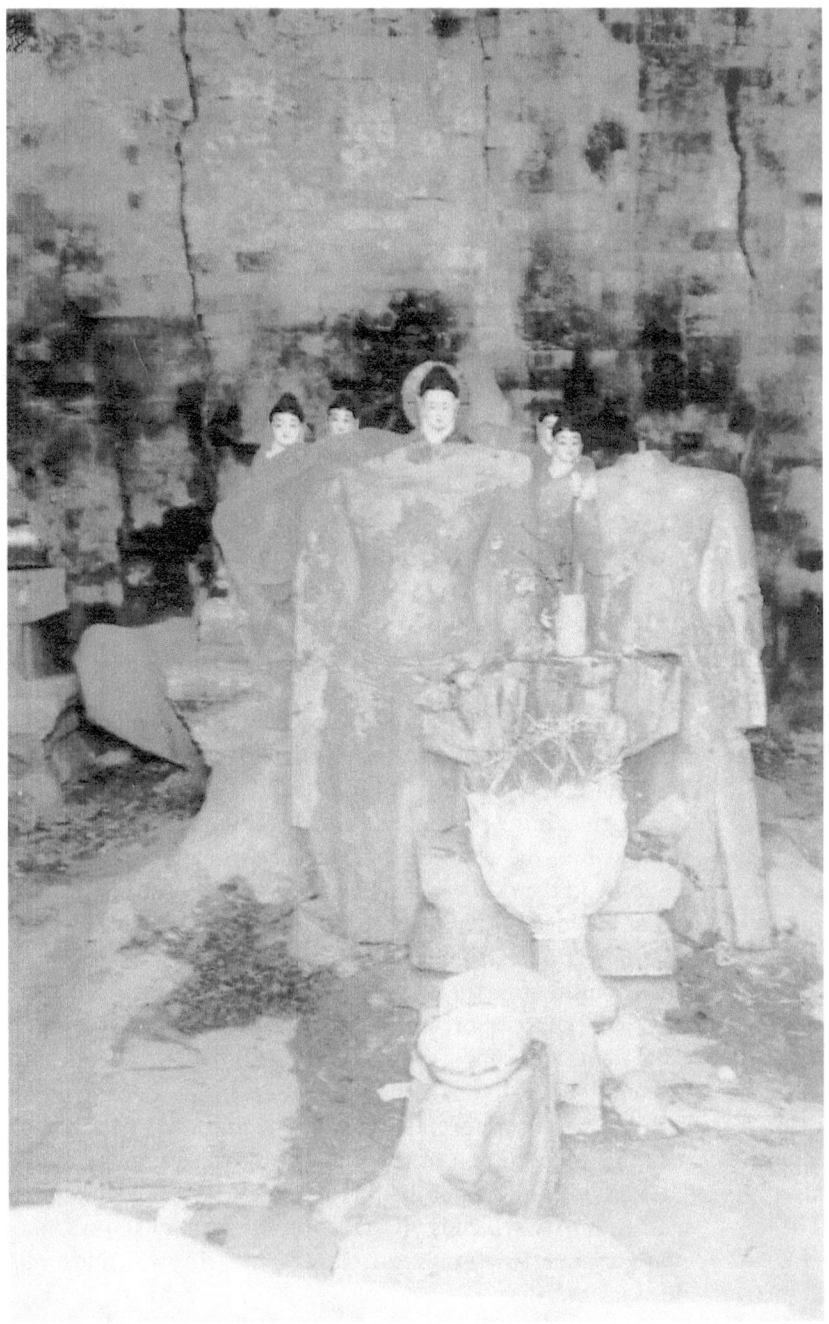

In the Temple of Pre Rup; tenth century; built by Rajendravarman II.

At the same time, there is a big difference between the daily life of the Cambodian people and the ideal life explained in the doctrines of Theravada Buddhism. The main beliefs of the religion created the society that people lived in and the artistic visualization of this religion has always remained very important. "Ideology is a critical thread in any social or political fabric. It is especially so in urban situations where diverse occupational groups, élites and commoners, different ethnic groups, etc., need to be bound together in peaceful coexistence. Ideologies may be expressed materially in the form of religious regalia, insignia of ethnic membership, or sumptuary items and laudatory art devoted to the legitimation of the élites' rule. Ideologies are often reflected in material items that function as signs or symbols designating behavior appropriate to the context in which they are used. These items, then, function as models of the complex ideologies, that is, as partial representations in which detail is economized in order that complex ideas and mental associations may be invoked by the observer."[23]

Taking the example of our research, one of the main components of the Cambodian culture is the power of the king, who has the quasi-divine power of a god on earth. The belief in karma and in the possibility of being reborn in future lives in different forms is one of the specifics of the development of the culture in Cambodia. The cultural archetype in Cambodia is connected closely with authority, and the government that represents power brings order and regulates all sorts of relations in society. God and the king are always right and are never contradictory. Such a belief in authority gives it the power of a miracle on the one hand and the readiness to follow it on the other. Therefore, there is a close connection between the people and their existence on one side and the visual reflection of these beliefs in the form of temples and statues on the other. The god-king is the main power on earth and is the center of life.

Such a hierarchical structure serves as the basis for all social relations—not only between a person and political power but also within the family between parents and children—and has established the background of the social system in Cambodia. Being a good servant to the king is like being a servant to God. Therefore, the idea of the authority of a god or king is a part of the religious cult of the society. It is the authority that is always right, has a solution to all problems, and will help in all situations. The loss of such authority, which is visualized in the form of statues, may be a cause of potential destruction to the cultural identity, which loses its cultural uniqueness.

Cambodia has already lost much of its cultural sources and sense of cultural belonging in the last three decades. Cambodian people have their

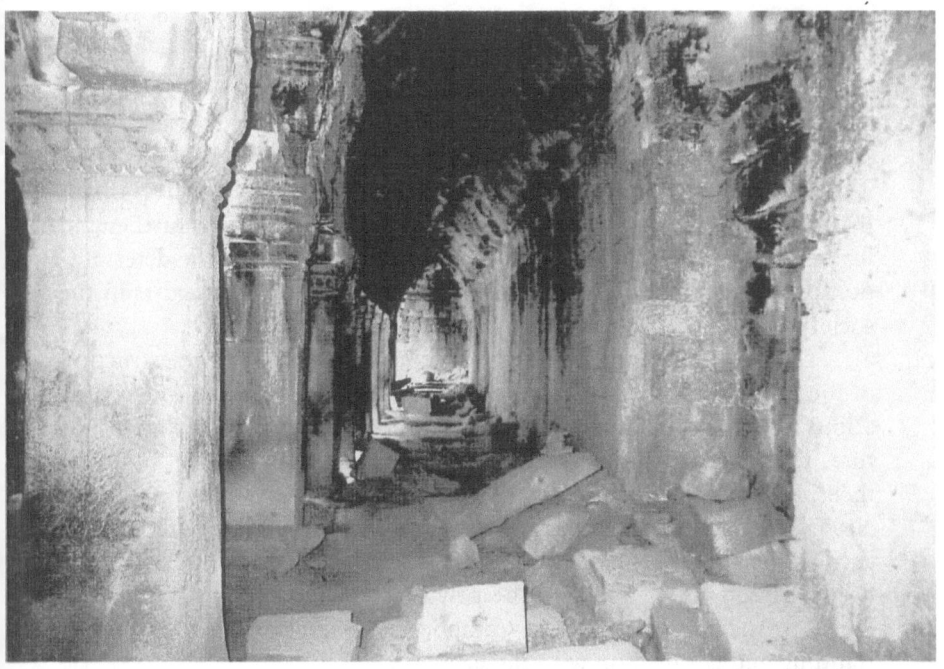

Temple of Ta Prohm.

own understanding of history and of what is good and what is bad, and they have their own prerogatives, gradations and placements of positive and negative historical features. The majority of Cambodians do not like the French and consider them occupants, although many of them do not even know the actual positive and negative consequences of the French protectorate. This is the modern perception of history. Modern society as a whole has lost many of its features and traditions. Most of the people, particularly those who live in towns or big centers, are not religious. Changes combined with social inequality produce a very hostile society. On the one hand, the old system of values has been eliminated; on the other hand, it has not been replaced with anything new or modern.

Many of the people who live in the countryside also think that the ancient statues are old and ugly and should be substituted with beautiful new carvings and sculptures that are much prettier, or they often just prefer to keep the temple, which may be used as a building. It means that people are losing touch with their cultural roots and their cultural identity. The loss of traditions causes the loss of culture, which may with time lead to the loss of civilization as a whole as the traditions and cultural connections between people and epochs disappear. It may also cause the loss of experience gained by the nation during its development, which reduces to zero the development achieved by the ancestors.

The roots of culture that are lost over time cannot provide new development in the culture; in other words, they cannot be reinnovated. They die away, sometimes without anybody noticing and sometimes quite visibly. Evidently each individual person has his own desires and necessities. By stepping away from tradition, however, the individual gets further and further away from the norms that exist and brings about the deterioration of himself as well as the whole system of culture that exists in the society.

The beginning of anything untraditional often causes the destruction of the cultural roots of the nation. Rarely is it a renovation. The unconscious choice of a human being reflects both his internal and external culture. The loss of tradition or culture is contagious. People start to follow their needs and the new ways by which they can be satisfied unconsciously. Needs can be very simple, such as food and shelter, or more complicated, such as social needs. Culture may be observed in the forms of how these needs are satisfied. Following the new lifestyle and the understandable desire to succeed, the modern Cambodian generation loses its understanding and connection with the past.

New elements developing in the social relationships between people that permit many of the things that were not permitted in the past create other forms and traditions that no longer require many of the previous needs. Modern Cambodia does not have much in common with the older civilization that was created many centuries ago and with the generations that later kept in touch with its culture. The decades of civil wars, dictatorship and now unending pillage of objects of art threaten to erase the traces of cultural identity, without which the nation cannot exist.

The acceptability of illicit trafficking of art by society and the participation of so many categories of the population in the pillage remove the last notions of morality—of what is possible and what is not possible—and create a cultural vacuum. This vacuum fills up the new generations that are not interested in traditions and ancestral roots; thus, the nation's cultural identity disappears. Loss of culture for the nation means the loss of the most important component without which society, even if it is technologically advanced, cannot function or continue its normal existence. The more objects of art that are lost for Cambodia, the more Cambodia loses touch with its culture. The new generations do not understand the creations of their ancestors or the importance of these creations for posterity.

It is interesting that in Angkor, one can see children playing with ancient stones that are small parts of sculptures, and it is evident that neither they nor their parents know the meaning of these small objects scattered around the place. Even the people who live in the villages in the territory of Angkor Wat do not understand the value of the stones. For them this culture is meaningless. In his interview, Pech Keo told me about his book that he published for children, in which he tried to explain the importance of the culture created by the ancient Khmer civilization and stressed correctly the necessity of educating children in this domain so that the next generation of Cambodian people will have a chance to understand their cultural roots of culture.

One of the antique dealers in Phnom Penh told me that she had been involved in the trade of ancient objects of Khmer art. Then she decided to stop. She thought that in the near future it would become less and less profitable and that the trade would gradually die out. Instead, she found it better to concentrate on making reproductions of antique pieces or producing souvenirs and silk to be sure that she'll maintain her share of the market.

After some time Cambodian culture will most certainly seek revival in its own country. However, this will be very difficult to achieve considering how many pieces of art have already left the country and continue to leave. One of the Cambodian film directors, Sok Sophal, has recently made a film *The Lohet Sela* (*Blood Stone*, Producers TVK, Cambodia) in which a man who participates in the pillage of a statue from Angkor gets killed with his family, punished by the spirits of the stone. What will also make the revival of culture more difficult is how deeply the cultural level or understanding of one's identity have fallen in such a society. In history it always takes very little time to destroy something and then it takes decades or even centuries to re-create. It is clear already that the re-collection of art and lost culture will take a long time, if it will be successful at all, considering how difficult it is to restitute objects of art that belong to Cambodia by law. However, even by losing much Cambodia will be able to recover its cultural identity that is so important for its survival.

The Jarai Tribe

While in Cambodia, I witnessed a case relevant to this discussion. A UNESCO employee found out that an antique dealer in Phnom Penh was holding an open auction of the Jarai wooden totems. The Jarai is a nomad tribe from the province of Rattamang in the northeastern part of Cambodia. As a part of their cult of the dead, they create wooden totems for

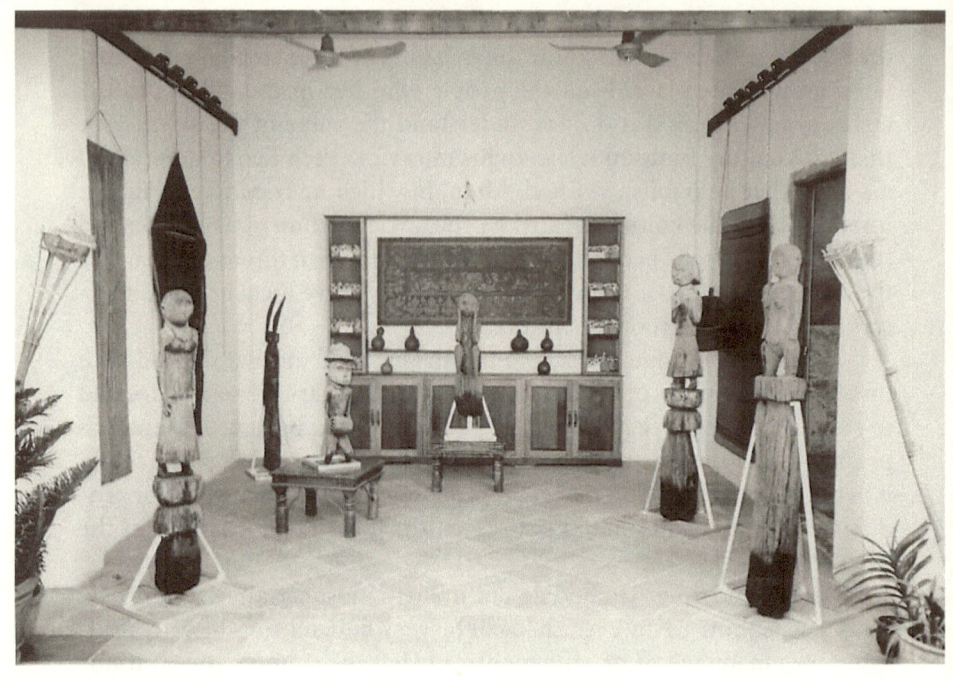

Display of Jarai totems.

their cemeteries. Each grave in the cemetery is surrounded by a small wooden fence with the totems on the sides or on the corner of the fence. Most of the totems represent the figures of the people, and there are also different carvings made out of wood. The tribal people in this part of the country are very poor, and once they have used the land for some time, they often migrate to another part of the province.

The photographs show six totems presented for sale. These are mainly wood carvings of male and female figurines, most probably representing male or female ancestors or popular spirits. One figure is in a seated position, representing a male who is holding his head with his hands behind his ears. The rest of the figurines—three female and one male—are in standing positions. The male figure has his arms half-folded and holds a drum at the level of a protruding navel. There is also a wooden sculpture carved from a single piece of wood with two horns of the same length. These totems, representing native art, possess an exceptional originality that gives more value to these rare objects.

To the eye of a person who does not know the culture of totems, they present just wooden figurines; however, for the tribal people each piece has its own symbolic meaning that gives certain information about the person or tribe in general. All of these pieces together also symbolize something, such as the rank of the family or the people buried in the grave. (All of the totems described here are grave or mortuary totems.)

The owner of the gallery displayed these totems. During the telephone conversation with the UNESCO official, he explained that while traveling in Rattamang province, he saw people from the Jarai tribe burning the cemetery. They were going to move to another land. The antique dealer asked them to sell him some of the totems, which he eventually bought for one hundred dollars. Therefore, according to him, he actually saved the totems from being destroyed. While it is true that the Jarai may migrate, they usually leave their cemeteries behind and do not burn them. However, it is also true that the totems were partially burned.

Within two days, UNESCO raised the question of the legitimacy of the auction and tried to contact various governmental officials because there are no laws to specify the behavior of various parties in such circumstances. It was interesting to see that the ministries, though concerned, were not really very interested in the auction of the cultural heritage of their country, which was going to take place right there in Phnom Penh. That could be a real problem for the protection of the totems. It is hard to follow the location of such objects of art once they are sold. Therefore, everybody understood that something should be done, but nobody knew what. For example, the antique dealer was visited by the representative of his embassy in Phnom Penh and promised not to sell the totems without prior permission from the authorities.

The Ministry of Culture was addressed by UNESCO. It was decided after some time that the statues could be sold at the auction, even to private collectors; however, the totems should remain in Cambodia. The auction was finally canceled. When I arrived in the evening at the antique shop where the auction should have taken place, it was closed. Nobody knew if the totems were there or not. The next day the dealer announced that they had not been sold and that he was planning to sell all of them to one of the foreign companies in Phnom Penh. That would mean that the complete lot would belong to a company based in Cambodia, which would make it easier to know the location of the totems and guarantee that the objects would remain in the country.

This situation showed the problem from different points of view. It clearly showed an absence of enforcement of law and lack of political will to intervene legally in the country. The Ministry of Culture took a few days to issue a statement that these objects should remain in the country. It is obvious that such a decision cannot be made each time for separate cases.

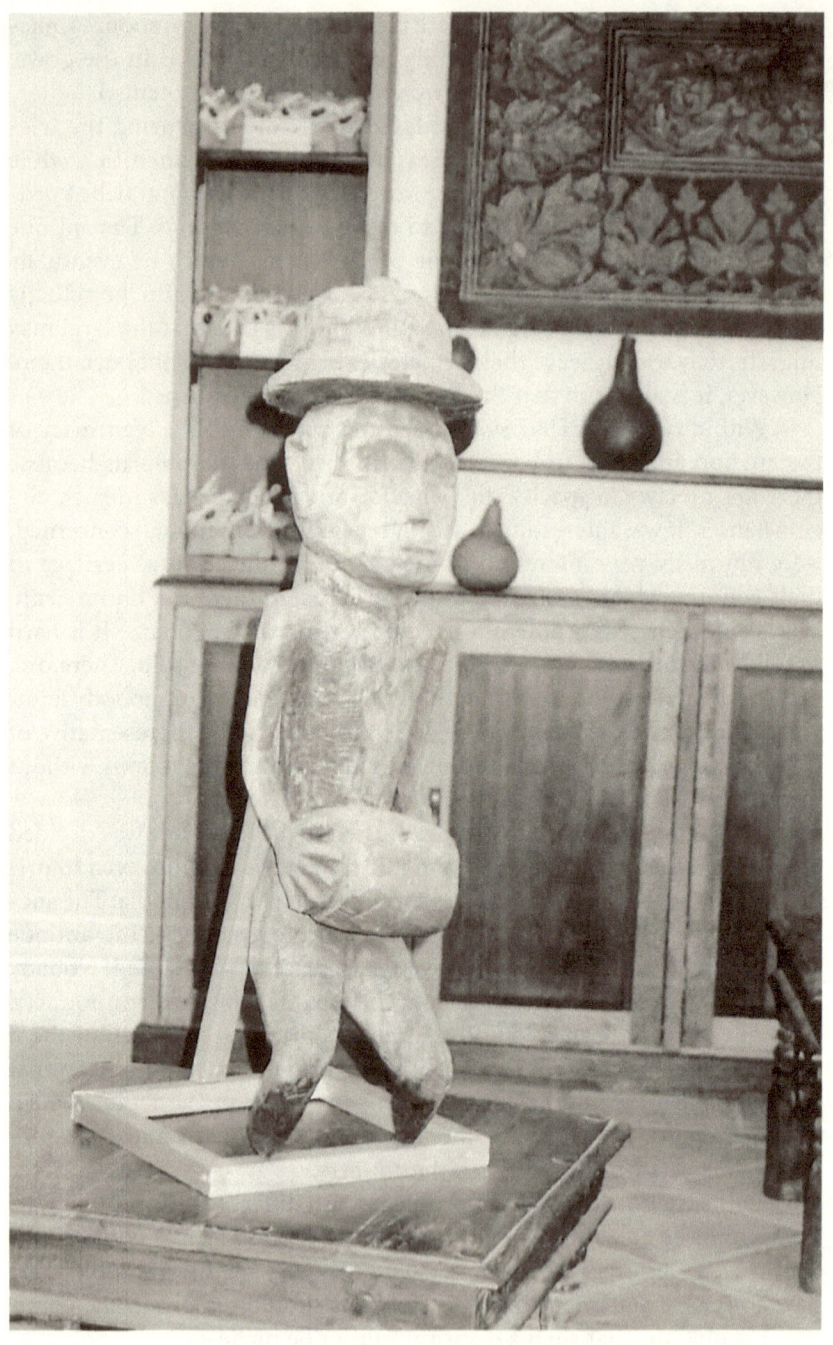

A totem of a man holding a drum.

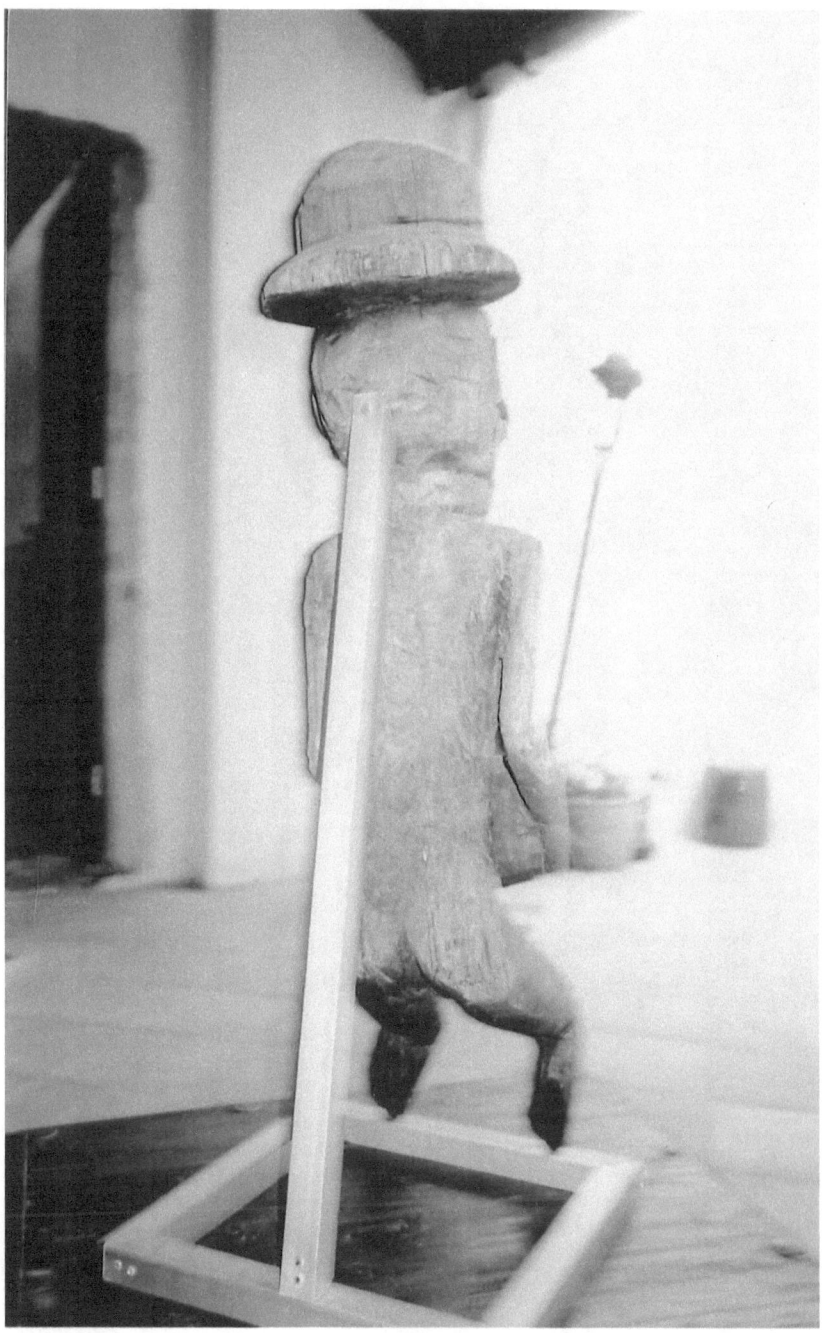

A totem of a man holding a drum.

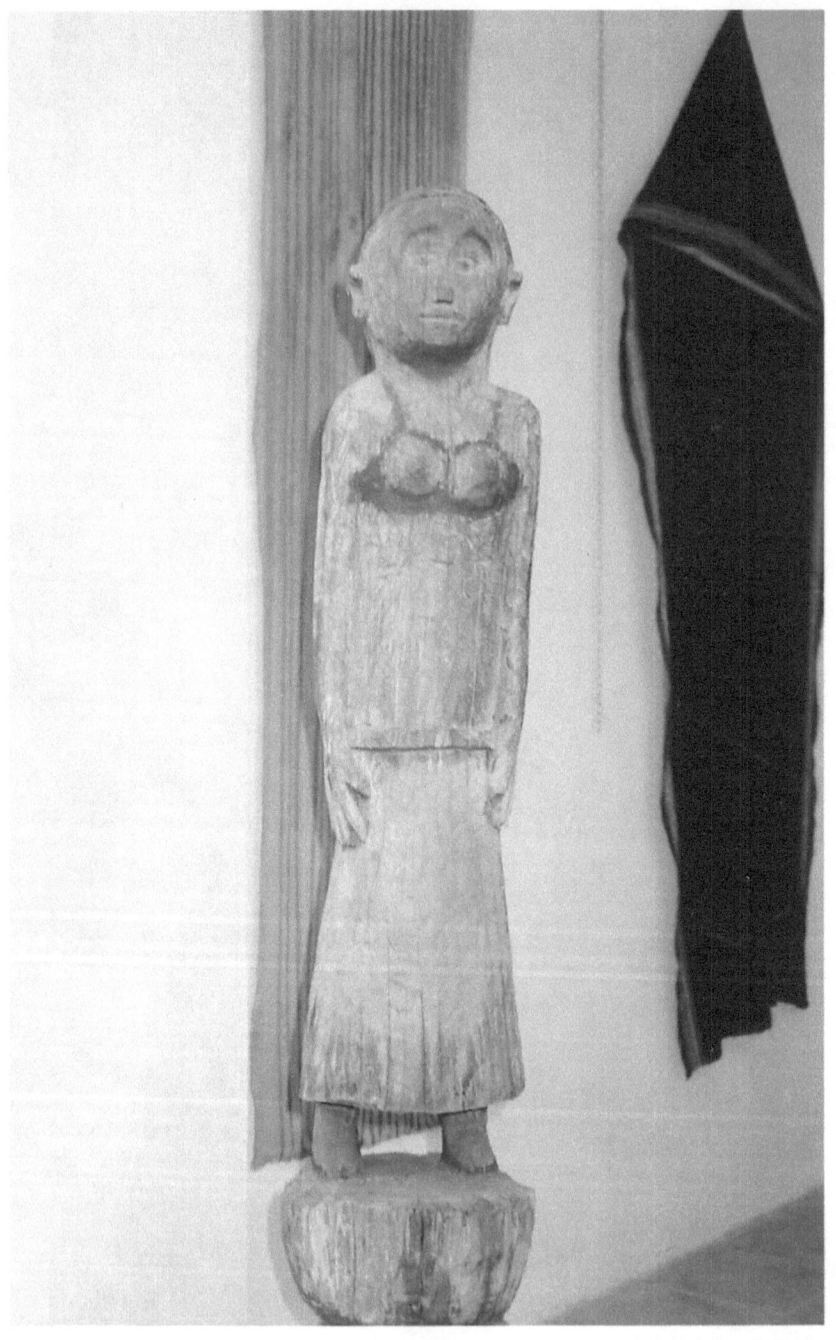

A totem of a woman.

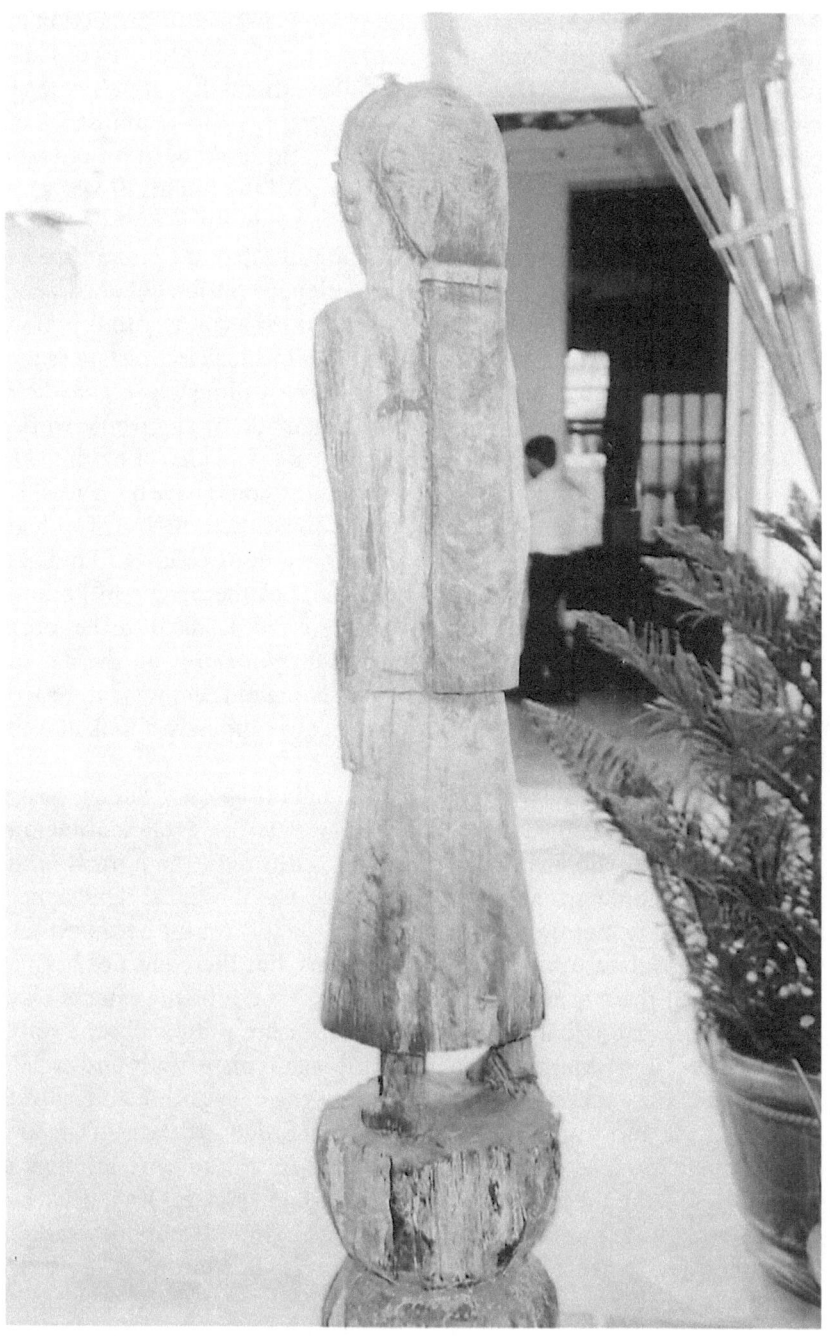

A totem of a woman.

Without law enforcement one cannot really discuss the protection of the cultural heritage of Cambodia. The reaction of the Ministry of Culture gave the impression that the Cambodians themselves were not very interested in taking action on the problem. Neither of the ministries of government organizations knew what to do in this case, what procedures should be followed, or what should happen with the totems. It was as if they were forced by UNESCO to do something about it.

The international organizations that are situated in Cambodia do a lot of good for the country, which lost experienced professional workers; for its economy; and for other things required for a country to function properly. However, they cannot do everything. In such circumstances the Cambodians themselves have to show themselves willing to preserve their culture; without their willingness the moves made by the whole world will not be sufficient to stop the trafficking of art. The idea of holding an open auction showed that politically such a thing could have been acceptable to the officials. Nobody would have stopped them if UNESCO had not found out about it. The totems could have been nicely and quietly sold by a foreigner to foreigners; even if most of the people in Phnom Penh knew about it, nobody was really interested. I talked to the journalists of the local newspapers, such as *Cambodia Daily*, on the day of the auction for the purpose of my research. None of them was interested in the auction and none of them wanted to come and have a look at it to see what was going on.

The culture of the Jarai tribe is practically unknown. Such a thing is understandable. If in Cambodia not very much research is done on Cambodia itself, who has time to study the culture of the nomad Jarai tribe whose people are not even considered Cambodians? The cemeteries of Jarai are mentioned sometimes in the local press because they are very unusual decorated with these totems, but there has not been a clear study of their history or tribal culture. No doubt the totems play a vital part in the tribal culture because they are practically the only known expression of Jarai art. They are important historically and architecturally as they present both facts and myths of Jarai life and reflect tribal legends and traditions that are not recorded otherwise. The art and forms of the totems are passed from generation to generation as a way of preserving these traditions and cultural heritage. Obviously the wooden totems do not survive for a long time in humid and hot weather and after a few generations need to be renovated. It means that after a few such sales the totems could disappear without a trace, making it more difficult for scientists to study the art and religious traditions of the tribe.

Conclusion

This research has tried to show that the trafficking itself as well as the dimensions of the illicit trafficking of art have numerous negative effects on Cambodia. They block many new and positive developments in the government and among the population and contribute to increasing corruption, bribery, and collaboration of many categories of the population with the traffickers, who want quick financial profits. Attempts to enforce the legal system in the field of the protection of cultural heritage are stopped all the time. The main area of deterioration is the cultural heritage itself, which is disappearing from the country on a daily basis in increasing proportions. Archaeological works also suffer as the valuable items disappear without trace from the country. Of course, this effect cannot be judged as negative without providing facts about the changes it brought to the country, but it is the trafficking of art together with other types of illicit activities and contraband that contribute to these consequences.

Among other negative effects are increased violence, underground activities and economic instability. Illegal trafficking of art is worsening the delegitimation process that occurs in Cambodia and increasing the lack of respect for the legal system. The continuation of trafficking effects certain variables within the social system of the country, such as the contribution to the establishment of an underground economy.

Archaeologically speaking, each artifact contains important and rare information that allows scientists to discover many details about the life of the ancestors. In a country like Cambodia that has many gaps in the study of its history due to a lack of evidence, these objects of art are the only witnesses that throw some light on the past. Their analysis provides the necessary data about the lifestyle, levels of social and industrial development, and other areas. Once the artifact is removed from the site, this information is lost and the object of art loses its historic value and becomes simply an object of aesthetic admiration. These artifacts are used by Cambodians for prayers and religious rituals. Once removed from the place of worship the statue loses the primary value for which it was created centuries ago by the Khmer ancestors and turns into an object of exchange value.

Some of the greatest dangers of the destruction of cultural heritage are that the country forgets its own culture, loses traditions, and loses cultural identity. The disappearance of culture is dangerous for the nation and may have the most negative consequences for the country in the future. Clearly it is in the hands of the Cambodian government and officials to reduce if not stop the trafficking. It is no wonder that many of

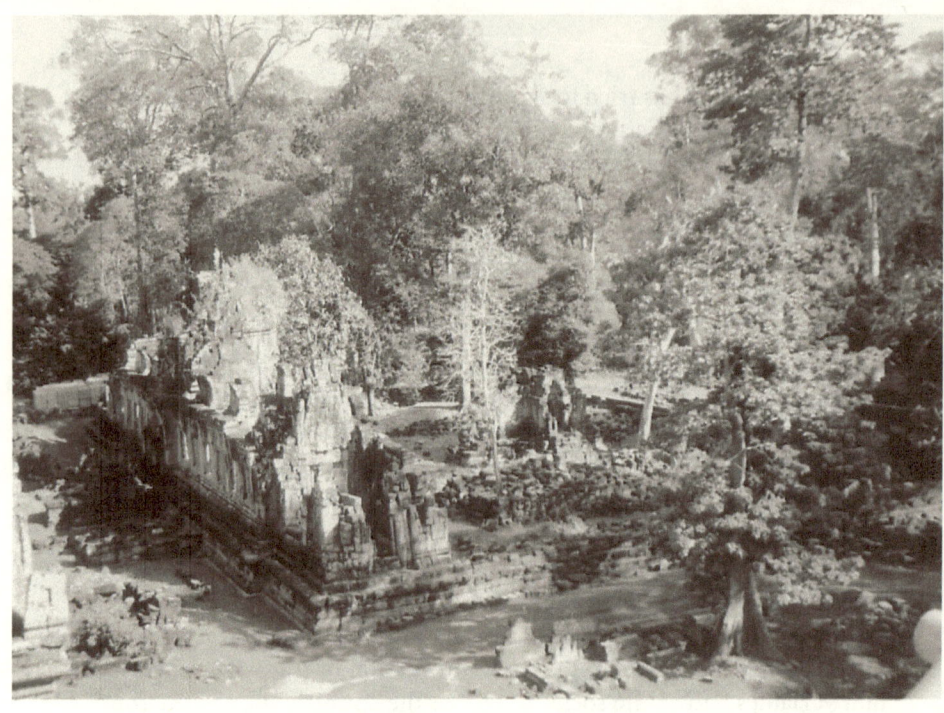

Temple in the area of Angkor Park.

them blame the military directly and openly discuss their involvement. The highest members of the government can lower the impact of trafficking on different areas of the country by introducing at least the most basic measures. Even if the trafficking of art is not stopped completely, it may be reduced and thus bring about positive consequences in politics, economy, archaeology and religion.

4

Conclusion

Policy Alternatives in Cambodia

It is obvious that the question of stopping or even reducing the illicit trafficking of art is more than complicated. Realistically speaking, it will be very hard to achieve any positive results or find any positive solutions to provide the desirable resolution of the problem. The analysis in the previous chapters showed that the question of smuggling art from the country is not an independent issue. On the contrary, it is intertwined with many different categories of problems in areas that are far from art: politics, economy, law, trade and many others. It is also clear that in a country like Cambodia it is hard to solve this issue when there are so many other basic problems that require urgent solutions.

I support the idea of many scholars who have worked on this issue that the problem starts on the side of demand, which is more powerful than any solutions to protect cultural heritage. At the same time, I am convinced that if anything can be done in this situation, it will come from the Cambodian government. Any efforts, even if they are small but have a realistic implication, taken by the Cambodian administration, judicial, military and other systems will by all means help to reduce art smuggling if not entirely stop it.

In this chapter, I will try to evaluate and determine the current policies of the Cambodian government as well as policy alternatives that could be considered by the policymakers undertaking the task of policy development and reevaluation. The chapter will start with an analysis of the governmental approach to the problem of illicit trafficking and with an attempt to understand whether this approach can be considered correct. This analysis will see the weak sides of the policies and will enquire whether the policymakers are on the right track. It will be followed by a brief critical analysis of the institutions in Cambodia that will permit us to see if the government is really able to implement its policies.

The discussion will continue with an in-depth analysis of the current policies developed and implemented by the government with the help of international institutions and organizations in the country, followed by a study of policy alternatives proposed for further study and implementation. Another section of the chapter is devoted to the description of the role of UNESCO in the country and its particular participation in this difficult problem. UNESCO's role cannot be underestimated.

I will end the chapter with a discussion of the future of illicit art trafficking in the world of globalization and of how these changes may alter and influence art smuggling worldwide in the twenty-first century. The appendix contains research made for this book on the restitution of Khmer objects of art. It offers a description of all the objects of art ever found outside Cambodia and proved to be of Khmer origin as well as all of the available cases in which the objects of art were returned to Cambodia. There is a detailed description of how and under what conditions they were returned to the country.

Finding a Correct Approach to the Issue of Illicit Trafficking of Art

The Cambodian government is facing an uneasy task from all points of view. It is not easy to find a realistic policy that will be an adequate measure for the protection of the cultural heritage of the country. Government policies should fit the current situation in the country and at the same time agree with legal, political, economical, moral and even psychological criteria. To start with, the problem of illicit trafficking should be well studied and researched in order for policymakers to be able to find measures that will be realistically effective. Illicit trafficking of art, as all other types of illegal activities, has particular characteristics that should be taken into account by the administrative system when creating and implementing these policies.

The list of such characteristics is numerous and includes the fact that the trade is transnational. Chapter I contains an analysis of how the objects of art may go to any of a number of transitional countries in the region of Southeast Asia after leaving Cambodia. They often change countries in this region and after that can be transported to importing countries such as Japan, countries in Europe, and the United States. Because demand plays a vital role in this trade, objects of art follow the consumer market. Therefore, the adoption of policies only in Cambodia will not stop the trafficking of art. To be effective, the policies must be reevaluated in all countries that are involved in the trade.

The task of making all countries concerned adjust their policies of trade in Khmer art to policies that would be helpful for Cambodia will be nearly impossible to achieve. All the governments and institutions involved have not only different policies but also different political goals and interests. For example, the establishment of new regulations concerning the import and trade of Khmer art in other countries will require the involvement of national, regional and international jurisdictions. It is a difficult task because it is too complicated to cope with from the bureaucratic point of view. It is equally difficult to imagine that all of these policies may be well coordinated and implemented. In many countries there is a rising concern that many of these policies will also be against the general consumers' interest. The mere idea of implementing these anti-market policies in many Western countries is hard to imagine.

Furthermore, the analysis in the first chapter showed that although not much is known about the structure of the trafficking itself, it is not a type of trade that is well structured. Trafficking of objects of art in the territory of Cambodia is not centrally organized and may take a sporadic character. This point causes many problems for effective policy implementation.

For example, we know for a fact that in the last two years the primary route through the Thai border has become less interesting for dealers who have taken on other routes via Singapore and other countries. However, the exact planning of these routes is not well known even now.

Another issue is that the identities of the leaders of the groups that participate in the pillage are not really known. The few people who were caught and jailed were just the executors of the planned operations whose identities were not important and whose imprisonment did not really change the state of affairs. Even if some of the leaders are caught and sentenced, the effect on the whole net of trafficking will not be particularly altered. For the same reason, negotiation with the main participants will not bring the desired effect either because these leaders do not control the entire trade.

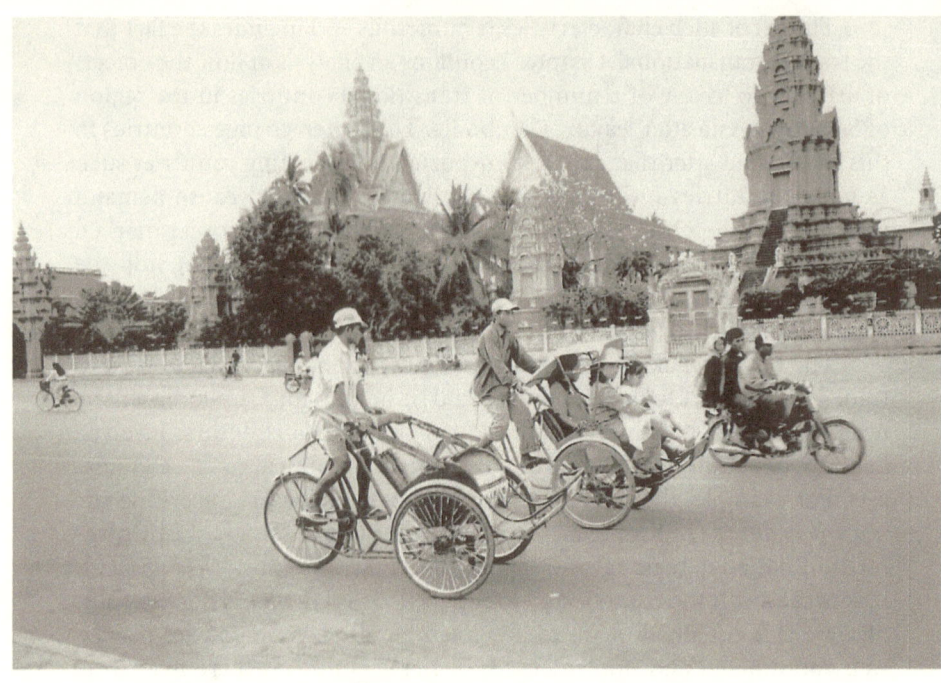

Motoriksha in front of the Wat Ounamlom; center of Phnom Penh.

It is important to mention here that although this research does not really focus on the criminal issue, that issue should be taken into account. Although illicit trafficking is a crime from the author's point of view, there is no real hard violence involved in it. Some other types of trafficking such as drugs or the slave trade involve severe offenses against humans. Here, objects of art, stones, vases or manuscripts are being looted. While stealing and transporting art from Cambodia the participants do not kill anybody; they do not commit murder or any similar offenses.

The more detailed structure of the trade was described in the first chapter. It is necessary to mention, however, that the areas of influence and jobs are well divided among the participants and they usually do not get involved in each other's spheres of influence. Therefore, destroying one or two of these groups will not eliminate the system completely. The spider net will remain intact, formed of independent groups and gangs.

Furthermore, considering the current situation of the Cambodian economy, industry, etc., the government obviously has other priorities. All the participants are so interested in making a bit of money in this affair that nobody will turn the looters over to the police for prosecution. The guards prefer to add an extra twenty dollars to their fifteen-dollar monthly salary rather than report the looters. It also means that many people are not very loyal to the legitimate system and to the administrative system. It is also true that many Cambodians do not see it as a damage to the society.

In the previous chapter we saw the example of the Jarai tribe that sold their totems to the antique dealer from Phnom Penh. The Jarai tribe is just one of the minorities in Cambodia who are not considered Cambodians. Do they have the right to sell the totems considering that they really sold them and the items were not stolen from the cemetery? Can they be prosecuted for that? Are they under Cambodian legislation? In this case, can the government legally prohibit such affairs or insist that the items remain in the territory of Cambodia?

Another example is that of the Cambodian peasants who so often assist the art traffickers. Many of them who live far from Phnom Penh or from the big administrative centers do not see the administration or the government as a real authority. Apart from that, many of them sincerely do not think they are committing an offense or are acting against the rules. Real implementation of the policies will require much work with the local and rural population. This is a very difficult task considering that it is a completely different way of thinking and approach to life.

It is also important to consider the financial issues. As in each trade that produces sufficient profits, it is difficult for the state to do something to stop people from making money this way. As the profit margin increases at each stage, so do the identities of the participants and the interest involved. Of course the biggest share is made outside the region of Southeast Asia. The attractive side of Cambodia compared with other countries is the low initial price of the objects of art. Sold at one thousand dollars, the prices may rise more than a hundred times in the United States. Therefore the interest coming from outside Cambodia is so strong and there are so many important middlemen involved that it is difficult to stop or even to slow down the trade. However, I believe that a certain reduction of the trade is possible.

Is Government Really Able to Implement Its Policies?

It is important to discuss the right approaches to policies and to evaluate current policies or propose alternatives. In the case of Cambodia, an important question to be asked, however, is whether the government is able to implement all of these policies. What makes the implementation of any kind of policies dealing with protection of art difficult in Cambodia is the problems with administrative, judicial and various types of insti-tutional systems. These systems are in such poor condition that they are not prepared to deal with the problem of illicit trafficking in Cambodia. In the last chapter, I looked at the condition of the judicial and economic systems in Cambodia. The level of the deligitimation process made it clear that the absence of laws makes it difficult to prevent trafficking on a legal basis. Further analysis of how trafficking creates an underground econ-omy and increases corruption, bribery and a paternalistic political system shows the difficulty the government has in implementing its own policies.

As often happens, issues of culture and art are considered important but are not the first priority. The government still has problems left over from the years of the Pol Pot regime and the Vietnamese occupation; for example, the Khmer Rouge are still active in certain areas of the country. There are other types of contraband that may be considered much more harmful for the Cambodian economy, such as which costs the country millions of dollars every year and brings about a much more harmful effect on the underground economy and money laundering. Many polit-ical and economic reforms as well as social improvement in the areas of education or health are required in the country before it will be possible to implement policies on the protection of cultural heritage to any extent.

For example, one of the urgent issues is the issue of security. The security of such objects as museums or temples becomes really compli-cated. All the guards have to be trained and need to go through training courses on a regular basis. For example, the National Museum of Arts in Phnom Penh, which is the main museum in the country, until recently lacked the most elementary things. Many of them were introduced only in the last few years and some such as police guards at night, an alarm sys-tem, fire alarms, a telephone or intercom system, a vehicle to be used in case of emergency, adequate locks, etc., are still lacking. Like the rest of the country, Phnom Penh often has problems with power cuts; in the case of electricity blackouts the staff use kerosene lamps.[1]

The objects are not really well protected; the museum that contains many of the rarest examples of Khmer art in the world cannot exhibit many of them for these reasons and keeps them in the basement. The museum needs a lot of financial investment, restoration, construction work and professional help such as restructuring the displays. The entrance fee has stayed at two dollars for years and cannot be considered a sufficient financial investment. It is possible that the Cambodian government can-not afford the financial refurbishment of its main museum or does not have good professionals to change the displays; in this case the museum could ask for foreign help. At the moment, the museum is helped by representatives of the French government, who provide advice on restoration, finances and artistic development.

It is true that one should consider the transnational character of the modern world and of this issue. The nature of the illicit trafficking of art explains the importance of the participation of the other countries concerned in this task. To what extent do these countries want and have the ability to change their systems? Many of these countries have limited possibilities to implement the measures. For example, the United States signed the agreement prohibiting import of Khmer art into the country, but it will expire soon.

There are also a few elements that have a deeper psychological background to be considered. Illicit trafficking of art exists on all continents and in all countries. The advanced countries of Japan, the United States and countries in Europe have numerous objects of art that are illegally imported and exported on a daily basis. It is a phenomenon that cannot be eliminated completely. Most of the countries have developed a set of policies that significantly reduce the quantity of objects of art that are traded illegally, but none of them has hundred-percent success.

Another important issue that should be considered is a critical look at the institutional system from the psychological point of view. It is understandable that such institutes as schools, wats, and the army are currently not in a good "form" from the administrative or functional point of view. The people who constitute these institutional bodies are not prepared to assist in policy implementation. Society is so weakened by the events of recent history and is so intensely corrupted that it cannot be relied on. On the contrary, the continuous trade of art attracts more and more participants, and from the social point of view it is not considered harmful. People surrounding potential participants do not condemn art smuggling. In the eyes of the neighbors, family or colleagues it is not a serious offense. The main support of the government comes from the foreign employees of NGOs and IGOs, who could give greater assistance than anybody else in this issue.

What is difficult about these issues is that they are not something that can be changed overnight. Even if the government implements some good and positive policies, the above issues prevent them from being well adopted in the society. Psychological issues take generations to be changed or get stabilized, which is not something that politicians or economists like. People who present the government interests usually seek changes now. None of them wants to waste time in finding solutions that will work only after a long period of time.

The government is planning to launch several important projects such as an inventory of art stock; however, experience shows that the accomplishment of a real complete inventory is a nearly impossible task. Even in Western countries the inventory of objects is not fully complete; the big museums, of course, have their inventories and catalogs, but the rest of the collections held in other institutions or by private individuals are not recorded. The reasons are the same as in Cambodia—the absence of professional help and financing that can be provided only by the help of international organizations.[2]

Evidently, impoverished Cambodia will need years to complete the inventory of the temples scattered all over the country. Because it is impossible to predict which objects will be stolen, a full inventory that is as detailed as possible and is focused on objects that may attract thieves is required. There is a need for professionals who will be able to use the necessary language and who possess a knowledge of various methods and analysis used in this field.

Even the simplest issues that generally can be done in the Western countries present a problem in Cambodia; for example, an Art Loss Register, was formed in 1991 by an organization based in the United Kingdom to organize a more efficient exchange of information on stolen art between countries. The requirement is to provide a good description and a photograph, which may often be problematic in Cambodia. Another issue is fees. The registration fee of each object is twenty pounds plus a recovery fee between two and five percent calculated on the value of the object.[3] Considering that Cambodia needs to register hundreds of objects of art, the fee of twenty pounds may be difficult to find. In the case of the Art Loss Register, Cambodia (with the help of UNESCO) was offered a big discount and much help. The example, however, is typical and illustrates the various financial difficulties Cambodia may have while trying to satisfy the most basic requirements.

Current Policies

The current policies in Cambodia are not very effective. There are many reasons for their ineffectiveness. The main one is probably that they do not suit the current situation in the country. Policy failure is clearly visible as the trafficking increased in 1990s, particularly from about 1995, when it got out of proportion. There is no visible support of the policy from any of the social, educational or religious sectors in the country. The traffickers find better and better ways to conduct their business and find new routes to smuggle their goods and transport them outside the country.

The early route known through Thailand is no longer much in use; the goods may be transported through Singapore, Vietnam, Laos, or by sea to all accessible ports. Trafficking is becoming more diversified and sophisticated.

The current policies in Cambodia include a set of policies developed by the government with the help of UNESCO and other international institutions. The policies were established in 1992, when Cambodia and UNESCO hosted its first regional workshop in Thailand in February 1992 and in Cambodia in July 1992 on Measures Against Illicit Traffic in Cultural Property, focused on looting objects of art from Cambodia. After the workshop, for the first time Cambodia started to introduce some of these measures against art trafficking. A brief description includes:

• the preparation and publication of educational and informative material on the issue of illicit trafficking of art in the Khmer language in order to provide some elementary and primary education for the general public

• the first steps to improve the security of the monuments, starting with strengthening the security in the museum of Phnom Penh with the help of the officials of ICOM

• further education for the public to increase awareness of the problem such as productions for public television in Cambodia on the measures against illicit trafficking, which could be broadcast regularly; the production of brochures and other published information in Khmer; the organization of a competition for a poster depicting the illicit trafficking of art for nation-wide distribution

• productions of traditional performing arts (A-Yai) to create awareness and increase cooperation in the rural areas

• education and information sessions for Buddhist monks

• a series of training sessions organized for customs officials by UNESCO: Cambodian journalists went on training sessions with UNESCO in order to be able to explain the issue in the press and media and four hundred fifty Cambodian police officers (a special unit of the Police of Cultural Heritage) who guard the area of Angkor temples are trained regularly with the help of the French police

• on an international level, the media and television prepare programs about illicit trafficking to be shown all over the world; restart the liaison with INTERPOL; the Art Loss Register for registration of five hundred to six hundred objects stolen from Angkor temples; preparation of computerized inventory with the help of the EFEO.[4]

During the last decade the government has been implementing all of these policies. The most important introductions are national legislation in 1996; the establishment of a special police unit of four hundred and fifty officers with the help of French police (SCTIP), UNESCO, and the Ministry of the Interior of France since 1994; and the establishment of an INTERPOL unit in Phnom Penh.[5] Many of them have been introduced with real difficulties. Much has been done by the French police to establish a unit of police for the protection of Angkor. The French have provided the police with all the necessary training and equipment such as uniforms, cars, petrol, mobile phones and motorbikes to survey the territory at night. All the police officers had to be given lessons on how to drive motorbikes.

A very urgent issue that is also very complicated is the issue of inventory. The first inventories were made by the French scholars from the EFEO at the beginning of the twentieth century when the temples were first discovered. An inventory of the temples, museums and storage rooms is very important and is absolutely necessary for the protection of monuments from theft. All the items to be inventoried must be photographed and described in detail. At the moment there is a complete inventory of the temples of Angkor and an inventory of Conservation d'Angkor, the storage room containing about five thousand statues mainly from the Angkor area.

The storage room has been attacked many times since the 1970s. The items have continued to disappear until recently and nothing could be done to start a proper search because there was no proof that the objects were coming from the Conservation D'Angkor. The difficulty of the inventory was that it contained many statues similar in nature, so they needed to be well described.

Another important inventory project that is being undertaken now by the EFEO and the French police is the inventory of the temples outside the territory of Angkor. The main concern here is financial. Such a project requires a lot of money, which the Ministry of Culture does not have, and it requires the participation and support of local governors. Often the temples are not even known to the local administration.

Many of the measures are of international character, which is very significant in this case. Cambodia is a party to all international conventions. An important step was the imposition by the United States government of the restrictions on the importation of Khmer cultural heritage into the United States. The agreement will come to an end soon and needs to be prolonged. The art dealers who say that it is against the legal trade of art and that the agreement should not be prolonged are pressuring the

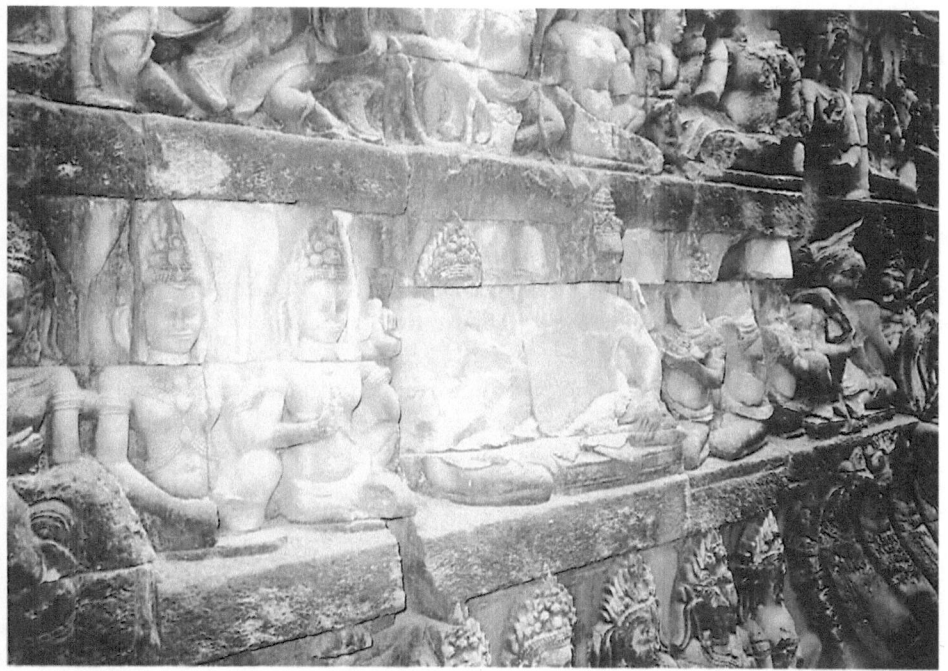

Terrace of the Leper King in Angkor Thom; end of the twelfth century; built during the reign of Jayavarman VII.

United States government. The stolen objects of art are registered in the Art Loss Register. Many films have been made recently on the topic of illicit trafficking of art from Cambodia. These films include documentaries made by National Geographic Television, the Franco-German Television Channel ARTE, and others.

The policies listed above show an enormous effort undertaken by the government. Unfortunately, the implementation of these policies has not given the desired result. The policy failure was highlighted by a significant increase in art trafficking from 1995. The suppressive policies and the increase of risk connected with trafficking have led to a rise in prices. Considering the nature of the trade, the higher risk and prices could make looting objects of art less attractive for the participants. They still, however, enjoy protection from the military and the initial prices remain low compared with the rest of the region, making it very profitable still to resell Khmer art outside Southeast Asia. What remains interesting is that there is no record of increased violence associated with the trafficking in Cambodia.

Many policies fail because the government cannot control or sustain them on the required level for a long period of time. The issue of inventories has lasted for years without being solved due to problems of a financial and organizational character. The information reported in newspapers and on television, even though extensive, is of a temporary character. It is quickly forgotten and does not give a desirable long-lasting effect. The backwardness of the judicial system does not allow for the implementation of many policies or finding a legal basis for them. The failure of policies implemented by other states is also evident. In the United States the art dealers demand cessation of the regulation prohibiting the import of Khmer art into the country; they claim that it is against the right of the legal trade.

An important reason for policy failure is the absence of data on trafficking. The gap in information makes it hard to create an effective policy that will have the desired short-term and long-term results. The question needs to be studied by professionals who specialize in similar problems, who know the structure of the trade, who know more about the trafficking itself, and who will be able to actually implement the law. Many policies are initiated by UNESCO and other foreign institutions and are not well executed later by the Cambodian ministries. They end up having a spontaneous character and become short-term actions.

The government realizes that the policies could be more efficient and should be changed. The majority of existing policies should be restructured in order to give good results. There are many possibilities to stop trafficking, and many people have their own ideas of what can be done to stop it. For example, an idea presented by some foreign art dealers explains that there should be a legal trade in art and that the prohibition of the art trade leads to the excessive looting of the objects of art from the country. Policies may be aimed indirectly at illicit trafficking, such as improving people's lifestyle in the rural areas, giving more financial support to the countryside, creating jobs for the peasants, and improving the conditions of soldiers.

Policy Alternatives

The Cambodian government has already undertaken many steps to prevent trafficking of objects of art. However, all of the policies mentioned in this chapter are evidently not efficient enough, which means that it is important to rework them or investigate alternatives. First of all, it is necessary for the government to raise questions about the current policies and analyze how efficient they are and whether they are really the best way to cope with the existing problems in this area. Problems that should be reconsidered are very numerous and include such issues as: Are the border checkpoints effective? How many objects of art have disappeared? How many people were caught transporting objects of art and what punishment has been meted out? It is also important to note that the Cambodian government needs the participation or as much involvement as possible of other countries, particularly Thailand. Unless countries like Thailand go along with Cambodian policies, the Cambodian government cannot introduce more effective measures to fight the trafficking of art.

The Cambodian government does have the possibility to influence its policy and to introduce measures that will make participants of trafficking realize that the continuation of their business is too risky even considering the potential profits. In theory it is possible to do that. The most logical way to do that would be to introduce stronger anti-trafficking laws that would reduce bribery and corruption. It is evident, however, that this choice as a measure of preventing looting of objects of art from Cambodia is not the most effective, at least in the near future. Even if we could imagine for a minute that the introduction of such laws were as successful as in many countries in the West, it would not stop completely the looting of the objects of Khmer art from Cambodia.

The government always has some policy alternatives available. A possibility that is rather unusual and is not used often in many countries, at least not on an official basis, is to negotiate with the traffickers. This idea could work to some extent in Cambodia and is not so illogical. As mentioned in Chapter I, many important participants or main organizers are known to the administrative authorities. It is believed that the main organizers of the trafficking web come from the Cambodian top military officials. In this case, if the correct approach is used, such negotiations could bring positive results. Reaching some kind of an agreement with some of the military representatives, if not with all of them, might reduce the trafficking of art in certain areas. It would be logical, however, to conclude that such negotiations would not bring a one hundred-percent result because it would not be possible to have successful negotiations with all of the participants.

What is also impossible to forget is that the participants of trafficking are committing a criminal offense. Stealing what is considered part of the cultural heritage of the country is a criminal offense. Because many of the participants have been involved in trafficking for a long time, it should be regarded as a series of criminal offenses, the authors of which need to be prosecuted and cannot be left unpunished.

This criminal offense, which is not prosecuted by the government, has numerous negative consequences for the country and its population. It would be morally wrong to engage in this kind of attitude for present as well as for future developments in the country. At the same time, negotiations or the introduction of certain government policies may soften the punishment and consider forgiveness or amnesty. Total amnesty, however, would be unacceptable and immoral, considering the present scale of art trafficking in Cambodia and the irrecoverable damage done to the cultural heritage of the country.

This has been already proved by numerous examples. Amnesty was granted to some of the criminals in similar situations in some countries of Latin America, but the situation was not well accepted by certain members of society and had a negative impact in general. On the other side, however, amnesty would be granted to many people who occupy important positions in society and whose opinion is important. The government can conduct negotiations now or at any time in the near future. These are immediate short-term measures that, if applied correctly, may bring the necessary effect and may also be used over a long period.

When introducing new policies, it is important to have both short-term and long-term measures. One of the drawbacks of the existing system is that all the measures are short-term and usually do not last for a long time. As part of other strategies, the government also may develop policies that will be effective in the long run. Such propositions may include international participation or the participation of international organizations. Many NGOs and IGOs are already present in the country and their role in how the country is run is very important. UNESCO, whose role in this country is vital, presents an important example. The importance of UNESCO policies in protecting the Cambodian cultural heritage cannot be overestimated. At the same time, Cambodia should strengthen its own institutions.

Participation of some nongovernmental institutions may facilitate certain issues. Such institutions include, for example, the participation of religion, such as the Head Body of Theravada Buddhism in the country, the Buddhist Council. As it was mentioned in the previous chapter, a Buddhist temple or wat occupies an important place in the Cambodian community. Therefore, the participation of religious leaders in this work could be beneficial. It is true that many members of the younger generation have different attitudes toward religion. Buddhism, however, as an institution remains very important and the efforts made by the religious representatives in Cambodia may be very effective.

Other nongovernmental participation may include work with the population by the administration and education in schools and universities. The goal of attracting all these nongovernmental institutions would be to change slowly the attitude of the people to the problem or to change social attitudes. The goal is definitely very hard to achieve. Only if the problem is addressed at the roots will effective changes take place. It is important to understand the opinion of the neighborhood or the village council or of colleagues at work about a particular issue. The change of attitude in this case may alter the generally accepted approach of groups and individuals and thus alter behavior.

Indeed, it is recognized that the issue of public awareness is very important and needs more attention. It is a known fact that in some villages the peasants managed to protect some of the statues from the temples that were systematically looted. The statues that were important for the local community and were under the threat of being looted by thieves were finally kept in their proper place. In some other countries where the level of art trafficking is as tragic as that of Cambodia, the local population has ended up helping more than those who were hired to do the service.

Such practices are common, for example, in India, where the local population is recruited to protect the temples; similarly, in Sicily the tombaroli (those who participate in illegal excavations) were hired as guards.[6]

Evidently, the involvement of the population in the protection of their cultural heritage offers some solution but does not solve the entire problem. The question of what measures can be taken to reduce the illicit trafficking of art remains important. In order to be able to find other alternatives we could try and rephrase the question: What can be done to reduce the demand for ancient Khmer art? One of the measures could be to authorize the export of some objects of art that are of minor value and are not so important for archaeological and historical reasons.

An example can be provided by pre-Angkorean vases, whose sale and eventual export could be permitted. If all the vases found could be registered, cataloged and researched, the museums would not need to keep all of them. In an ideal world, with an adequate system that is not corrupt, these vases could be put on legal, official sale. Export certificates could be issued and such an action would bring additional revenue to the government.

Another example can be provided by the museum of Phnom Penh, which has been attacked on a number of occasions because there were inadequate locks. If the staff could sell one or two objects of art from their collection and install a normal security system, they could manage to protect many of the objects of art that would otherwise be stolen from the

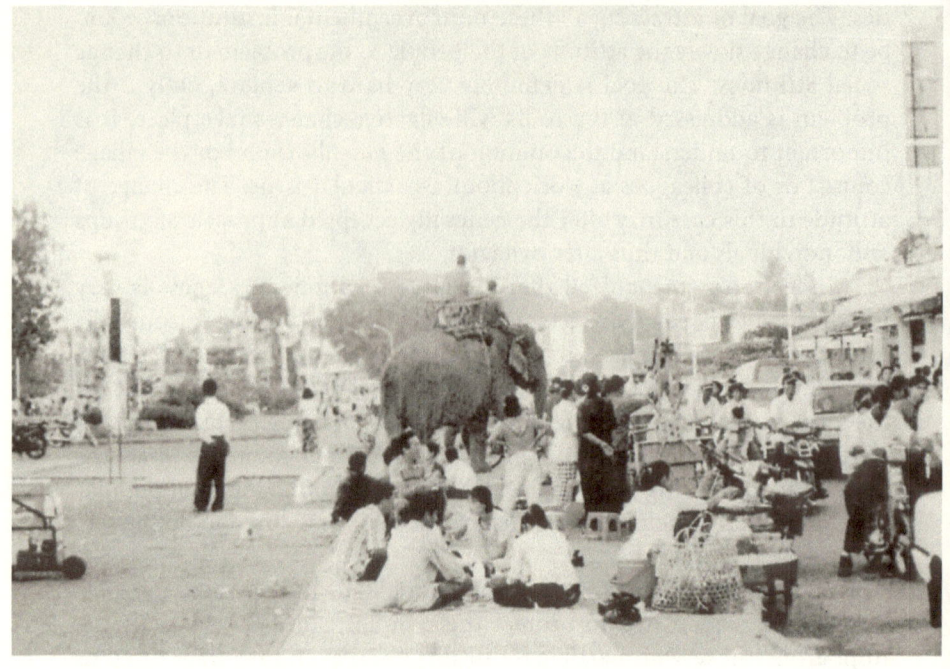

Sisowath Quay, the central street of Phnom Penh.

museum. However, they do not have the right to do that, nor have any procedures been developed for this purpose. In Cambodia, however, it would be difficult even to organize a committee to make an honest selection of minor items or items that exist in several copies. On many occasions the acceptance of decisions on items like statues could vary, which would create the precedents of sale of rare objects of art.

Big achievements in the field of protection of cultural heritage were the agreement between Cambodia and the United States in December 1999 and a bilateral agreement with Thailand at the beginning of 2001. Both agreements indicate a positive shift and improvement of policies. They have caused a reduction in the importation of objects of art to the United States and a significant reduction of trafficking over the Thai border. The agreement with Thailand, for example, is very efficient. It is a bilateral agreement that is very effective because it works in everybody's interest.

In the case of the agreement with Thailand, Cambodia's objects of art are better protected and it is more difficult for the traffickers to cross the border, while Thailand preserves other goods that cross the border, for example, cars. In this case bilateral agreements are more efficient than regional or international ones because they are more precise and involve two countries and their very particular problems. It is evident that the arrangement of similar agreements with other countries could be a very efficient start in policy implementation and could be one of the realistic long-term possibilities of improving the issue of trafficking.

The unfortunate conclusion of this chapter, however, is that Cambodia cannot propose many effective measures to stop the trafficking immediately. The government alone cannot cope with the trafficking as well as with the increasing number of objects of art that leave the country. The helplessness of the government is due to the lack of many factors within the infrastructure of the country, which have already been discussed here on a number of occasions. The government cannot implement many policies primarily because of the drawbacks of its systems.

It means that in the near future, the government cannot take any measures that will be as effective as could be desired. The gap between the social groups in Cambodia continues to widen. The current generation is better off than the previous one but still has been largely affected by previous historical and social crises and continues to go through many crises and problems. It can not now pay much attention to the problems of cultural heritage.

It is evident that the participation of other countries, which is so important, is starting to work but is still very far from ideal. The antique shops in the Bangkok River City antique market are still very active and are not going to cease their existence in the near future. The government of Thailand is ready to cooperate, but that cooperation does not mean that it will be easier to return or achieve restitution of objects of art that still cross the border or are found in Thailand.

The same is true for other countries that accept Khmer art. Galleries in Hong Kong and Singapore flourish as much as they did before, displaying the art acquired in Cambodia. However, without the participation of other countries, Cambodia will not be able to solve its problems and reduce the looting of art. It is up to the government of Cambodia to implement some measures that will interest the countries in the region and increase their participation.

The Role of UNESCO and Other International Organizations

Cultural property has always been a silent victim of armed conflicts regardless of its geographical place, time or historical situation. A vast number of castles, temples, archaeological sites, and museums as well as sculptures, paintings and other objects of art have been practically or completely destroyed during hostilities. Sometimes they have been permanently removed from their country of origin. A few examples are worth mentioning: the large scale looting of objects during World War II in Europe; irreparable damage to Cambodian monuments and museums during the past twenty years; the destruction of cultural heritage in the former Yugoslavia, Afghanistan and Somalia.[7]

Many IGOs and NGOs have offices in Cambodia. The practice shows that, notwithstanding the frequent critiques of these institutions, Cambodia is one of the countries in which they all serve a very good purpose. Without the presence of some of them such as Handicap International or the Red Cross, Cambodia cannot even be imagined after the hardship it has been through over the last thirty years. UNESCO occupies a very important and often central role in many affairs related to science and culture and the development of legal and political structures on a governmental level. In the area related to this book, the role of UNESCO is vital. After more than twenty years of abandonment, UNESCO has launched an international appeal for support of Cambodia and particularly of Angkor.

UNESCO is one of the first and primary organizations to restart restoration projects in Angkor. It organized teams of Japanese archaeologists and scientists from other UNESCO member countries to work in Angkor. The project in Angkor started in 1994, and UNESCO provides the main fundraising and financial organization for the restoration of the site.[8] UNESCO is not alone in its participation in restoration projects in Angkor. A large part of the job is done by the EFEO and the World Monuments Fund, which are restoring the Temple of Preah Khan. Teams are also sponsored by the German, Chinese, Italian, Hungarian and other governments.

UNESCO has helped to organize an ICC in Angkor to help coordinate the various projects and work of different teams in Angkor. UNESCO is acting as the Standing Secretariat on this Committee, which is cochaired by the French and Japanese governments, which are the main donors in this restoration. The committee also includes APSARA[9] and representatives of the Cambodian government. UNESCO also often helps to solve the conflicts arising between the different parties and teams participating in the restoration of Angkor. In the UNESCO headquarters office in Paris the Department of Protection of Cultural Heritage has a separate unit focused on Cambodia, mainly on Siem Reap and Angkor, to coordinate most of the activities in the territory of Angkor. There is also a department specializing in international law and the protection of cultural heritage.

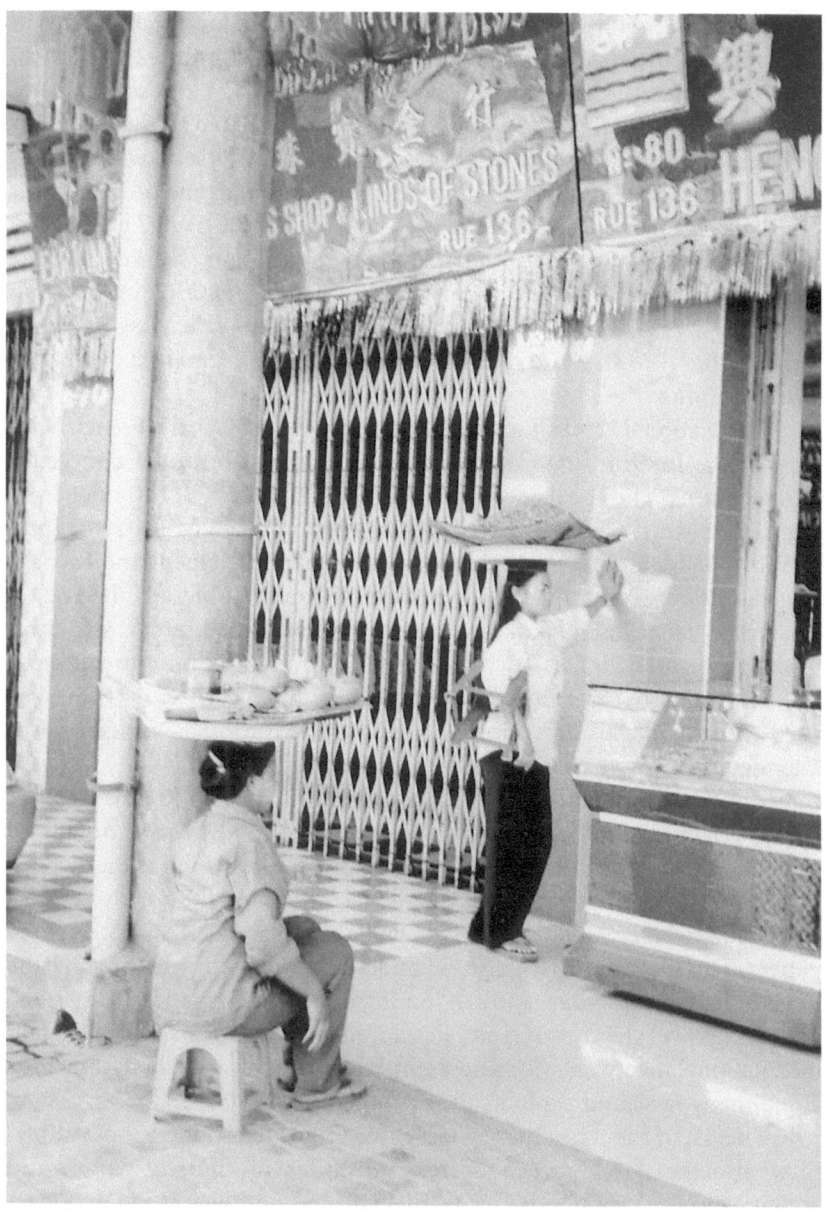

Two mango vendors near the jewelry shop.

In Cambodia UNESCO has an office in Phnom Penh and, until the beginning of this year, had an office in Siem Reap. UNESCO helps Cambodia with legislation in the area of protection of cultural heritage. For example, the employees and advisors of UNESCO help the country write and implement legislation. UNESCO organizes conferences and workshops in Cambodia and Paris on this issue. UNESCO has also published a few books, if not to say the only existing books related to this problem; some are based on the conferences held on the issue of the illicit trafficking of art from Cambodia (National Workshop on the Means of Preventing the Illicit Traffic in Cultural Property held in Phnom Penh, July 20–24, 1992) and some were written independently by scholars who specialize in this area (*Looting in Angkor: One Hundred Missing Objects, Preventing the Illicit Traffic in Cultural Property. A Resource Handbook for the Implementation of the 1970 UNESCO Convention, Angkor: A Manual for Past, Present and Future.*

The National Workshop was organized by UNESCO, the French Ministry of the Interior, the Cambodian Government and other concerned organizations. The speakers and participants included: B. Bruguier from the EFEO; Mr. Heymes, a representative of the French Ministry of Interior; Mr. Biswas, a representative of ICOM; Etienne Clément and Richard Engelhardt, representatives of UNESCO; Mr. James Coble, a United States Customs Attaché in Bangkok; and others. The participants addressed most of the problematic issues, such as the state of museums, monument security, informational and educational measures, and measures that could be used to fight illegal trafficking. Altogether the National Workshop was attended by more than one hundred twenty participants.[10]

Another conference was held at UNESCO on The Preservation of Cultural Heritage in Cambodia on November 27, 1999. It was organized by APSARA and The Friends of Angkor. Many speakers, such as Pierre Baptiste from the Guimet Museum; Claude Jacques, a UNESCO adviser; Mr. Paringaux from *Le Monde*; and Assia Bedjaouri from UNESCO presented papers. The topics of discussion included the work done in Angkor, the most urgent current-day issues of looting and vandalism that go on in the temples all over the country, and developments in the legislative field and international involvement. The presentations, which varied in nature, provided many facts and explained the problems.

The list of the participants in the two events mentioned above shows to what extent UNESCO organizes and unites all kinds of people and activities to help Cambodia protect its cultural heritage. It involves participation of experts like Claude Jacques, a UNESCO consultant; Bruno Brougier, a researcher at the EFEO; journalists; representatives of the Guimet Museum; Gilbert Heymes, a representative of the French Police; and representatives of ICOM. UNESCO coordinates all the activities in this area.

One of the most important events was organized in October 1999 with the Ministry of Interior Affairs. For the first time it involved the participation of all Cambodian provincial authorities and police who saw the global scale and the deteriorating effects of trafficking of art, which they did not realize themselves. It was practically a discovery for the most of them.

Another event organized in Cambodia took place at the beginning of March 2001, the Intergovernmental Committee for Promoting the Return of Cultural Property to its Countries of Origin or its Restitution in Case of Illicit Appropriation.[11] The committee developed and adopted the measures, the implementation of which is indispensable for solving problems with illicit trafficking of art in cases like Cambodia. For example, the ninth session of the Intergovernmental Committee (Paris, September 16–19, 1996) "adopted, among other recommendations, Recommendation No. 6 concerning an international code of ethics for art dealers.... The motivation behind the drafting of this Code was to provide a harmonized version of numerous national dealers' codes relative to illicit traffic, to avoid problems that some existing provision in such codes have revealed, and to give international recognition to dealers who adopted it."[12]

The Committee helps to advance work on computerized databases of stolen or missing artworks. It helps many countries to conduct inventories of cultural objects and create an international database of this kind. The Committee assisted the technical meetings organized for this purpose in Prague, Czech Republic, November 4–6, 1996; Washington, DC, November 17–18, 1997; and Lyon, France, September 23–24, 1998. These meetings were attended by UNESCO, the FBI, the Art Loss Register, OCBC, and UNIDROIT.[13] The questions of illicit trafficking are constantly addressed in World Heritage Committee sessions,[14] which try to develop measures to stop the trafficking.

A separate word should be said about APSARA. APSARA performs a controlling function of all the work done in Siem Reap on behalf of the Cambodian government. It introduces projects and develops most of the existing measures of protection on the national and international level. Its multiple projects include the promotion of tourism, the protection and promotion of cultural heritage in Cambodia, the improvement of the Cultural Heritage Police in Angkor, and various projects on urban planning in this area. A large community of people lives in the territory of Angkor itself and in Siem Reap. The lives of these people need much change and coordination, considering tourism, restoration works on the territory of Angkor, and other issues this community faces while living next to and within one of the biggest monument compounds in the world.

The problems faced by APSARA, however, reflect the general problems already presented in this chapter, such as the lack of qualified personnel; the lack of coordination of work between the organizations, the
participants of which have many different agendas; and political problems
between the various ministries and within the government.[15]

UNESCO constantly helps Cambodia in the areas of training, communication, legislation and education. It continues to help to improve
security in the museums and storehouses with the help of ICOM and other
relevant organizations. It also assists in the creation of inventories and has
published various materials such as the book *Looting in Angkor. One Hundred Missing Objects*[16] that was prepared with the help of ICOM and the
EFEO and contains photographs and descriptions of the most precious
statues stolen from Cambodia.[17]

Perspectives of the Illicit Trafficking of the Objects of Art in the World of Globalization

The potential development and possible changes in the illicit
trafficking of art in the world of globalization are current-day issues. The
new tendencies of internationalization brought into the world have
changed many approaches that existed and were predefined before. The
increased multiplicity of linkages and interconnections between states
means an international society that is much more interlinked than before.
The events that take place in one part of the world may have a previously
unexpected impact in some other part of the world that may be quite far
away.

Everybody realizes that the world in which we live is changing every
day. Many issues are acquiring a transnational character and are becoming interlinked. The direct impact of globalization on the modern world
is observed primarily in the issues of trade, finance, telecommunications,
transport and multinational institutions, the influence of which may often
be as great as those of the independent states. Because the issue of illicit
trafficking of art is a transnational affair and has a direct connection with
the above issues, it is possible to imagine that it is going through certain
changes in today's world.

The people who participate in it are adjusting the process of art
trafficking to this interchanging world and to the new potential it may
offer to facilitate, enlarge and make the trafficking of art more global and
convenient for its participants. At the same time the officials, who look at

it from the other point of view and try to safeguard their cultural heritage, realize and understand the changes in the world although they cannot get adjusted to them as quickly as participants in art trafficking.

The analysis given in the previous chapters showed that all the models and measures that were introduced against illicit trafficking of art to date have proved to be powerless and ineffective against the constant increase of art smuggling in Cambodia and elsewhere. We could see in the example of Cambodia a significant increase in the looting of art from 1996. In fact, the increase of the art trafficking could be analyzed from much earlier.

The last thirty years have shown a constant increase in illegal art smuggling. Similar instances that took place at the end of the nineteenth century and the first half of the twentieth century in Cambodia were of a different proportion than art smuggling in the 1970s (or 1960s in Latin America). The participants in art smuggling and smugglers participating in other types of illicit activities are very skillful at using the new possibilities that globalization can offer.

Indeed, the process of globalization has facilitated the processes in many areas of life. An example is the operation of money transfer or money laundering that is much easier than it used to be with new financial developments and multiple offshore banks opened all over the world that provide endless possibilities for the participants. Computerized transfers; increased globalization of trade; and greater regional, economic, and financial unification between various countries undoubtedly facilitate operations for the dealers.

Another example is new transportation possibilities and lower costs. There are more flights, roads, and routes of sea transportation, and the general cost is much lower than it used to be. At the same time the participants in art smuggling are more dispersed, their number is increasing, and it is getting more and more difficult to follow them in order to prove the issue of illegality and to prosecute them.

The shipment of objects of art from Cambodia, through Singapore, to Bangkok, and then to New York is almost impossible to trace for a number of reasons. For example, ships received at Bangkok port from Singapore are never checked. A regular ship nowadays may often be the property of a company from one country, licensed to another, hired by somebody else, under a flag of a fourth state, and controlled by a person who never even saw this ship or the merchandise on the ship, whose name is not mentioned in any of the documents, and whose location can be based on any of the five continents. These are just a few examples of new trends for the illicit trafficking of art in the globalized world.

Of course, art trafficking has not yet become a worldwide issue of vital importance. There are many other types of illegal activities, such as the arms or drug trade, whose influence on the destruction of the world's human or financial factors is much more important. The human and financial sacrifices in these two examples are much more global in the worldwide economy, trade, politics, and other spheres. However, the issue of art smuggling still exists. It occupies its place in the same niche with the rest of the activities of a similar type. Its transnational character and increasing scale are evident and will be dangerous if they continue to develop in the same manner in the future.

The trade in Khmer objects of art involves the participation of people from dozens of countries on all the continents who are interested in developing this trade, making it more international and more efficient, and increasing their turnover and profit margins. It is the participants in this kind of business themselves who help to make this world globalized and make all the states more interlinked with each other by and for their activities. They are interested in minimizing and reducing the difficulties of communication, transportation, and finances.

On the other hand, officials from all kinds of administrative institutions and organizations—often multinational organizations trying to follow this trade and implement measures to reduce it—are not capable of catching up with the intensity globalization offers. They understand current changes and even issue laws and regulations, for example, the international conventions introduced by the member states to reduce art trafficking. Many of these attempts, however, remain strictly theoretical. In practical terms they are always one step behind the art smugglers. Officials lack the necessary instruments to make policies more effective, in contrast to participants in the trafficking of art, who are organized, have their ways of dealing and doing business, and know their rights and are able to produce politically and legally correct explanations of their activities.

The defense side usually lacks serious analysis that is necessary to investigate the motives of the opposite side, to collect information on the structure of their activities, and to understand the strategy and environment in which participants of the illegal trafficking of art operate. In addition, the participants usually have access to very advanced tools of operation offered by the world of globalization such as new technologies, more advanced means of transportation and financial flexibility.

Therefore, the question of to what extent the government and official institutions may have lost their control of certain issues within their domestic policy is valid. Can it be considered that the military in Cambodia who probably participate in art trafficking plays the role of governmental actors representing their country (by being in the government). Or do they more represent themselves and the government cannot do anything about it either nationally or internationally?

The issue of globalization has not yet taken its full and completed form. It is more a phenomenon of the twenty-first century, which is only just beginning. Many issues in the world economy and politics need to be changed before this process will become really global, and one can only imagine what the world will really look like at the end of the twenty-first century. Many issues still remain from the past such as the north-south conflict, with the widening gap between wealth and poverty. The countries that play a much less important role in international affairs are practically always the countries that are culturally exploited, while the Western countries that are enriched by the art taken from the Third World countries are always advocated. The smaller and poorer states always have a lesser degree of control over the worldwide state of affairs.

Notwithstanding this issue, however, one thing is certain—that there is a swift change in the global environment. The rapid changes in technology that offer unprecedented capabilities and the role social forces play in the modern world have an unprecedented effect on the various relations that can no longer be controlled by the states or forces that controlled them some thirty years ago.

Appendix: Restitution of Khmer Art

With the scale of illicit trafficking of art going on in the country, Cambodia hardly manages to achieve restitution of any of the objects of art that surface in Thailand, the United States or any other countries. The main problem is that there is no evidence that the objects of art belong to Cambodia. Even though the expression of Khmer culture is unique and does not repeat itself in other cultures, the absence of evidence eliminates the possibility of restitution. Therefore, the cases in which objects of art have been returned are very unique. The research conducted for this chapter showed that over one hundred pieces of Khmer art were returned to the country as of April 2001. It is the biggest example of the restitution of objects of art in the world.

The restitution of objects of art takes a long time and much effort on the part of the UNESCO office in Cambodia and Cambodian officials. Most of the objects found were stolen from the storage rooms in Siem Reap; the inventory numbers of the objects of art are coded as DCA. Most of them were found because of the book *Looting in Angkor. One Hundred Missing Objects*[1] that provides photographs, descriptions, and inventory numbers of the statues missing from DCA.

All these pieces of art were kept in the DCA before 1970 and cataloged by French scholars from the EFEO who worked there at that time. After the EFEO left Cambodia at the beginning of the 1970s, the DCA was attacked on a number of occasions and many statues disappeared. Here is the list of objects that were located in other countries and proved to be of the Khmer origin. Only some of the objects listed here were returned; the rest of the cases are still under negotiation.

1. The biggest restitution ever, and the most recent, was the restitution of the part of the wall of Banteay Chmar found by Thai police on the border between the two countries. Only part of the wall was found (38 feet, 11.5 meters) and consisted of 117 pieces. Even though it was recognized by Thai authorities that the wall belonged to the temple of Banteay Chmar it stayed in Thailand for over a year, until all the formalities were completed. It was displayed for some time in Thailand as a courtesy of the Cambodian government.[2]

Six more artifacts were returned with the 117 pieces of the temple wall (altogether 123 objects of art). The artifacts seized in Thailand in November 1994 included three eighteenth century demons heads, one eleventh century garuda head and two other garuda heads.[3]

2. Another famous case that was much discussed in the media was the restitution of a head of Shiva (DCA 5729) by the Metropolitan Museum of Fine Art in New York. The curator of the Asian Department of the Museum, Martin Lerner, returned the Head of Shiva, which was a part of the collection of the Metropolitan Museum. The item was identified by the curator from the book *Looting in Angkor. One Hundred Missing Objects*[4] in 1994 and was identified by Bruno Dagens while visiting the Metropolitan Museum. He confirmed that it was stolen from Conservation d'Angkor. The head was returned in 1997.[5]

3. The restitution of two more objects is now being discussed. The head (DCA 5602) was sold in Hong Kong in the 1980s, located on the American Market in 1996 and at the moment is in the Metropolitan Museum of Fine Arts. The sandstone head (DCA 1664) was sold at Sotheby's London on June 10, 1985, and at the moment is in the Honolulu Academy of Arts.[6]

4. A female torso (DCA 1429) was stolen at the beginning of the 1980s from the DCA and was handed to the Cambodian authorities in December 1993 by Jean-Michel Beurdeley, a Parisian antique dealer. A twelfth century statue was bought by the Beurdeley Gallery in Asia, sold in France to a private collector and recognized later (in 1982) by one of the staff members of the Guimet Museum as one of the statues of the Temple of Bayon.[7] The gallery refunded the buyer and the statue was kept in France until relations between the two countries were normalized.

5. A female torso (DCA 7081) was sold at Sotheby's on June 2, 1992, and located in Switzerland in January 1995; negotiations are now under way for its return.

6. An Angkor sandstone statue found by American customs officers in September 1994 was seized from an art dealer in San Francisco and returned to the Cambodian authorities in July 1996.[8]

7. Out of twenty-four objects found in Thailand between 1990 and 1994:

> • thirteen from the collection of Lek's Gallery. These were resti-
> tuted.[9] The articles were returned on October 14, 1996, after being
> stored for a few years in the National Gallery of Thailand, dur-
> ing an official ceremony attended by the Minister of Culture of
> Cambodia and Thai officials. It was the first case of Thailand
> returning articles found in River City in Bangkok.[10] The objects
> of art were returned six years after the Thai police had seized
> them in a shop. Roland Eng, the Cambodian Ambassador to
> Thailand, called this decision "an important symbolic gesture."[11]
>
> • four objects from Mr. Wichai Phnolarach Collection.
>
> • seven objects from Mr. Ya Majpochamarn Collection. These
> eleven objects were not returned although Bruno Dagens
> confirmed the origin of the most of them with certainty.

8. An object sold at Sotheby's in London in October 1993 was returned to the country. The Khmer Grey Sandstone Three-Faced Head was a part of the Ruluos Temple Group,[12] formerly owned by the owner of the antique gallery Mrs. Taniewska-Elliott.[13],[14] In return for the restitution, she and her husband were invited to visit Cambodia to participate in the ceremony of restitution and travel in Cambodia, and she was compensated for legal and transportation costs, which amounted to a little over one thousand dollars.

9. An object sold in Sotheby's New York has inventory number DCA 7081. It was identified by Bruno Dagens and the demand for its restitution was filed by the Cambodian government on October 10, 1995. Negotiations are still going on.

10. Twenty-nine objects were seized by the Thai police during January and February 1995 in Aranyaprathet near the border. Since 1995, official negotiations between the two countries' Ministries of Foreign Affairs have been going on. It has been proved that the objects could have come only from Cambodia and their origin has been confirmed, but so far this has not produced any results.

11. Out of four objects seized by the Dutch customs offices in October 1995, two were identified of being of Cambodian origin and returned to Cambodia with the agreement of their owner.[15]

12. Objects found in the Malikka Gallery in Bangkok in April 1996 are under negotiations.

13. Lapidary Stela inscriptions in Khmer found in Bangkok, Thailand in May 1996 were returned.

14. In November 1996, a Western tourist returned twenty-six ancient pots that he bought in the 1980s in Cambodian markets to Cambodia. All the pots date between tenth and twelfth century and will be kept in the National Museum of Phnom Penh.[16]

15. Another two artifacts were returned in April 2000 by an American private collector. The sculptures, a Shiva head from the ninth century and a Tevaroup figure from the eleventh century and said to be from Banteay Chmar, were returned to the Cambodian Embassy in Washington by Pratapaditya Pal.[17]

16. By far the two biggest cases of artifacts seized by Thailand happened on a ship docked in Bangkok, when Thai customs authorities seized twenty-nine wooden crates (more than eight tons) of Cambodian statues.[18] They were believed to have been loaded on a ship in Sihanoukville (a Cambodian port), taken to Singapore and taken from there to Bangkok.

17. Another case was in Auytthaya province where smugglers found nearly four hundred objects.[19] The return of the objects of art is under negotiation.

The seventeen cases mentioned above present complete information on objects that were either located or successfully returned to Cambodia, which happened only in nine of the cases: one, two, four, six, seven, eight, thirteen, fourteen, and fifteen. In the rest of them, even if the origin of the statue is identified and proved by the experts and Cambodia has all the necessary documents proving the origin of the objects of art, negotiations can take years before completion.

For example, in the case of the Head of Shiva that was part of the collection of the Metropolitan Museum, negotiations for its return took more than three years. Each time it is a lengthy process that involves many different parties and institutions. The absence of proof and the lack of professionalism on the Cambodian side increase the length of the negotiations. In many cases UNESCO employees take it upon themselves to lead negotiations and complete formalities. On a few occasions, private owners wanted to return objects of Khmer art they acquired in Asia. There are even some cases, not mentioned here, in which the objects of art turned out to be fakes and were not accepted by the Cambodian authorities.

Only in a few of these cases were the objects of art returned by the individuals themselves or discovered by customs officers. Situations in which UNESCO or Cambodian authorities are informed about sales of Khmer art in Europe or in America take place very often. The sale of objects of Khmer art in galleries, for example in New York, however, cannot be stopped or prevented. One cannot prove that these articles were brought into America illegally or were stolen from Cambodia, even though it is widely known that all objects of Khmer art found outside of Cambodia most probably left the country illegally.

In seven of the seventeen cases the objects of art were found in Thailand. Cases sixteen and seventeen mention hundreds of objects of art (eight tons in one case and nearly four hundred objects in the other) discovered in 1999 in Bangkok and Auytthaya, which is astonishing by the scale, openness, and lack of persecution of the participants, who could be traced by the Thai authorities. However, most pieces of Khmer art discovered in Thai galleries have not yet been returned to Cambodia, such as in case seven, when twenty-four objects of art were seized by the Thai authorities between 1990 and 1994. Only eleven had been returned in 1996. It was the first-ever case of restitution between the two countries. The other thirteen still remain in Thailand and after all these years negotiations have not been completed.

In eight of the seventeen cases, the objects of art were found in the West and were noticed either in auction houses or in art galleries. Auction houses usually cannot disclose the owner of the pieces of art. The solution left for the Cambodian authorities is to buy the piece of art, which is usually too expensive. Again, the provenance of the object of art is difficult to question.

In museums the explanatory note concerning the object usually says that it was a gift of an individual to a museum, a clause that cannot be questioned legally. Unfortunately for Cambodia, there were not many inventories before the 1970s and most of the documents and photos that existed were lost or burned during the following twenty years. Those who worked with the EFEO before the 1970s even remember seeing many of the registered inventories on the subjects that are now displayed in museums all over the world, but now that the documents are gone, nothing can be proved.

During the act of restitution the returning party usually gets something in return. With the museums it is usually an agreement of exchange of some pieces of art. In return for a Head of Shiva the Metropolitan Museum got a few pieces of Khmer art of lesser importance. In general with museums the agreement of restitution may be followed by the exchange of pieces of art, a display of pieces of art, or possibly a long-term loan. The restitution of 123 pieces of art from Thailand (case one) was preceded by an exhibition of these pieces in Thailand. During the restitution of a three-faced Shiva head by Mrs. Taniewska-Elliott, the couple was invited to visit Cambodia. Cambodia always tries to find a compromise that will be acceptable for both sides. It must be kept in mind that financial arrangements, even the cost of two airplane tickets, may be difficult to achieve for one of the ministries responsible for restitution, the Ministry of Culture or Ministry of Foreign Affairs.

Undoubtedly Cambodia faces many problems with the return of its cultural heritage, which is getting more and more dispersed throughout the world, displayed in museums, sold in auction houses or lost in private collections. Restitution in most cases is largely impossible, even in cases that seem to be unquestionable in essence, i.e., there is a documented proof available that the object belongs to a certain temple or place in Cambodia. No doubt in certain cases where there is an absence of proof, the object cannot be returned even if its provenance is evident. There is no solution to help the country to accelerate the return of its cultural heritage, which continues to leave the country at an alarming rate.

The question of restitution, if approached on an international basis, could be solved more efficiently than just sporadic efforts undertaken by countries separately. Addressing the question in the mass media and publications could often help. What was evident in the seventeen cases described above is that most of the objects of art were discovered through the book *One Hundred Missing Objects* published by ICOM and UNESCO.

The theft of more than forty meters of the temple wall of Banteay Chmar was so much discussed in the press that when the Thai officers discovered the truck containing 117 pieces of the wall on the border, they expropriated it. The Thai authorities returned it to Cambodia. Worldwide exposure of the problem makes publication one of the most effective and realistic solutions for the moment but, hopefully, not the only one available.

Notes

1. The Illicit Traffic of Art from Cambodia

1. Chandler, David. *A History of Cambodia.* Colorado: Westview Press, 1996, p. 9.
2. Osborne, Milton. *Politics and Power in Cambodia.* Australia: Longman, 1973, p. 13.
3. Gibson, Michael. "Ten Centuries of Khmer Art." *The World & I.* June 1997, pp. 106–107.
4. Report by the World Monuments Fund. "The Conservation and Preservation of the Angkor Sanctuary, Cambodia." *International Round Table of Experts on the Preservation of the Angkor Monuments*, Bangkok June 5–8, 1990, pp. 1–10.
5. Chandler, David. Op. cit., pp. 50–52.
6. A title of Sanskrit scholars studying sacred Hindu and Buddhist scripts.
7. Chandler, David. "Seeing Red: Perceptions of Cambodian History in Democratic Kampuchea." In Chandler, D., and Kiernau, B., eds. *Revolution and its Aftermath in Kampuchea: Eight Essays.* Yale University: Southeast Asia Studies, Monograph series No. 25, 1983, pp. 42–44.
8. Dagens, Bruno. *Angkor, la Foret de Pierre.* N. p.: Découvertes Gallimard Archéologie, 1989, p. 21.
9. Hugues de, Varine-Bohan. "The Rape and Plunder of Cultures: An Aspect of the Deterioration of the Terms of Cultural Trade between Nations." *Museum International.* XXXV, 3. 1983, pp. 152–157:153.
10. Loti, Pierre. *Un Pèlerin d'Angkor.* La Nompareille Éditions Paris. 1989.
11. Greenfield, Jeanette. *The Return of Cultural Treasures.* Cambridge: Cambridge University Press, 1996, pp. 282–283.
12. Morand, Paul. *Journal Inutile.* 1968–1972. N. p.: Gallimard, 2001, p. 606. (Appropriation of the bas-reliefs from the temple of Banteay Srei in 1923 cannot be considered a theft because the temple was abandoned and without an owner. However, the colonial authorities who confiscated the above-mentioned bas-reliefs upon their arrival in Phnom Penh had to necessarily prove this confiscation by condemnation of Malraux to three years of prison, which was reduced to one year of suspended sentence according to the judgment of the Court of Justice of Saigon October 8, 1924. It was only in 1925, under the government of Edouard Herriot, that the law on the protection of the ancient monuments of Indochina was introduced.)
13. Protection and Conservation of the Historical Monuments and of the Objects of Art of French Indochina.
14. Dagens, Bruno. Op. cit., p. 84.
15. Ibid., pp. 86–100.
16. Roy, Jules. *Les Années Déchirement. Journal 1925–1965.* N.p.: Albin Michel, 1998, pp. 318–321.
17. Osborn, Milton. Op. cit., pp. 14–15.
18. From the interviews in Phnom Penh.

19. Martin, Marie Alexandrine. *Cambodia: A Shattered Society*. California: University of California Press, 1994, pp. 21–22.

20. Ledgerwood, J., Ebihara, M. M., and Mortland, C. "Introduction." Ebihara M. M. et al., eds. In *Cambodian Culture Since 1975. Homeland and Exile*. Ithaca and London: Cornell University Press, 1994, p. 1.

21. Interview with Pich Keo, Pnom Penh.

22. Ledgerwood, J. Op. cit., pp. 2–3.

23. Preston, Douglas. "The Temples of Angkor Still Under Attack." *National Geographic*, Vol.198, No. 2, August 2000, p. 87.

24. From interviews with the antique dealers in Phnom Penh.

25. Ana, Phann. "Thieves Loot Four Temples in Angkor Wat." *Cambodia Daily*. 21.06.1999, p. 12.

26. Ana, Phann. "Thieves Loot Four Temples in Angkor Wat." *Cambodia Daily*. June, 21, 1999, pp. 1, 12.

27. Sepul, René. "Pour financer la guérilla Khmer Rouge." *La Gazette d'été*. July 19, 2000, p. A1.

28. Pomonti, Jean-Claude. "La Thaïlande tente de freiner le Trafic d'Antiquités Khmères." *Le Monde*. August 14, 1999. http://www.lemonde.fr/article/0,2320,18752,00.html.

29. Pathan, Don. "Security Ends Looting at Cambodian Temple." *The Nation*, June 23, 1999, p. A2.

30. Chandara, Lor. "Five Arrested for Theft of Angkor Heads." *Cambodia Daily*, February 28, 1995, p. 6.

31. Chantra, Kimsan. "Culture Officials Say Relic Looting on Rise." *Cambodia Daily*. November 24, 1999, p. 14.

32. de Roux, Emmanuel, and Paringaux, Roland-Pierre. *Razzia sur l'art*, "Cambodge. Le massacre des dieux de pierre." N. p.: Fayard, 1999, pp. 231–252: 240–241. Roland-Pierre Paringaux, who worked in Cambodia and Thailand, has talked on numerous occasions with the art dealers in the River City who, until recently, were rather open about the provenance of the objects they sell and about the means of obtaining them.

33. Burchard, Hank. "Cambodian Art: Angkor's Way." *The Washington Post Weekend*. July 18, 1997.

34. Ishizawa, Yoshiaki. "Etat actuel des monuments angkoriens." *Dossier Histoire est Archéologie*. No. 125 March 1998, pp. 102–103. (Everything around here is worsened by the brutal changes...at the edge of the Southern basin, in the bushes and wild grass that reached the height of a man, we had discovered fragments of about thirty statues of Buddha and of other deities, beheaded torsos, heads and other parts, broken and dispersed all over the place. It is possible that they were taken there for the purpose of destruction.)

35. Interview with Pich Keo, Phnom Penh.

36. Interview with Roland-Pierre Paringaux, Paris.

37. Vickery, Michael. *Kampuchea. Politics, Economics and Society*. London: Frances Pinter, 1986, p. 132.

38. Pomonti, Jean-Claude. Op. cit., pp. 1–2.

39. Boua, Chanthai. "Observations of the Hung Samun Government." In Chandler, D., and Kiernau B., eds. Op. cit., pp. 274–279.

40. Interview with Roland-Pierre Paringaux, Paris.

41. UNESCO Report on the Temple of Banteay Chmar. Unpublished.

42. The World Heritage List is the list of protected and endangered sites all over the world. Inclusion on the list means protection and security for the monument, provided by the UNESCO and other international organizations.

43. Lokeshvara is a divine combination of Shiva and Aalokitesvara.

44. Gysembergh, Benoit. "Les pilleurs du temple perdu." *Match Document*, p. 22.

45. Agence France Presse. "Banteay Chmar Looters Said to be Soldiers." *Cambodia Daily*. January 25, 1999, p. 15.

46. Sukphisit, Suthon and Thaitowat, Nusara. "Stolen Arts." *Bangkok Post*. February 28, 2000, pp. A1, A2.

47. Fawthrop, Tom. "The Raiders of Banteay Chmar." *Phnom Penh Post*. May 14–27, 1999. The Ministry of Culture stated that they had six reports in the year 1998 mentioning military officials participating in the looting of art and so far none of them had been brought to justice.

48. de Roux, Emmanuel, and Paringaux, Roland-Pierre. Op. cit., pp. 246–247.

49. Revise, Nicolas. "Officials Fear Stolen Artifacts are Heading West." Agence France Presse. *Cambodia Daily*. August 2, 1999, pp. 1, 13.

50. de Roux, Emmanuel, and Paringaux, Roland-Pierre. Op. cit., pp. 241–242.

51. Sesser, Stan. "Chipping away Art Theft." *The Asian Wall Street Journal*. December 5, 2000, p. 8.

52. Interview with Pich Keo, Phnom Penh.

53. Vincent, Steven. "The Looting of Cambodia." *Art & Auction*. October 1994, p. 129.

54. Samnang, Ham. "City Official Denies Looting of Island Pagoda." *Cambodia Daily*. February 28, 2000, p. 14.

55. World Bank Report, 1999.

56. Serey, To. "County Hunters Pillage Ancient Temple Site, Official Says." *Cambodia Daily*. February 14, 1996, p. 14.

57. McPhillips, Jody. "Looting Threatens Pre-Angkorian Cemetery." *Cambodia Daily*. December 4, 2000, pp. 1, 18.

58. de Roux, Emmanuel, and Paringaux, Roland-Pierre. Op. cit., p. 240. "Qu'une tête angkorienne pouvait être échangée contre un bol du riz..."

59. Covington, Richard. "Turning the Tide." *Discovery*. May 1997, p. 47.

60. Interviews with antique dealers in Phnom Penh.

61. Roy, Jules. *Les Années Déchirement. Journal 1925– 1965*. N. p.: Albin Michel, 1999, p. 19. For her I have stolen a bunderilla for prayers from the highest pediment, placed in front of the most distinguished Buddha. My heart was beating. Until I returned to my hotel, I kept the bunderilla well hidden under my shirt, like a bird that would have picked my flesh with her claws and beak, and I hurried to take it out in my room. But there, it had lost all its mystery.

62. Form of a Shiva as a phallic symbol.

63. Roberts, Matthew. "Italian Released after Detention for Art Theft." *Cambodia Daily*. February 24, 1995, p.7.

64. Faulder, Dominic. "Sandstone Cops. Two princesses press a bold initiative." *Asiaweek*. August 13, 1999, p. 27.

65. Interview with Christoph Pottier, architect at EFEO, February 2001.

66. Roeun, Van. "Artifacts Looting Continuing." *Cambodia Daily*. March 23, 1999, p. 7.

67. Report of Royal Angkor printed in *Cambodia Daily*. December 13, 1996, pp. 19–20.

68. Sesser, Stan. Op. cit. Interview with Tamara Teneishvili, December 5, 2000.

69. Vincent, Steven. "The Looting of Cambodia." *Art and Auction*, October 1994, p. 129.

2. The "Demand" Side of the Story

1. Lowenthal, David. *Possessed by the Past:* *The Heritage Crusade and the Spoils of History*. New York: The Free Press, 1996, pp. 248–249.

2. Rollet-Andriane, Louis-Jacques. "Precedents." *Museum International. XXXI*, 1, 1979, pp. 4–7: 4, 5.

3. Ede, James. "The Antiquities Trade: Towards a More Balanced View." In Tubb, Kathryn Walker, ed. *Antiquities Trade or Betrayed, Legal Ethical and Conservation Issues, an Archetype Publication in Conjunction with UKIC Archaeology Section*. 1995, p. 213.

4. Leyten, Harrie. "International Cooperation in the Fight against Illicit Traffic." In Leyten, H., ed. *Illicit Traffic in Cultural Property: Museums against Pillage*. Amsterdam: Royal Tropical Institute, 1995, pp. 73–74.

5. de Roux, Emmanuel, and Paringaux, Roland-Pierre. Op. cit., p. 241.

6. Ibid., pp. 242–243.

7. Bator, Paul M. *The International Trade in Art*. Chicago: University of Chicago Press, 1981, pp. 36–40.

8. Marks, Peter. "Antiquities Market Should be Open, Honest." *The Wall Street Journal*. January 9, 1995.

9. Teicholz, Nina. "U.S. Committee Does more Harm than Good for Antiquities." *Cambodia Daily*. January 29, 2001. p. 14.

10. Elia, Ricardo J. "Conservators and Unprovenanced Objects: Preserving the Cultural Heritage or Servicing the Antiquities Trade." In Tubb, Kathryn Walker, ed. Op. cit., p. 247

11. Ede, James. Op. cit.

12. Eisenberg, Jerome, M. "Ethics and the Antiquity Trade." In Tubb, Kathryn Walker, ed. Op. cit., pp. 218–219.

13. Bouwman, Wim. "The International Market." In Leyten, H., ed. Op. cit., p. 63.

14. Meyer, Karl E. *The Plundered Past. The Story of the Illegal International Traffic in Works of Art*. New York: Atheneum, New York, 1973, p. 100.

15. Pearce, Susan, W. *On Collecting. An Investigation into Collecting in the European Tradition*. London and New York: Routledge, 1995, p. 335.

16. Belk, Russell, W. *Collecting in a Consumer Society*. London and New York: Routledge, 1995, p. 10.

17. Meyer, Karl E. *The Art Museum: Power, Money, Ethics*. New York: William Morrow, 1979, p. 202.

18. Melikian, Souren. "A degree of destruction is unprecedented in the history of the

world—and yet I support collecting." *The Art
Newspaper*, No. 52. p. 101.

19. In his book, Belk, op. cit., compares
collectors with librarians who see their task in
protecting books from the readers rather than
providing access to them. (p. 75)

20. Meunsterberger, Werner. *Collecting: An
Unruly Passion*. Princeton, 1994, pp. 25–26.

21. The quotation was cited by Cranwell
Andrew. *The Price of Age: An Investigation into
the Illicit Trade of Antiquities*. Unpublished
dissertation, May 1999. http://www.museum-
security.org/cranwell:index.html

22. Elia, Ricardo. "The World Cannot Afford
Many More Collectors With a Passion for
Antiquities." *The Art Newspaper*. No. 41. p. 99.

23. Ellis, Richard. "The Antiquities Trade:
A Police Perspective." In Tubb, Kathryn
Walker, ed. Op. cit., p. 223.

24. DCA is an inventory made at Conservation d'Angkor. It means that the object was
stolen at one point directly from storage in
Siem Reap. The item referred to was in the
book *One Hundred Missing Objects. Looting in
Angkor* published by ICOM and UNESCO,
listing the most well-known objects of art that
were in storage with the inventory number
DCA and were stolen from Conservation
d'Angkor. This publishing helped to discover
and even return a few items and is the only
one of its kind listing some of the objects
missing with the photograph and a full
description.

25. Prasuchantip, Somprasong. "A Treasure
Trove of Thai Antiquities Abroad." *Kinnaree*.
February 2000, pp. 108–109.

26. Vogel, Carol. "Indictments Revitalize
Art Inquiry." *Herald Tribune*. May 4, 2001, p.
13.

27. Boyce, Debra, and Soenthrith, Saing.
"1,200-Year-old Head Makes its Way Home."
Cambodia Daily. December 12, 1996, p. 20.

28. Hoving, Thomas. *The Chase, the Capture: Collecting at the Metropolitan*. New York:
Metropolitan Museum of Art, 1995, p. 1.

29. Meyer, E. Karl. Op. cit., p. 20.

30. Sozanski, Edward F. "Khmer Sculpture
Melds Sensuality and Religiousness." *The
Philadelphia Inquirer*. August 3, 1997.

31. Robinson, Simon, and Labi, Aisha.
"Endangered Art." *Time*. June 18, 2001, p. 74.

32. Torres de Arauz, Reina. "Museums and
the Containment of Illicit Traffic." *Museum
International*. XXXIV. February 1982, p. 134.

33. Covington, Richard. "Stones from the
Jungles." *Discovery*. May 1997, p. 52.

34. Leyten, Harry. "International Cooperation in the Fight against Illicit Traffic."
Leyten, ed. Op. cit., p. 75.

35. Wilson, David. "It's Simply out of the
Question." *UNESCO Sources*. No. 28,
July–August 1991, p. 11.

36. Cook. B. F. "The Trade in Antiquities:
Curator's View." In Tubb, Kathryn Walker ed.
Op. cit., pp. 181–182.

37. Somers-Cocks, Anna. "The Getty
Museum Retreats from the Antiquities Market." *The Art Newspaper*. No. 54. December
1995, p. 92.

38. Boardman, John. "Don't just Berate the
Thieves: Look at the Museums and Excavators
too." *The Art Newspaper*. No. 54. December
1995, pp. 96–97.

39. O'Keefe, Patrick. "Museum Acquisition
Policies and the 1970 UNESCO Convention."
Museum International. 50 January 1998, p. 21.

40. Vincent, Steven. "Who Owns Art?" *Art
& Auction*. January 1995, p. 84.

41. O'Keefe, Patrick. *Trade in Antiquities:
Reducing Destruction and Theft*. Paris:
UNESCO, 1997, p. 9.

42. Ibid., pp. 101–102

43. Vincent, Steven. Op. cit., p. 122.

3. Impact of Illicit
Trafficking

1. Eyo, Ekpo Okpo. "A Threat to National
Art Treasures. The Illicit Traffic in Stolen Art."
In, Isar, Raj, ed. *The Challenge to our Cultural
Heritage: Proceedings of the Conference on Cul-
tural Preservation, Washington, 8–10 April,
1984*. London: Smithsonian Institution Press,
Washington, D. C. Paris: UNESCO. 1984, pp.
203–213.

2. Fraoua, Ridha. "Note de Mission."
Report to UNESCO after the mission to Cambodia. (The judicial instruments on the issues
of regulation, promotion and protection of
the cultural heritage have not been much
applied in practice. In addition, the legal rules
on the protection of cultural heritage are not
observed.)

3. Fraoua, Ridha. Op. cit. (The employees whose job is to ensure the regulation and
protection of the cultural heritage of Cambodia are not very effective. They lack political
willingness, qualified personnel, and sufficient
financial means, which no doubt cause this
situation.)

4. There is also an argument that the inscription on the World Heritage List attracts too much unnecessary attention to the monument, which puts it in greater danger and makes it more difficult for the state to protect it.

5. World Bank Report, 1997.

6. Sambath, Thet, and Chon, Gina. "Hun Sen, Thai Foreign Minister Target Border Smuggling." *Cambodia Daily*. February 4, 2000, p. 13.

7. News Briefing. "Agreement Reached on Border Checkpoints." *Cambodia Daily*. December 1, 1999, p. 10.

8. Sambath, Thet, and Mockenhaupt, Brian. "Artifacts, Border Top Agenda for Thai PM." *Cambodia Daily*. June 14, 2000, p. 8.

9. Sambath, Thet. "Military Officials Urge Border Finalization." *Cambodia Daily*. February 28, 2000, p. 14.

10. Chandara, Lor. "Millions Lost to Smuggling, Government Claims." *Cambodia Daily*. August 17, 1999, p. 1, 2.

11. According to the World Bank Report, foreign direct investment has decreased from $150.8 million in 1995 to $125.5 million in 1999.

12. One of the examples is IMF, which closed its office in 1996 and pulled out funding.

13. Maeda, Yuko, and Kimsong, Kay. "PM Slams Customs Corruption, Pledges Smuggling Crackdown." *Cambodia Daily*. December 22, 1999, pp. 1, 12, 14.

14. Renfew. "Introduction." In Tubb, Kathryn Walker ed. Op. cit., p. XVII.

15. The mythical mountain sacred to Hindus and Buddhists that is the center of the world and a dwelling place of the Hindu God Shiva.

16. Jacques, Claude. Speech at UNESCO Conference in October 1999.

17. All the examples cited in this chapter were collected during the trip to Cambodia.

18. McIntosh, Roderick, and McIntosh, Susan Keech. "Dilettantism and Plunder: Illicit Traffic in Ancient Malian art." *Museum International*. XXXVIII. January 1986, p. 50.

19. McIntosh, Roderick and McIntosh, Susan Keech. Op. cit.

20. McPhillips, Jody. "Protecting Kbal Spean." *Cambodia Daily*. August 12–13, 2000, pp. 15, 16.

21. Johnson, Kay. "Controlling Phnom Kulen." *Cambodia Daily*. September 2–3, 2000, p. 11.

22. Ley, John F. *Australia's Protection of Movable Cultural Heritage, 1991 Report on the Ministerial Review of the Protection of Movable Cultural Heritage Act 1986 and Regulations*. Canberra: Australian Government Publishing Service. July 1991, p. 13.

23. McIntosh, Roderick and McIntosh, Susan Keech. Op. cit., p. 52.

4. Conclusion

1. Biswas, S. S. "Working Group on Museums and Monument Security." *Proceedings of the National Workshop on the Means of Preventing the Illicit Traffic in Cultural Property in Cambodia*. Phnom Penh. July 20–24, 1992.

2. Monreal, Luis. "Problems and Possibilities in Recovering Dispersed Cultural Heritages." *Museum International* XXXI, 1, 1979, pp. 22—25: 53.

3. www.artlossregiter.com

4. Report, Tokyo Inter-Governmental Conference on Angkor, October 12–13, 1993.

5. www.apsara-authority.org

6. UNSDRI. *The Protection of the Artistic and Archaeological Heritage. A View from Italy and India*. Publication No. 13. March 1976, p. 14.

7. Clément, Etienne. "Protection of Cultural Property." In Maley, William, ed. *Shelters from the Storm: Developments in International Humanitarian Law*. Australian Red Cross. 1995, pp. 271–279.

8. Prott, Lyndel, V. "From Admonition to Action: UNESCO's role in the Protection of Cultural Heritage." *Nature and Resources*, vol. 28, N.3, 1992 p.5.

9. Authority for the Protection and Management of Angkor and the Region of Siem Reap.

10. Clément, Etienne. "The Aims of 1970 UNESCO Convention." In Tubb, Kathryn Walker, ed. Op. cit., p. 42.

11. The committee was established in 1978. It depends on the UNESCO General Assembly and advises on issues that are not covered by the 1970 Convention (mainly matters of colonization). So far only two cases has been presented to the committee: the case of the restitution of the Greek marbles of the Pantheon and the case of the restitution of the sphinx from Turkey. The session takes place every two years; the last one took place in Paris in 1999. This one took place in Phnom Penh.

12. Report of the Tenth Session of the

Intergovernmental Committee for Promoting
the Return of Cultural Property to its Countries of Origin or its Restitution in Case of
Illicit Appropriation. Tenth Session. January
25–28, 1999.

13. Information Document on the Databases Concerning the Illicit Traffic in Stolen
Cultural Property. Paris: UNESCO. 1999, pp.
1–3.

14. World Heritage Committee, Twenty-
first Session. Naples, Italy. December 1–6,
1997.

15. Vann, Molyvann. *Angko:. A Manual for
the Past, Present and Future.* Phnom Penh:
APSARA. 1998, pp. 162–205.

16. ICOM, EFEO, UNESCO. *Looting in
Angkor: One Hundred Missing Objects.* Paris :
ICOM. 1997.

17. Clément, Etienne. op. cit.

Appendix. Restitution
of Khmer Art

1. ICOM, UNESCO, EFEO. Op. cit.

2. Thaitawat, Nusora. "Stolen Artifacts
Handed Back." *Bangkok Post.* March 1, 2000,
p. 4.

3. Agence France Presse. "Thailand
Returns Looted Art." *Cambodia Daily.*
November 20–21, 1999, p. 3.

4. Associated Press. "Thailand to Return
Cambodian Temple Wall." *Cambodia Daily.*
July 12, 1999, p. 15.

5. Ana, Phann. "Stolen Temple Carvings
to be Returned Soon." *Cambodia Daily.* June
22, 1999, p. 10.

6. DPA. "Thailand to Return Temple Artifacts." *Cambodia Daily.* November 11, 1999, p.
8.

7. Sukpanich, Tunya. "Rendering to Cae-
sar." *Bangkok Post,* July 1999.

8. ICOM, UNESCO, EFEO. Op. cit.

9. Vogel, Carol. "Tracing Path of Artworks

Smuggled out of Asia." *The New York Times.*
April 23, 1997.

10. ICOM, UNESCO. Op. cit., pp. 10–11.

11. Agence France Presse. "Stolen Khmer
Statue Returned." *Cambodia Daily.* December
7, 1993, p. 4.

12. Eisenberg, Jerome M. "New Khmer
Temple Site Discovered as Several Stolen
Sculptures are Returned to Cambodia." *Min-
erva.* June 1997.

13. Vittachi, Imran. "Thailand Returns
Stolen Artifacts." *Phnom Penh Post.* October
4–17, 1996, p. 16.

14. Ngo Laura. "Two Ancient Artifacts
Returned to Museum." *Cambodia Daily.* October 15, 1996, p. 8.

15. Agence France Presse. "Thais Return 13
Sculptures." *Cambodia Daily.* September 24,
1996, p. 9.

16. Rizzi, Claudia. "Stolen Artifact to
Return Home." *Cambodia Daily.* April 10,
1996, p. 16.

17. Wilson, Chris Oliver. "Couple Return
Looted Artifact to Jungle Shrine." *Daily Tele-
graph,* December 1, 1996.

18. Boyce, Debra, and Soenthrith, Saing.
"1,200-Year-old Head Makes its Way Home."
Cambodia Daily. December 12, 1996, p. 20.

19. Swatsawang, Nussara. "Dutch Customs
Seize Three Antique Buddha Statues Destined
to be Sold in Central Holland." *Bangkok Post*
March 5, 1998.

20. Soenthrith, Saing. "26 Ancient Pots
Returned by Westerner." *Cambodia Daily.*
November 27, 1996, p. 20.

21. Deutsche Presse Agentur. "U.S. Collector Returns Stolen Artifacts of Angkor Temples." *Cambodia Daily.* April 12, 2000, p. 9.

22. "Customs Raid Nets 8-tonne Haul sent
from Singapore." *Bangkok Post.* July 6–7, 1999,
p. 8.

23. Associated Press. "Thais Seize Tons of
Stolen Cambodian Artifacts." *Cambodia Daily.*
July 6, 1999, p. 2.

Bibliography

Books

Art Trade

Bator, Paul. *The International Trade in Art.* Chicago: University of Chicago Press, 1981.

Fahy, Anne, ed. *Collections Management.* London and New York: Routledge, 1995.

Tubb, Kathryn Walker. *Antiquities Trade or Betrayed, Legal Ethical and Conservation Issues, an Archetype Publication in Conjunction with UKIC Archaeology Section.* London, 1995.

van Rijn, M. *Hot Art, Cold Cash.* London: Little, Brown, 1993.

Watson, P. *Sotheby's: Inside Story.* London: Bloomsbury, 1997.

Collecting Antiquities

Belk, Russell W. *Collecting in a Consumer Society.* London and New York: Routledge, 1995.

Cabonne, P. *The Great Collectors.* London: Cassell, 1963.

Fahy, Anne, ed. *Collections Management.* London and New York: Routledge, 1995, pp. 122–125.

Griffiths, T. *Hunters and Collectors.* Melbourne: Cambridge University Press, 1996.

Hoving, Th., and Bothmer, D. *The Chase, the Capture: Collecting at the Metropolitan.* New York: Metropolitan Museum of Art, 1995.

Lach, D.F. *Asia in the Making of Europe.* 2 vols. Chicago: University of Chicago Press, 1994.

Lowenthal, David. *Possessed by the Past: The Heritage Crusade and the Spoils of History.* New York: The Free Press, 1996.

Messenger, P.M. *The Ethics of Collecting Cultural Property: Whose Culture? Whose Property?* Albuquerque: University of New Mexico Press, 1999.

Meunsterberger, Werner. *Collecting: An Unruly Passion*. Princeton University Press, 1994.

Meyer, Karl Ernst. *The Art Museum: Power, Money, Ethics*. New York: William Morrow, 1979.

Ortiz, G. "In Pursuit of the Absolute." In *In Pursuit of the Absolute: Art of the Ancient World from the George Ortiz Collection*. London: Royal Academy of Arts, 1994.

Pearce, Susan. *On Collecting. An Investigation into Collecting in the European Tradition*. London and New York: Routledge, 1995.

Legislative Texts

Askerund, P., and Clément E. *Preventing the Illicit Traffic in Cultural Property. A Resource Handbook for the Implementation of the 1970 UNESCO Convention*. Paris: UNESCO, Division of Cultural Heritage, 1997.

Clément, Etienne. "The Aims of the 1970 UNESCO Convention. On the Means of Prohibiting and Preventing the Illicit Import, Export and Transfer of Ownership of Cultural Property and Action being taken by UNESCO to Assist in its Implementation." In Tubb, Kathryn Walker, ed. *Antiquities Trade or Betrayed, Legal Ethical and Conservation Issues, an Archetype Publication in Conjunction with UKIC Archaeology Section*. London, 1995, pp. 38–44.

Clément, Etienne. *Pillage and Illicit Trafficking in Cultural Objects: International Conventions and Cooperation, Ta Nei Training Programme*. Siem Reap: ICCROM, 1999.

Fraoua, R. *Le Trafic Illicite des bien Culturels et leur Restitution*. Fribourg: Editions Universitaires, 1985.

Phelan, Marylyn E. *Scope of Due Diligence Investigation in Obtaining Title to Available Artwork*. Seattle: Seattle University Law Review, 2000. Vol. 23, Winter 2000, Number 3.

Prott, L.V., and O'Keefe, P.J. *Handbook on National Regulations Concerning the Export of Cultural Property*. Paris: UNESCO, 1988.

Prott, L.V., and O'Keefe, P.J. *National Legal Control of Illicit Traffic in Cultural Property*. UNESCO Doc. CLT-83/WS/16, 1983.

Prott, Lyndel V., and Specht, James. *Protection or Plunder: Safeguarding the Future of our Cultural Heritage*. Canberra: Australian Government Publishing Service, 1989.

Sullivan, Anne M. C. "Law and Diplomacy in Cultural Property Matters." In Fahy, Anne, ed. *Collections Management*. London and New York: Routledge, 1995, pp. 97–121.

Thornes, R. *Protecting Cultural Objects Through International Documentation Standards: A Preliminary Survey*. Santa Monica: Getty Art History Information Program, J. Paul Getty Trust, 1995.

Illegal Trafficking of Objects of Art

Bourguignon, A., et Choppin, *L'Art Volé*. Paris: Éditions La Découverte, 1994.

Broodie, N., Doole J., and Watson, P. *Stealing History: The Illicit Trade in Cultural Heritage*. Cambridge: The McDonald Institute for Archaeological Research, 2000.

Broodkin, Lisa J. *The Economics of Antiquities Looting and a Proposed Legal Alternative.* Col. L. Review. 1995.

Chatelain, Jean. *Means of Combating the Theft of and Illegal Traffic in Works of Art in the Nine Countries of the EEC.* Brussels: Commission of the European Communities, 1976.

Cranwell, Andrew. *The Price of Age: An Investigation into the Illicit Trade of Antiquities.* Unpublished Dissertation, May 1999. *http://www.museumsecurity.org/cranwell/index.html*

de Roux, E., and Paringaux R-P. "Cambodge. Le massacre des dieux de Pierre." *Razzia sur l'art.* Fayard, 1999. pp. 231–252.

Eyo, Ekpo Okpo. "A Threat to National Art Treasures, The Illicit Traffic in Stolen Art." In Isar, Raj, ed. *The Challenge to our Cultural Heritage: Proceedings of the Conference on Cultural Preservation, Washington, 8–10 April, 1984.* London: Smithsonian Institution Press, W. D. C. Paris: UNESCO, 1984, pp. 203–213.

Greenfield, J. *The Return of Cultural Treasures.* Cambridge, England: Cambridge University Press, 1996.

ICOM, EFEO. *Looting in Angkor: One Hundred Missing Objects.* Paris: ICOM, 1997.

Ley, John F. *Australia's Protection of Movable Cultural Heritage, 1991 Report on the Ministerial Review of the Protection of Movable Cultural Heritage Act 1986 and Regulations.* Canberra: Australian Government Publishing Service, 1991.

Leyten, H., ed. *Illicit Trade in Cultural Property: Museums against Pillage.* Amsterdam: Royal Tropical Institute, 1995.

Meyer, Karl Ernst. *The Plundered Past.* New York: Atheneum, 1973.

O'Keefe, Patrick J. *Commerce des antiquités: Combattre les Destructions et le Vol.* Paris: UNESCO, 1999.

O'Keefe, Patrick J. *Trade in Antiquities: Reducing Destruction and Theft.* Paris: UNESCO; London: Archteype, 1997.

O'Keefe, Patrick J., and Prott, L.V. *Law and The Cultural Heritage.* Vol. 3: *Movement.* London: Butterworths, 1989.

Pal, H.B. *The Plunder of Art.* New Delhi: Abhinav, 1992.

Palmer, Norman, ed. *The Recovery of Stolen Art. A Collection of Essays.* Cambridge MA: Kluwer Law International, 1998.

Schick, Jürgen. *The Gods Rre Leaving the Country. Art Theft from Nepal.* Bangkok: White Orchids Books, 1998.

Weihe, H.K. "Licit International Traffic in Cultural Objects." *International Journal of Cultural Property.* 1995, pp. 4–81.

Khmer Art

Boissolier, Jean. *Le Cambodge.* Paris: Editions A & J Pickard, 1966.

Chou Ta-Kuan. *Notes on the Customs of Cambodia.* Bangkok: Social Science Association Press, 1967.

Cohen, J. L., and Kalman B. *Angkor: The Monuments of the God-Kings.* New York: Harry N. Abrahams, 1975.

Cambodia

Boua, Chanthai. "Observations of the Hung Samun Government." In *Revolution and Its Aftermath in Kampuchea: Eight Essays.* Eds. Chandler, D., and Kiernau, B. Yale University Southeast Asia Studies, Monograph series No. 25, 1983.

Chandler, D. "Seeing Red: Perceptions of Cambodian History in Democratic Kampuchea." In Chandler, D., and Kiernau, B. eds., *Revolution and its Aftermath in Kampuchea: Eight Essays.* Yale University: Southeast Asia Studies, Monograph series No. 25, 1983.

Chandler, D. *The Tragedy of Cambodian History: Politics, War and Revolution Since 1945.* New Haven: Yale University Press, 1991.

Chandler D., and Kiernau B., eds. *Revolution and its Aftermath in Kampuchea: Eight Essays.* Yale University: Southeast Asia Studies, Monograph series No. 25, 1983.

Chandler, David. *A History of Cambodia.* Oxford: Westview Press, 1996.

Charn, Y. J., and Sprangens, J. *Obstacles to Recovery in Vietnam and Kampuchea. U.S. Embargo of Humanitarian Aid.* Boston: Oxfam America, 1984.

Dagens, Bruno. *Angkor, la Forêt de Pierre.* N.p.: Découvertes Gallimard Archéologie, 1989.

Ebihara, M. M., et al. *Cambodian Culture Since 1975, Homeland and Exile.* Ithaca and London: Cornell University Press, 1994.

Garrett, W. *The Temples of Angkor: Will They Survive?* Washington, D.C.: National Geographic Society, 1982.

Ghosh, M. *A History of Cambodia, from the Earliest Times to the End of the French Protectorate.* Calcutta: Calcutta Oriental Books Agency, 1968.

Held, S., and Claude, Jacques. *Angkor Vision de Palais Divins.* Paris: Hermé, 1997.

Jacques, C. *Angkor.* Milan, Paris: Bordas, 1990.

Jelen, Janos, and Hegyi, Gabor. *Angkor and the Khmers, Brutality and Grace.* Budapest: Gutenberg Publishing and Printing Ltd., 1991.

Kosikov, I. G. *Ethnic Processes in Kampuchea.* Moscow: Science, Head Publishers of Eastern Literature, 1988.

Ledgerwood, J., Ebihara M., and Mortland, C. "Introduction." In Ebihara, M. M. et al., eds. *Cambodian Culture Since 1975, Homeland and Exile.* Ithaca and London: Cornell University Press, 1994.

Mabbett, I., and Chandler, D. *The Khmers.* Blackwell, 1996.

MacDonald, Malcolm. *Angkor and the Khmers.* Singapore: Oxford University Press, 1987.

Marcucci, J. "Sharing the Pain: Critical Values and Behaviours in Khmer Culture." In Ebihara, M. M. et al., eds. *Cambodian Culture Since 1975, Homeland and Exile.* Ithaca and London: Cornell University Press, 1994.

Martin, Marie Alexandrine. *Cambodia: A Shattered Society.* California: University of California Press, 1994.

Moore, Elisabeth. "Myanmar and Cambodia: The Needs of Local and Foreign Tourists." In Nurryanti, Wiendu, ed. *Heritage, Tourism and Local Communities.* Gadjah: Mada University Press, 1999. pp. 99–108.

Morand, Paul. *Journal Inutile. 1968–1972.* N. p.: Gallimard, 2001, p. 606

Myrdal, Jan, and Gun, Kessle. *Angkor: An Essay on Art and Imperialism.* London: Chatton and Windus, 1971.

Nordom, Sihanouk. *Ombre Sur Angkor.* Phnom Penh: Sangkum Reastr Niyum, 1968.

Osborne, Milton. *Politics and Power in Cambodia.* Australia: Longman, 1973.

Osborne, Milton. *Southeast Asia. Introductory History.* 7th ed. Australia: Allen & Unwin, 1996.

Ray, Nick. *Cambodia.* 3rd ed. Paris: Lonely Planet Publications, 2000.
Roy, Jules. *Les Années Déchirement. Journal 1925–1965.* N. p.: Albin Michel, 1999.
Vann, Molyvann. *Angkor: A Manual for Past, Present and Future.* Phnom Penh: APSARA, 1998.
Vickery, M. *Kampuchea: Politics, Economics and Society.* Boulder: Lynne Rienner, 1986; London: Frances Pinter, 1986.
Yang, Sam. *Khmer Buddhism and Politics from 1954 to 1984.* Newsington, CT: Khmer Studies Institute, 1987.

Reports

Biswas, S. S. "Working Group on Museums and Monument Security." *Proceedings of the National Workshop on the Means of Preventing the Illicit Traffic in Cultural Property in Cambodia.* Phnom Penh, 20–24 July, 1992. UNESCO.
Clément, Etienne. "The 1970 UNESCO Convention on the Means of Prohibiting the Illicit Import, Export and Transfer of Ownership of Cultural Property. *Proceedings of the National Workshop on the Means of Preventing the Illicit Traffic in Cultural Property in Cambodia.* Phnom Penh, 20–24 July, 1992. UNESCO.
Clément, Etienne. "Protection of Cultural Property." In Maley, William, ed. *Shelters from the Storm: Developments in the International Humanitarian Law.* Australian Red Cross. 1995.
Clément, Etienne. "Public Information and Educational Measures against Illicit Traffic in Cultural Property." *Proceedings of the National Workshop on the Means of Preventing the Illicit Traffic in Cultural Property in Cambodia.* Phnom Penh, 20–24 July, 1992. UNESCO.
Cole, James L. "U.S. Assistance under the Convention on Cultural Property Implementation Act." *Proceedings of the National Workshop on the Means of Preventing the Illicit Traffic in Cultural Property in Cambodia.* Phnom Penh, 20–24 July, 1992. UNESCO.
Council of Europe. "The Art Trade." *Report of the Committee on Culture and Education.* Parliamentary Assembly Doc. 5834, 1988.
EFEO. "Conservation in Angkor, 1907–1972." *The Proceedings of the International Round Table of Experts on the Preservation of the Angkor Monuments in Bangkok.* 1990, p. 12.
Emson, James. Report, Art Loss Register. UNESCO, n.d.
Engelhardt, Richard. "Closing Remarks." *Proceedings of the National Workshop on the Means of Preventing the Illicit Traffic in Cultural Property in Cambodia.* Phnom Penh, 20–24 July, 1992. UNESCO.
Fawthrop, Tom. "The Raiders of Banteay Chmar." *Phnom Penh Post.* May 14–27, 1999, p. 9.
Fraoua, Ridha. "Compte rendu du group de travail sur les mesures législative." *Proceedings of the National Workshop on the Means of Preventing the Illicit Traffic in Cultural Property in Cambodia.* Phnom Penh, 20–24 July, 1992. UNESCO.
Fraoua, Ridha. "Invention." *Proceedings of the National Workshop on the Means of Preventing the Illicit Traffic in Cultural Property in Cambodia.* Phnom Penh, 20–24 July, 1992. UNESCO.
Heymes, Gilbert. "Compte rendu du group de travail sur la formation des policiers."

Proceedings of the National Workshop on the Means of Preventing the Illicit Traffic in Cultural Property in Cambodia. Phnom Penh, 20–24 July, 1992. UNESCO.

Institute of Art and Law. "Art Export Licensing and the International Market." *Papers from a Seminar held in London on 19 March 1996.* Leicester: Institute of Art and Law, 1996.

Institute of Art and Law. "Title and Time in Art and Antiquity Claims." *Papers from a Seminar held in London on 13 November 1995.* Leicester: Institute of Art and Law, 1995.

INTERPOL. *Theft of Cultural Property and Illicit Traffic in it.* Report submitted by INTERPOL to UNESCO, 1985, p. 13.

Jacques, Claude. *Des Inscriptions Kméres en vente chez les Antiquaires de Bangkok.* Report interior pour UNESCO. June 4, 1996.

Keo, Pich, and Soubert, Son. "Rapport sur l'atelier national sur les moyens d'empecher le traffic illicit des biens culturels." *Proceedings of the National Workshop on the Means of Preventing the Illicit Traffic in Cultural Property in Cambodia.* Phnom Penh, 20–24 July, 1992. UNESCO.

"Main Recommendations of the Workshop." *Proceedings of the National Workshop on the Means of Preventing the Illicit Traffic in Cultural Property in Cambodia.* Phnom Penh, 20–24 July, 1992. UNESCO.

National Workshop on the Means of Preventing the Illicit Traffic in Cultural Property in Cambodia. Phnom Penh, 20–24 July, 1992. UNESCO.

O'Keefe, P.J. "Provenance and Trade in Cultural Heritage." *University of British Columbia Review,* Special Issue (1995): 259.

Regional Workshop on the Convention on the Means of Prohibiting and Preventing the Illicit Import, Export and Transfer of Ownership of Cultural Property. Organized by UNESCO in cooperation with SEAMEO-SPAFA, Jointien, Pattaya, Thailand, February 24–28, 1992.

A Report on a Symposium on the Return of Cultural Property held at the Africa Centre, 21 May 1981. Commonwealth Art Association, 1981.

"Safeguarding and Development of Angkor." For the Intergovernmental Conference on the *Safeguarding and Development of the Historical Area of Angkor.* Tokyo, October 1993.

Soubert, Son. "Invention." *Proceedings of the National Workshop on the Means of Preventing the Illicit Traffic in Cultural Property in Cambodia.* Phnom Penh, 20–24 July, 1992. UNESCO.

United Nations Social Defense Research Institute (UNSDRI). *The Protection of the Artistic and Archaeological Heritage; A View from Italy and India.* Rome: UNSDRI, 1976.

UN Department of Public Information. *The United Nations in Cambodia 1991–1995.* New York: United Nations, 1995, p. 352.

UNESCO. *Consultation on Illicit Traffic of Cultural Property.* Paris. March 1–4, 1983.

UNESCO. *Report by the Director-General on the Conservation of the Monuments of Angkor.* Paris, 1993, p. 10.

UNESCO. *Report of Director-General on the Implementation of Safeguarding Activities on the Site of Angkor.* Paris, 1994, p. 4.

UNESCO Office for Cambodia. *UNESCO Office for Cambodia: Annual Report 1994.* Phnom Penh: UNESCO, 1994, p. 145.

UNESCO. *Intergovernmental Committee for Promoting the Return of Cultural Prop-

erty to its Countries of Origin or its Restitution in Case of Illicit Appropriation. Report by Secretariat. 9th session. 1996, p. 10.

UNESCO. *Rapport de mission à Singapore.* Singapore, January 5, 1997.

UNESCO. *Intergovernmental Committee for Promoting the Return of Cultural Property to its Countries of Origin or its Restitution in Case of Illicit Appropriation,* Report by Secretariat. 10th session. Paris, January 25–28, 1999.

UNESCO. *Intergovernmental Conference for the Safeguard and Development of the Archaeological Zone of Angkor.* Tokyo: UNESCO, October 1993.

Watts, K. *Report of the Kampuchea Needs Assessment Study.* New York: UNDP, August, 1989.

World Heritage Committee, 16th session, Santa Fe, U.S.A., 7–14 December 1992.

World Heritage Committee, 17th session, Cartagena, Colombia, 6–11 December 1993.

World Heritage Committee, *World Heritage Committee and the Prevention of Illicit Traffic of Cultural Property.* 21st session. Naples: 1997, p. 7.

World Monuments Fund. *From the Draft Report on the Conservation and Preservation of the Angkor Sanctuary, Cambodia.* Bangkok: UNESCO, 1990, p. 20.

Articles

Illicit Trafficking of Art in Cambodia and Other Countries

"Agreement Reached on Border Checkpoints." *Cambodia Daily.* December 1, 1994, p. 10.

Ana, Phann. "Thieves Loot Four Temples in Angkor Wat." *Cambodia Daily.* June 21, 1999, pp. 1, 12.

"Banteay Chmar's Looters said to be Soldiers." *Cambodia Daily.* January 25, 1999, p. 15.

Bhidtlipanya, Boonnarong. "Customs Raid Nets 8-tonne Haul sent from Singapore." *Bangkok Post.* July 6–7, 1999.

Binns, Graham. "Let the Marbles go Home!" *UNESCO Sources.* No. 28. July–August 1991.

Chandara, Lor. "Five Arrested for Theft of Angkor Heads." *Cambodia Daily.* February 28, 1995, p. 6.

Chandara, Lor. "Ministry of Culture Discusses Smuggling." *Cambodia Daily.* March 24, 2000, p. 13.

Chantara, Kimsan. "Cultural Officials Say Relic Looting on Rise." *Cambodia Daily.* November 24, 1996, p. 14.

Chaumeau, Christine. "Biggest Angkor Loot Haul Seized after Stand-off." *Phnom Penh Post.* September 21–22, 1997, pp. 1, 4.

Clément, Etienne. "Towards Coordination of Efforts to Combat Illicit Traffic. UNESCO Intergovernmental Committee meets in Athens." *Museum International* XLIV, 1, 1992, pp. 32–33.

Coggins, C. C. "A Licit International Traffic in Ancient Art: Let There be Light." *International Journal of Cultural Property.* 1995, pp. 4–61.

des Portes, Elisabeth. "ICOM and the Battle Against Illicit Traffic of Cultural Property." *Museum International.* No. 191, Vol. 48, No. 3, 1996.

des Portes, Elisabeth. "Patrimoine artistique, moral et politique." *Le Monde.* January 14, 1997.

Deutsche Presse Agentur. "Cambodian, Thai Suspects in Banteay Chmar Stone Theft." *Cambodia Daily*. January 28, 1999, p. 8.

"Don't Let Cambodia's Past become a History." *Cambodia Daily*. December 12, 1996, pp. 3, 5 and December 13, 1996, p. 19.

Dudar, Helen. "Making a Dent in the Trafficking of Stolen Art." *IFAR*. April 22, 1997.

Folder, Dominic. "The Sandstone Cops. Two Princesses Press a Bold Initiative." *Asiaweek*. August 13, 1999, p. 27.

Franklin, Romain. "Angkor, Temple du Pillage." *Liberation*. February 1, 1999, p. 39.

Franklin, Romain. "Bapùon, Puzzle de 300,000 Pierres sans More d'Emploi." *Liberation*. February 1, 1999, p. 38.

Gysembergh, Benoit. "Les pilleurs du temple perdu." *Match Document*. pp. 21, 22, 119.

Hladik, J. "The Theft of History." *UN Chronicle*. No. 3. 1998, pp. 76–79.

Ishizawa, Yoshaki. "Etat actuel des monuments angkoriens." *Dossier Histoire et Archéologie*. No. 125, March 1988, pp. 102–105.

Johnson, Kay. "Controlling Phnom Kulen." *Cambodia Daily*. September 2–3, 2000, p. 11.

"King Blasts Logging Art Theft Problems." *Cambodia Daily*. October 22, 1996, p. 8.

Lamant, Pierre. "Après Angkor." *Dossier Histoire et Archéologie*. No. 125, March 1988, pp. 94–97.

"Maic Sarun Mom Horn, 68 ans, Gardien des Trésors d'Angkor Borei." *Cambodge Soir*. April 25, 2000.

Matthiesen, P. "Archaeological Looting Unacceptable." *The Art Newspaper*. March 1997.

McDowell, Robin. "Angkor Looting on Rise as Economy Declines." *Cambodia Daily*. November 14, 1996, p. 14.

McIntosh, Roderick J., McIntosh, Susan Keech. "Dilettantism and Plunder: Illicit Traffic in Ancient Malian Art." *Museum International*. XXXVIII, January 1986, pp. 49–57.

McPhillips, Jody. "Looting Threatens Pre-Angkorian Cemetery." *Cambodia Daily*. December 4, 2000, pp. 1, 18.

McPhillips, Jody. "Protecting Kbal Spean." *Cambodia Daily*. August 12–13, 2000, pp. 15–16.

McPhillips, Jody. "Public Access. Military and Police Officials, Businessmen, Scramble for Slice of Angkor." *Cambodia Daily*. September 2–3, 2000, pp. 8–9.

Melikan, S. "Protecting the World's Heritage." *International Herald Tribune*. October 24–25, 1998.

Monreal, Luis. "Problems and Possibilities in Recovering Dispersed Cultural Heritages." *Museum International* XXXI, 1, 1979, pp. 22–25.

O'Keefe, Patrick J. "Museum Acquisitions Policies and the 1970 UNESCO Convention." *Museum International* 50, January 1998, pp. 6, 20, 24.

Pathan, Don. "Security Ends Looting at Cambodian Temple." *The Nation*. June 23, 1999, p. A2.

Pathan, Don. "Thailand Joins Cambodian bid to Protect Temples." *The Nation*. July 20, 1999.

Pomonti, Jean-Claude. "La Thaïlande tente de freiner le Trafic d'Antiquités Khmères." *Le Monde*. August 14, 1999.

Prasuchantip, Somprasorg. "A Treasure Trove of Thai Antiquities Abroad." *Kinnaree*. February 2000, pp. 106–112.
Preston, Douglas. "The Temples of Angkor Still Under Attack." *National Geographic*. August 2000. Vol. 198, No. 2. pp. 82–103.
Revise, Nicolas. "Le Cambodge appelle à sauver ses Temples du Pillage." *Agence France Presse*. February 26, 1999.
Revise, Nicolas. "Officials Fear Stolen Artifacts are Heading West." *Cambodia Daily*. August 2, 1999, pp. 1, 13.
Rizzi, Claudia. "State-of-Emergency Declared to Stem Antique Smuggling." *Cambodia Daily*. September 22, 1995, p. 13.
Roberts, Matthew. "Italian Released after Detention for Art Theft." *Cambodia Daily*. February 24, 1995, p. 7.
Rochigneux, Grégoire. "Angkor, Temple du Pillage." *Libération*. February 1, 1999.
Rochigneux, Grégoire. "Banteay Chmar: des pierres du temple repérées à Bangkok." *Cambodge Soir*. January 21, 1999, pp. 1, 5.
Rochigneux, Grégoire. "Une menace plane au-dessus de Koh Ker." *Cambodge Soir*. December 27, 2000.
Rochigneux, Grégoire. "Le Musée expose les bas-reliefs anachés à Banteay Chmar." *Cambodge Soir*. April 3, 2000.
Rochigneux, Grégoire. "Les Pillages stoppes, on attend toujours le retour des bas-reliefs. " *Cambodge Soir*. June 23–24, 1999.
Rochigneux, Grégoire. "Thieves sell Antiquities." *Phnom Penh Post*. May 14–27, 1999, pp. 6–8.
Rochigneux, Grégoire. "L'UNESCO évoque Banteay Chmar." *Cambodge Soir*. January 27, 1999, pp. 1, 5.
Roeun, Van. "Artifacts Looting Continuing." *Cambodia Daily*. March 23, 1999, p. 7.
Rollet-Andriane, Louis-Jacques. "Precedents." *Museum International* XXXI, 1, 1979, pp. 4–7.
Roux, Arnaud. "Archaeologists Praised for Work around Palace at Angkor Thom." *Cambodia Daily*. January 29, 1996, p. 16.
Sambath, Thet, and Mockenhaupt, Brian. "Artifacts, Border Top Agenda for Thai PM." *Cambodia Daily*. June 14, 2000, p. 8.
Sepul, René. "Angkor la pillée. Les Mafias se servent dans les temples de ce Patrimoine de l'humanité." *La Gazette de l'été*. July 19, 2000.
Serey, To. "County Hunters Pillage Ancient Temples Site, Official Says." *Cambodia Daily*. February 14, 1996, p. 14.
Sesser, Stan. "Chipping away Art Theft." *The Asian Wall Street Journal*. December 5, 2000, p. 1, 8.
Sozanski, Edward F. "Khmer Sculpture Melds Sensuality and Religiousness." *The Philadelphia Inquirer*. August 3, 1997.
Sukpanich, Tunya. "Stop the Treasure Looting." *Bangkok Post*. July 18, 1998, p. 12.
Sukphisit, Suthon. "On the Trail of Stolen Heritage." *Bangkok Post*. August 19, 1996.
Sukphisit, Suthon. "Reclaiming a Lost Heritage." *Bangkok Post*. August 3, 1996.
Sukphisit, Suthon, and Thaitawat, Nusara. "Stolen Arts." *Bangkok Post*. February 28, 2000.
Torres de Araùz, Reina. "Museums and the Containment of Illicit Traffic." *Museum International* XXIV, February 1982, pp. 134–136.

Turnbull, Robert. "Temples of Gloom." *Far Eastern Economic Review*. August 31, 2000, pp. 52–54.

Vachon, Michel, and McPhillips, Jody. "New Documentary Unearths the Looting of Cambodia's Past." *Cambodia Daily*. December 20, 2000, p. 16.

Varine-Bohane, Hugues de. "The Rape and Plunder of Cultures: An Aspect of the Deterioration of the Terms of Cultural Trade Between Nations." *Museum International* XXXV, 3, 1983, pp. 152–157.

Vincent, Steven. "The Looting of Cambodia." *Art & Auction*. October 1994.

Wilson, David. "It's Simply Out of the Question." *UNESCO Sources*. No. 28. July–August 1991.

Art Trade in Cambodia and Other Countries

Benhamou-huet, J. "Le boom du marché asiatique." *Les Echos*. January 24–25, 1997, p. 42.

Benthal, J. "An Interview with Sir Robert and Lady Sainsbury." *Anthropology Today*. 1989. 5, 1:2–5

Boardman, John. "Don't just Berate the Thieves: Look at the Museums and Excavators too." *The Art Newspaper*. No. 54. December 1995.

Burchard, H. "Cambodian Art: Angkor's Way." *The Washington Post Weekend*. July 18, 1997.

"Les Collectionneurs sont les véritables pillards." *The Art Newspaper*. No. 10. January 1995, p. 104.

Covington, R. "Turning the Tide." *Discovery*. May 1997, pp. 47–52.

Ede, J. "A Licit Trade in Antiquities Would Protect Sites." *The Art Newspaper*. No. 70. May 1997.

Elia, R. "The World Cannot Afford Many More Collectors With a Passion for Antiquities." *The Art Newspaper*. No. 41. October 1994, p. 19.

Gibson, M. "Ten Centuries of Khmer Art." *The World and I*. June 1997.

Groslier, Peter White. *National Geographic Magazine*. May 1982, p. 577.

Iwamoto, Yutaka. "Angkor Wat and its Problems." *The Toyogakiyutsu Kenkyu: The Journal of Oriental Studies*. No. 24 (1) pp. 192–218.

Josephson, J. "Are Collectors Destroying our Cultural Heritage?" *IFAR Journal*, Vol.1, No. 1, Spring 1998:17–19.

Marks, Peter. "Antiquities Market Should be Open, Honest." *The Wall Street Journal*. January 29, 1995.

Melikon, Souren. "A Degree of Destruction Unprecedented in the History of the World–and yet I Support Collecting." *The Art Newspaper*. No. 52. October 1995, p. 27.

Merryman, J. H. "A Licit International Trade in Cultural Objects." *International Journal of Cultural Property*.1995, pp. 4–13.

Prott, Lyndel V. "UNIDROIT Draft Convention Focuses on Purchases." *Museum International* XLII, 4, 1991, pp. 221–224.

Somers-Cocks, Anna. "The Getty Museum Retreats from the Antiquities Market." *The Art Newspaper*. No. 54. December 1995.

Teicholz, Nina. "U.S. Committee does More Harm than Good for Antiquities." *Cambodia Daily*. January 29, 2001, p. 14.

Vincent, Steven. "Who Owns Art?" *Art & Auction*. January 1995, pp. 83, 85, 87, 122.

Cambodia—Politics, Economics

Ana, Phann. "Government, Thailand begins Border Talks." *Cambodia Daily*. July 6, 2000, p. 6.

Associated Press. "Thais to Cooperate on Border." *Cambodia Daily*. November 8, 1999, p. 14.

Chandara, Lor. "Millions Lost to Smuggling, Government Claims." *Cambodia Daily*. August 17, 1999, pp. 1, 2.

Chandara, Lor. "Smuggling Costs Government $800,000 a Month." *Cambodia Daily*. November 12, 1998, p. 8.

Maeda, Yuko, and Kimsong, Kay. "PM Slams Customs Corruption, Pledges Smuggling Crackdown." *Cambodia Daily*. December 22, 1999, pp. 1, 14.

McPhillips, Jody. "Tourism Potential Huge, but Problems Remain." *Cambodia Daily*. April 8–9, 2000, p. 3.

Nov, Ana. "Thailand Donates to Help Degraded Temple." *Cambodia Daily*. October 31, 2000, p. 7.

Sambath, Thet. "Military Officials Urge Border Finalization." *Cambodia Daily*. February 28, 2000, p. 14.

Sambath, Thet, and Chon, Gina. "Hun Sen, Thai Foreign Minister Target Border Smuggling." *Cambodia Daily*. February 4, 2000, p. 13.

Sisovann, Pin, and Watson, Rachel. "PMs take Aim at Smuggling." *Cambodia Daily*. July 9, 1998, p. 10.

Restitution of Objects of Art to Cambodia

Agence France Presse. "Stolen Khmer Statue Returned." *Cambodia Daily*. December 7, 1993, p. 4.

Agence France Presse. "Thailand Returns Looted Art." *Cambodia Daily*. November 20–21, 1999, p. 3.

Agence France Presse. "Thais Return 13 Sculptures." *Cambodia Daily*. September 24, 1996, p. 9.

Ana, Phann. "Stolen Temple Carvings to be Returned Soon." *Cambodia Daily*. June 22, 1999, p. 10.

"Appel à Lutter contre le démantèlement du Patrimoine." *Cambodge Soir*. No. 710. March 2, 1999, pp. 1, 4.

A.S.C. "Sotheby's définit un code de bonne conduit." *Le Journal des Arts*. No. 52, January 16, 1998.

Associated Press. "Thailand to Return Cambodian Temple Wall." *Cambodia Daily*. July 12, 1999, p. 15.

Associated Press. "Thais Seize Tons of Stolen Cambodian Artifacts." *Cambodia Daily*. July 6, 1999, p. 12.

Boyce, Debra, and Soenthrith, Saing. "1,200 Year-old Head makes its Way Home." *Cambodia Daily*. December 12, 1996, p. 20.

Chandara, Lor. "Artifacts Returned to Museum." *Cambodia Daily*. November 13, 1996, p. 16.

Chandneary, C. "Khmer Artifacts may Finally be Coming Home." *Bangkok Post*. April 11, 1995.

Culture Without Context. Issue 4, Spring, 1999. *The Newsletter of the Illicit Antiquities Research Center*.

Culture Without Context. Issue 5, Autumn, 1999. *The Newsletter of the Illicit Antiquities Research Center.*

Culture Without Context. Issue 6, Spring, 2000. *The Newsletter of the Illicit Antiquities Research Center.*

Eisenberg, J. M. "New Khmer Temple Site Discovered as Several Stolen Sculptures are Returned to Cambodia". *Minerva.* June 1997.

Munthit, Ker. "Army Recovers Artifacts Stolen by Rebels." *Cambodia Daily.* May 10, 1999, p. 14.

Ngo, Laura. "Two Ancient Artifacts Returned to Museum." *Cambodia Daily.* October 15, 1996, p. 8.

Osthanon, Prapasri. "Cambodia to Receive Stone Artifacts." *Nation.* September 16, 1996, pp. A1, A6.

Reuters. "Ta Mok's Ancient Loot Trucked to Museum." *Bangkok Post.* May 10, 1999.

Rezzi, Chandra. "Stolen Artifact to Return Home." *Cambodia Daily.* April 10, 1996, p. 16.

Soenthrith, Saing. "26 Ancient Pots Returned by Westerner." *Cambodia Daily.* November 27, 1996.

Le Soir, March 18, 1997, p. 15.

Sukpanich, Tunya. "Returning Stolen Artifacts." *Bangkok Post.* July 18, 1999, pp. 3–4.

"Thailand to Return Temple Artifacts." *Cambodia Daily.* November 11, 1999, p. 8.

Thaitawat, Nusora. "Stolen Artifacts Handed Back." *Bangkok Post.* March 1, 2000.

Thaitawat, Nusora. "Long Wrangles over Artifacts." *Bangkok Post*, July 1999.

Thaitawat, N., Sawatsawang, S., Sukpisit, S. "Artifacts Returned to Phnom Penh." *Bangkok Post.* September 24, 1996.

"U.S. Collector Returns Stolen Artifacts of Angkor Temples." *Cambodia Daily.* April 12, 2000, p. 9.

Vittachi, Imran. "Thailand Returns Stolen Artifacts." *Phnom Penh Post.* October 4–17, 1996, p. 16.

Vogel, Carol. "Tracing Path of Artworks Smuggled out of Asia." *The New York Times.* April 23, 1997.

Restitution of Art (Examples of Other Countries)

"Art Institute of Chicago Returns Khmer Lintel to Thailand." *Museum International.* XLI, 2, 1989.

De Silva, R.H.D.H. "Return and Restitution of Cultural Property. Viewpoints: Sri Lanka." *Museum International* XXXI, 1. 1979, pp. 22–25.

ICOM. *Ad. Hoc. Committee for the Return of Cultural Property, Preliminary Study of Three National Situations in Regard to the Return of Cultural Property to its Country of Origin (Mali, Bangladesh, West Samoa)*, 1980.

Lenioud, J-M., and Schmitt, J-M. "Patrimoine: pertes et profits." *Le Journal des Arts*, No. 34, March 1997.

P. Pott, and Sutaarga, M. A. "Arrangements Concluded or in Progress for the Return of Objects: The Netherlands-Indonesia." *Museum International.* XXXI, 1, 1979, pp. 38–42.

Sawatsawang, N. "Dutch Customs Seize Three Antique Buddha Statues." *The Bangkok Post.* 1998.

"Statement Presented by the Democratic Socialist Republic of Sri-Lanka Concerning the Restitution of Significant Cultural Objects from Sri-Lanka." *Museum International.* 1980.

Legislative Texts

International Conventions

1970 UNESCO Convention on the Means of Prohibiting and Preventing the Illicit Import, Export and Transfer of Ownership of Cultural Property adopted by the General Conference at its Sixteenth Session Paris, 14 November 1970.

ICOM Code of Professional Ethics.

INTERPOL CRIGEN Art Forms.

List of States Parties to the 1970 UNESCO Convention.

Object Identification Checklist.

Statutes of the UNESCO Intergovernmental Committee.

The Convention Concerning the Protection of the World Cultural and Natural Heritage (World Heritage Convention, Paris, 1972).

The Hague Convention for the Protection of Cultural Property in the Event of Armed Conflict 1954.

The ICOM Handbook of Standards.

The Nairobi Convention Annex XI Concerning Assistance in Action Against the Smuggling of Works of Art, Antiquities and Other Cultural Property, adopted by the Customs Cooperation Council (Now The World Customs Organization) in Nairobi, June 9, 1977.

The World Customs Organization.

UN Model treaty for Bilateral cooperation for the Prevention of Crimes that Infringe on the Cultural Heritage of People in the For of Movable Property.

UNESCO Recommendation Concerning the International Exchange of Cultural Property.

UNESCO Recommendation for the Protection of Movable Property.

UNESCO Recommendation on International Principles Applicable to Archaeological Excavations, "New Delhi Recommendation," 1956.

UNESCO Standard Form concerning Requests for Return and Restitution, January 1986, Intergovernmental Committee for Promoting the Return of Cultural Property to its Countries of Origin or its Restitution in Case of Illicit Appropriation.

UNIDROIT Convention on Stolen or Illegally Exported Cultural Objects.

U.S. Information Agency on the Protection of Cultural Property.

Cambodian Legislation

Agreement between the Government of the Kingdom of Cambodia and the Government of the Kingdom of Thailand. 1999.

Document preparing for the return of artifacts to the government of Cambodia. November 19, 1999.

Law on the Protection of Cultural Heritage. Vann Molyvann. *Angkor: A Manual for Past, Present and Future.* Phnom Penh: APSARA, 1998.

Legislation and measures against illicit trafficking in cultural property (Cambo-
    dia).
National Heritage Protection Angkor of Cambodia (NHPAC).
Royal Decree concerning the Hotel Zone. Vann Molyvann. *Angkor: A Manual for
    Past, Present and Future*. Phnom Penh: APSARA, 1998.
Royal Decree establishing a National Authority for the Protection and Manage-
    ment of Angkor and the Region of Siem Reap, named APSARA. Vann Moly-
    vann. *Angkor: A Manual for Past, Present and Future*. Phnom Penh: APSARA,
    1998.
Royal Decree establishing Protected Cultural Zones in the Siem Reap/Angkor
    Region and Guidelines for their Management. Vann Molyvann. *Angkor: A Man-
    ual for Past, Present and Future*. Phnom Penh: APSARA, 1998.
Royal Decree establishing the Supreme Council of National Culture. Vann Moly-
    vann. *Angkor: A Manual for Past, Present and Future*. Phnom Penh: APSARA,
    1998.
Sub Decree establishing the Special Police Corps for the Protection of Cultural
    Heritage. Vann Molyvann. *Angkor: A Manual for Past, Present and Future*. Phnom
    Penh: APSARA, 1998.
Texte législatif relatif an classement, à la conservation et à la protection des mon-
    uments historiques et des objets d'art de l'Indochine Française. Hanoi, 1925.
    Journal Officiel 1925. 1422.
The Supreme National Council of Cambodia. Decision of February 10, 1993 on
    the National Heritage Protection Authority of Cambodia.
U.S. Emergency Import Restriction on Khmer Stone Archaeological Material.

Thai Legislation

Loi relative à la réglementation des ventes aux enchères et à la vente des antiqui-
    tés, B. E. 2474. 1931.
Loi relative aux monuments anciens, aux antiquités, aux objets d'art et aux musées
    nationaux, B. E. 2504. 1961.

Films

Beyond Angkor. Director Pierre Stiné. France 2, Turner and Turner, CNRS Images.
    2000.
Franco-German Television Channel ARTE with APSARA, a documentary on the
    fight against the traffic of Khmer cultural goods.
Journey to Angkor: The Essence of the Khmer Culture. By Van Eight Co., Ltd. 1997.
Looting in Angkor. National Geographic Television and APSARA. 1997.
The Lohet Sela (*Blood Stone*). Director Sok Sophal. Producers TVK. Cambodia.
    2000.

Interviews

Keo, Pich, Ex-Director of Conservation d'Angkor, Ex-Director of the National
    Museum in Phnom Penh, Professor of Archaeology in the Institute of Fine Arts
    in Phnom Penh, February 8, 2001.
Paringaux, Roland-Pierre, journalist at *Le Monde*, February 2, 2000

Sites on the Internet

http://www.archaeology.org
http://www.artloss.com
http://www.coolectors.org/doc.thefts.htm
http://www.e.usia.gov/education/culprop
http://exchanges.state.gov/education/culprop
http://www.fbi.gov/art.htm
http://www.icom.org
http://www.interpol.com
http://www.museum-security.org
http://www.saztv.com
http://www.trace.co.uk/index-frame.htm
http://www.usdoj.dov/usncb/cultural.htm
http://www.worldbank.org

Index

www.ingramcontent.com/pod-product-compliance
Lightning Source LLC
Chambersburg PA
CBHW020904180526
45163CB00007B/2620